DUNKIRK

Also by Norman Gelb

The Berlin Wall

Scramble

Less Than Glory

The British

Irresistible Impulse

Enemy in the Shadows

DUNKIRK

The Complete Story of the First Step in the Defeat of Hitler

Norman Gelb

William Morrow and Company, Inc.
New York

Library of Congress Cataloging-in-Publication Data

Gelb, Norman.
    Dunkirk : the complete story of the first step in the defeat of
Hitler / Norman Gelb.
        p.   cm.
    Bibliography: p.
    Includes index.
    ISBN 0-688-07793-5
    1. Dunkerque (France), Battle of, 1940.   I. Title.
D756.5.D8G44   1989
940.53—dc20   89-32357
                                                               CIP

Printed in the United States of America

First Edition

1 2 3 4 5 6 7 8 9 10

BOOK DESIGN BY NICOLA MAZZELLA

For Amos,
my son and friend

Contents

War reveals dimensions of human nature both above and below the acceptable standards of humanity.
—J. Glenn Gray, *The Warriors: Reflections on Men in Battle*

PART ONE

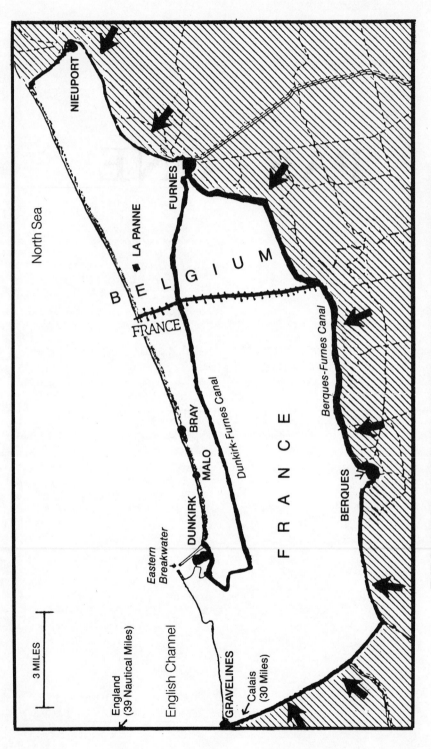

North Sea

NIEUPORT

LA PANNE

FURNES

B E L G I U M

FRANCE

Berques-Furnes Canal

BRAY

MALO

Dunkirk-Furnes Canal

DUNKIRK

BERQUES

F R A N C E

Eastern
Breakwater

3 MILES

England
(39 Nautical Miles)

English Channel

GRAVELINES

Calais
(30 Miles)

THE DUNKIRK PERIMETER DEFENSE WHEN FIRST ESTABLISHED

Dunkirk

At dawn on May 10, 1940, the armies of Nazi Germany bolted from behind the borders of their country to begin a march of conquest across Western Europe. Spearheaded by a formidable armada of tanks and closely supported by the most powerful fleet of attack aircraft ever assembled, they set out to accomplish what German armies had failed to achieve in the First World War a generation earlier—to crush France and humble Britain.

Though braced for the attack, Allied defenses—outmatched, outmaneuvered, and overwhelmed—quickly crumbled under the onslaught. In less than three weeks, Adolf Hitler, the emotionally charged, ideologically driven German dictator, achieved the most extraordinary military triumph of modern times. Not only was the French army, previously deemed the most indomitable fighting machine in the world, on the verge of collapse, but the British Expeditionary Force, which had been sent across the English Channel to help stop the Germans, was trapped against the sea at Dunkirk on the northwest coast of France.

Disaster loomed for the forces resisting the Nazi menace. Hitler's conquests had been relentless. Austria, Czechoslovakia, Poland, Denmark, Holland, and Luxembourg had already fallen to him. Most of Belgium had been overrun and its surrender was imminent. Norway was about to succumb as well, and even the proud French were heading for a humiliating capitulation.

In London, senior government officials and top military officers were astounded by the rapidity and magnitude of the Ger-

man rampage across northern France and by the peril suddenly
and without warning facing the British Expeditionary Force.
The BEF comprised almost all of Britain's combat-ready troops,
cadre, and experienced officers. The realization that it was
trapped with its back to the sea and had little hope of breaking
out was staggering. The war had just begun, but Britain was
about to be left without an army.

It was grimly accepted that virtually all of the army's heavy
equipment, which had accompanied the BEF to France, was ir-
retrievably lost. But plans were hastily patched together to try to
save some of the troops. Ships and boats were assembled to
shuttle across the English Channel to bring as many as possible
back to England from Dunkirk. But German bombers had been
blasting the city's port facilities for days, rendering them well-
nigh useless. And onrushing German ground forces were just a
few miles from the city. Not even the most optimistic of British
leaders believed the evacuation could be successful. At best, it
was thought, a comparatively small number of men—maybe
thirty thousand out of ten times that number—could be lifted
off before the German trap snapped closed. Some senior British
officers were convinced that practically none of the men would
get away.

A National Day of Prayer for the troops across the Channel
was ordained in Britain, prompting some of them who learned
of it to conclude that they were already written off as doomed.
Government aides advised that the British public, which had
been shielded from the details by censorship, should be apprised
of the situation so that when the worst finally occurred it would
not come as too devastating a shock.

A German invasion of Britain was believed to be in the
making, and those who already knew of the BEF's plight feared
that the country might be left minus the wherewithal to repel it.
Winston Churchill, newly named prime minister and scorned by
a number of the senior figures in London as a political dilet-
tante, the wrong man for the job, warned the House of Commons to brace itself for "hard and heavy tidings."

Some thought those tidings would be too hard and heavy to
bear. Junior government minister Harold Nicolson and his wife,
writer Vita Sackville-West, contemplated suicide. Though not
normally given to morbid sentiments, senior Foreign Office official Sir Alexander Cadogan was disheartened enough to con-

fide in his diary, "I should count it a privilege to be dead if Hitler rules England." As fears mounted for the fate of the British army at Dunkirk, a senior cabinet minister, exasperated by Churchill's determination to fight on no matter what the cost, urged that efforts be made to secure "honorable" peace terms from the German dictator, leaving him to consolidate his European gains before resuming his conquests.

What was happening was having a profound impact well beyond the countries and armies immediately involved. Much more was to be decided at Dunkirk than would be immediately realized. The two nations which would ultimately determine the outcome of the war were greatly affected by the consequences. The American government was led to believe that Britain was in such deep trouble that a government submissive to Hitler might conceivably take charge in London. Pressure was building up in Washington for the United States to reconcile itself to unchallenged Nazi domination of Europe if the British, without an army, were in fact forced to their knees. Instead of rushing badly needed war supplies to the struggling western democracies, preparations were made to dispatch great numbers of U.S. troops to Latin America, where Hitler was believed to be planning to follow up his European triumphs with incursions in the Western Hemisphere. At the same time, the U.S. government seriously considered annexing the British West Indies for American national security purposes.

In Moscow, Soviet officials also watched developments with growing anxiety. The Soviet army had been crippled by the execution or imprisonment of most of its officer corps on trumped-up treason charges during grotesque purges orchestrated by Soviet ruler Joseph Stalin. Despite the nonaggression treaty Stalin had signed with Hitler the previous year, the German Fuehrer had repeatedly insisted that the destruction of Soviet communism and the conquest of Russia were among his priority objectives. With France on the verge of collapse, if Britain was also humbled, no adversary would remain to distract Hitler from turning his ferocious attentions eastward.

The story of Dunkirk is therefore one of many dimensions. At its core, it is the tale of the great escape, of the transformation of a massive defeat for the British army into what would ultimately prove a disaster for the German forces which had driven it into a seemingly terminal trap. It is an account of how a monumental maritime rescue operation was pieced together in short order with limited understanding of what was involved and with practically no chance of success—and how it succeeded. On a personal level, it is a tale of contrasts—of clarity and confusion, true grit and deep despair, prodigious ingenuity and dazzling incompetence, selfless camaraderie and blind panic, all ingredients of one of the most extraordinary exercises in survival ever undertaken.

What follows in these pages is also an account of how it all came to pass. It is about lessons unlearned, warnings ignored, and mistakes repeated. It is about governments and generals fumbling and blundering their way toward what was about to become the greatest conflagration the human race has ever known, a war which might have turned into an even greater calamity had the ten days of Dunkirk not occurred or if they had ended differently.

Prelude

In the years before, the countries of Europe, still recovering from the ravages and grief of the First World War, had inexorably been drawn once more toward catastrophe. In Germany, at the heart of the continent, ominous perpetrations and pronouncements signaled the approaching crisis.

Germany had been battered into abject submission by the United States, Britain, and France in that earlier "Great War." It had also been so severely penalized in the peace treaty that had followed that it seemed certain that a very long time would pass before it could again emerge as a major power. The German army had been reduced to skeletal proportions. Germany had been forbidden to construct any weapons which could be used for aggressive purposes. It had been forbidden to build a military air force and was required to slash the size of its navy. It had been made to surrender more than one-tenth of its total territory in which 10 percent of its population lived and from which much of its natural resources were extracted. It had been forced to give up its extensive colonial empire—at a time before colonialism was generally considered wicked. It had been required to make huge, crippling cash reparation payments for the damage done in the war. As a nation it was ruined. As a military power it was nonexistent. That its forces would in the not too distant future be capable of closing in on routed and trapped armies of their former conquerors in the infernal pandemonium of Dunkirk was unimaginable.

But even before a postwar generation had grown to maturity, Germany had recovered and become an armed, swaggering colossus. More than that, it had become a bully and a menace, a threat to the other nations of Europe and, it seemed, to the United States as well. The image of the swastika, the insignia of Adolf Hitler's Nazi party, had risen in its midst like a demonic talisman symbolizing a sinister crusade based on ruthlessness, racist mumbo jumbo, fanatical national vainglory, and territorial aggression. A truculent, malignant mood, underscored by police-state terror, convulsed the land which had given the world the wonders of Beethoven, Goethe, and Albert Einstein.

Hitler had made no secret of his determination to expand the borders of Germany at the expense of its neighbors. The soil of Europe, he had earlier written, "exists for the people who possess the force to take it." Visitors to Germany's industrial hubs could see armament factories churning out the instruments of war in defiance of Versailles Treaty prohibitions. Visitors to German North Sea ports saw shipyards fully stretched building submarines and other warships. But when it came to contemplating the possibility of one day having to defend themselves against a recently prostrate but ever more powerful, ever more threatening Germany, most people were blinded by vivid recollections of the anguish and devastation of the earlier conflict.

More than ten million had been killed in the First World War and more than twenty million had been wounded. A generation of young men had been decimated. Countless women had been widowed and countless children had been left fatherless. The dead were still mourned, and the maimed—many still selling matches and shoelaces on street corners—were a constant reminder of what war meant. Vast national resources had been squandered. National economies had been crippled. The destruction of property had been immense. A replay of such a cataclysm was unthinkable.

In the popular imagination in the western democracies, no distinction was made between preparing for defense and heading for war. The Oxford University students who, as Hitler positioned himself to dominate Europe, resolved overwhelmingly not to fight for king or country aired not only the views of Britain's privileged young elite. They shared the much more widely held conviction that no development, no circumstance, no cause, no provocation could possibly justify another resort to arms.

Peace societies proliferated across Britain. They held count-less peace meetings, peace demonstrations, and peace parades. Thousands of people throughout the land enrolled in a Peace Pledge Union. Books, plays, songs, magazine and newspaper ar-ticles, and sermons galore denounced the futility of war and the absurdity of rearmament.

While not enamored of the Nazis, some influential British figures thought it important not to upset Hitler as he went about transforming and militarizing his country. Discounting his openly expressed expansionist aspirations, they feared that if af-fronted, he might turn to war to resolve bitterness and frustra-tion left over from the previous conflict. Geoffrey Lawson, editor of the London *Times,* told a friend, "I spend my nights in taking out anything [from the newspaper] which I think will hurt [German] susceptibilities."

Even among Britons who were appalled by Hitler and hor-rified by Nazi brutalities, some were reluctant to be overly crit-ical. They deeply regretted that the Germans had been dealt with vindictively by their conquerors at the end of the First World War. They believed that because Germany had been treated so harshly, it was natural for it to strive to regain its dignity, its self-respect, and perhaps even some lost territory. It was not unreasonable to maintain that the international climate would remain dangerously unstable until Germany was strong and proud again.

Not all who sought to appease Hitler subscribed to such reasoning. Many were profoundly worried by the emergence of the German tyrant and particularly by the growth of German military might. But they dreaded Soviet communism, which had been convulsing Russia for the better part of two decades and had been promoting violent upheaval elsewhere, more than they did the Nazis, who were comparatively new upon the scene. They feared that if Germany was slapped down and humiliated once more, the Soviet Union and its threat to western values would come to dominate much of Europe (which is how things eventually turned out).

Besides, who would do the slapping down? Britain couldn't do it by itself. By the time the Hitlerian menace became unmis-takable, British armed forces were outmatched in size and tech-nology by the Germans. Nor did the German threat fully occupy Britain's attention. The world's leading imperial power, it had

other pressing concerns, including the Japanese threat to its imperial domain in the Orient and an Italian threat to its interests
in the Mediterranean.

Bordering Germany and therefore even more fearful of the
consequences of another war, France also showed no sign of
wanting to challenge Hitler. The Soviet army, its officer corps
emasculated by political purges, could not be expected to take
on that task. As for the United States, where isolationist sentiment prevailed and where many people considered the British
Empire a tyrannical institution, unworthy of support, Prime
Minister Neville Chamberlain believed, "He would be a rash
man who based his calculations on help from that quarter."
Even later, when Britain felt it was left with no alternative but
to go to war with Germany, Chamberlain confided, "Heaven
knows I don't want the Americans to fight for us. We should
have to pay too dearly for that if they had a right to be in on the
peace terms."

Chamberlain was also haunted by the consequences for
Britain, its economy deep in depression doldrums, if it had to
finance another conflict. Economists calculated that if it went to
war again, it would soon be unable to pay for imported food and
raw materials it required to survive. During the earlier war,
Britain, like France, had been able to borrow from the United
States to sustain its war economy. But in its determination to
keep America neutral this time, and in its bitterness over unpaid
past loans, Congress had decreed that no such largess by the
American government would again be permitted.

The trench-scarred terrain of northern France had been the
main western battlefield of the First World War. One in every ten
Frenchmen in uniform—almost one and a half million—had been
killed and another million had been maimed. What had been a
prosperous country had been ruined. Coal mines had been flooded
and steel plants destroyed. Much of the country's railway network
had been shattered. Sections of some of its cities and towns had
been flattened. Vast areas of countryside had been so devastated
that millions of acres of productive farmland had been made
barren. Not since the Black Death of the Middle Ages had the
country suffered so grievously.

The prospect of another war was contemplated with horror
everywhere in France. Soldiering, once an honored profession in

the country, had come to be viewed with scorn. War stories, formerly laced with glory, now were tinged with gloom and despair. The number of candidates for enrollment in the elite military academy at Saint-Cyr had fallen sharply and French children had even stopped playing at being soldiers.

But as next-door neighbors of the headstrong Germans, the French were nervously aware of how exposed they were. They were doubly jittery because, more than the other victorious First World War powers, they had called at war's end for vanquished Germany to be severely punished. Their leaders had been the most insistent in demanding massive reparations from the Germans to compensate for the war's devastation. Now, with Hitler embarked on a campaign to redeem German pride and honor, the French feared Teutonic vengeance. Half the size and with two-thirds the population of Germany, France felt like a boy who, with a gang of friends, had beaten up the neighborhood bully but now feared having to face that bully, who was stronger and angrier than before, all by himself.

The rise of Hitler in Germany during the 1930s coincided with great domestic turbulence in France. An epidemic of violent street clashes between rightist and leftist mobs undermined political stability in the country, distracting attention from the growing danger across the border. A ceaseless political gavotte in Paris, where governments rose and fell with unnerving frequency, made the formulation of a consistent policy toward Germany difficult. In addition, France was stricken with an epidemic of industrial strikes which aroused the ire of its middle classes, intensified class antagonisms, and further diverted attention from questions of national security.

Nevertheless, senior figures of all political persuasions in the country realized that, unlike Britain, France could not rely on a natural barrier to frustrate an invasion by its increasingly bellicose neighbor. Aversion to war notwithstanding, the people of France accepted that they could not afford to share the presumption widely held among British peace activists that to take a moral stand would persuade an adversary to do likewise. They knew they had to be ready if the blast of cannon was heard once more along their frontiers.

However, the strategic imagination of French military and political leaders was clouded by the horrific experiences of the Great War. Their overriding objective in strategic planning was to spare the country a recurrence of the previous conflict's slaughter and havoc. It might become necessary to engage in battle, but the main objective would be not to vanquish the enemy but to keep him at bay, barred from entry onto French soil. Preparations for armed conflict were to be defensive rather than offensive, static rather than mobile. Thus was spawned the infamous Maginot Line.

Considered as formidable as a line of battleships at anchor, the Maginot Line, named after a former French minister of war, was one of the most extraordinary fortifications in history. It contained "every resource of material and design known to military science." Built of steel and concrete, up to seven levels deep, with interior as well as exterior defenses in case of unlikely enemy penetrations, it snaked along the Franco-German border all the way from Switzerland to Belgium. Once it was in place, direct military approach to France from Germany was believed blocked. It was conceded that the Germans might poke through the line here and there. But such spearheads would be quickly pinched off and smothered by covering forces. Two hundred miles of France's northern frontier, its border with Belgium, were without such fortifications; fixed defenses there were to be strengthened later. But the Belgians, guarding those northern approaches to France from Germany, were expected to provide a barrier of their own against German aggression.

The existence of this formidable defensive wall generated a stupefying complacency among French generals. With the initiative handed as a long-term gift to the Germans, those generals had nothing to do but wait for the enemy to strike. As France rearmed, its military leaders offered the War and Treasury ministries in Paris little meaningful advice on armament priorities, except that the defensive wall should be maintained and strengthened. The sixty-seven-year-old commander in chief of the French army, General Maurice Gamelin, had little idea what the next war might involve and didn't intend to worry about it. Dismissing the two instruments that were to seal France's fate, Gamelin declared, "Aircraft do not decide the outcome of a battle," and "Armored divisions are too heavy and cumbersome; they may penetrate our lines, but the lips of the gash will close behind them and we shall crush them with our reserves."

The French had begun rearming soon after word spread of Germany's clandestine military buildup. Munitions and equipment were manufactured in abundance. But no one knew where to deploy them. Much of the matériel went into storage and stayed there. After France was forced to capitulate, the Germans were amazed at what they found—millions of artillery shells still warehoused in army ammunition dumps and tens of thousands of bombs in aviation depots.

Committed to a defensive strategy, France was denied the possibility of fashioning a flexible military response as the German challenge developed step by step. Full mobilization was to be decreed as a warning to the enemy when the moment of extreme danger neared. But as that moment did approach, mobilization was seen as signifying a headlong rush into the war the French people and their leaders dreaded, so even that option was held in check. Instead of a warning, the signal given Hitler was a green light.

Underlying the failure of Britain and France to join in blocking what they both had reason to fear greatly—the resurgence of Germany as the most powerful single European power, and a vengeful one at that—was a fundamental affinity gap between them. American presidential adviser Adolf Berle quipped that the British had made "the mistake of living next to the French for several hundred years and not understanding them." It wasn't only British xenophobia which led Englishmen to maintain that "the wogs begin at Calais." The French and their ways had always baffled the British. Britons weren't sure whether to be dazzled by French chic and flair or disdainful of French emotionalism and delusions of grandeur. This failure in comprehension was hardly one-sided. The French were as perplexed by the British as the British were by them. They were torn between admiring British style and imperturbability and resenting British conceit and priggishness.

The British were annoyed with the French for having been insistent on punishing the Germans so harshly after the First World War that Central Europe had been fundamentally destabilized. The French reacted with contempt for British moralizing on the subject and grumbled over Britain's apparent indifference to German rearmament. Competition between London and Paris for influence and control in the oil-rich Middle East also generated friction between the two countries. However, as Germany grew more menacing, the French, seeking but finding no reliable alternative, came to rely on alliance with Britain as the cornerstone of their foreign policy and to invoke Britain's disdainful refusal to be panicked by Hitler as an excuse for their own inaction.

Nevertheless, the two countries continued to operate on different wavelengths, almost literally. Until shortly before the actual outbreak of war, no detailed staff consultations took place between their senior military men. The first time such consultations actually did take place, no interpreters were on hand and neither of the senior officers present fully understood what the other was saying.

The major power with most to fear from Nazi Germany was the Soviet Union. Not only had Hitler earlier laid claim to Russian territory as "living space" for Germans, to be incorporated into his Reich, but he continued to make no secret of coveting Soviet land, particularly the vast fertile fields of the Ukraine.

In addition to its military weakness, during the 1930s the Soviet Union was under pressure in a different part of the world. An aggressive, militaristic Japan had already occupied Manchuria and was now perched menacingly on a long stretch of the Soviet Union's eastern frontier. Serious border incidents had erupted, involving thousands of troops, air attacks, and large numbers of casualties. Reeling from famine, agricultural collapse, and industrial dislocation as it staggered from one fumbling five-year plan to another, the Soviet Union was terrified by the possibility of having to fight not one war but two, on fronts thousands of miles apart.

Since its inception shortly after the Russian Revolution, the Kremlin-run Communist International (Comintern) had strenuously promoted working-class overthrow of capitalist governments. Now Stalin ordered a sharp turnabout in policy. He set about trying to establish an effective collective security alliance against Nazi Germany. The Soviet Union joined the League of Nations, which it had previously scorned as an imperialist tool. Maxim Litvinov, Stalin's westernized, genial foreign minister, was dispatched to Paris, London, League headquarters at Geneva, and elsewhere to promote concerted defensive precautions against German aggression. Communist parties around the world were instructed to cease their clamor for the overthrow of bourgeois governments.

But loathing of communism and distrust of the Soviet
Union were too deeply implanted for Stalin's about-face to
arouse much sympathy in the countries he was trying to woo.
Most of their leaders reflexively recoiled against overtures from
the Kremlin. It was suspected that Stalin's motive was to divert
German territorial appetites their way rather than his. No doubt
the thought did cross his mind.

Distrust of the Soviets was fueled by what was seen as Russian treachery in the First World War. Many senior figures in
Britain and France personally recalled how the Bolsheviks, once
they had seized power during that war, unilaterally made peace
with the Germans and deserted the field of battle. The German
High Command was then able to shift a million troops from the
pacified eastern front to reinforce those locked in bloody combat
with the Allies on the western front. What good was an alliance
with an ally who had previously demonstrated that he could not
be trusted? Besides, Stalin's purges of military personnel cast
doubt on the usefulness of an alliance with Russia. The execution or imprisonment of a long list of the most senior Soviet
officers stunned foreign observers. Chamberlain had "no belief
whatever in [Russia's] ability to maintain an effective offensive,
even if she wanted to."

For the most part, the United States was spared Europe's
sense of once more being drawn toward murderous armed conflict. Americans had enough of their own worries not to want to
take on those of Europe as well. The economic depression
which had set in with the Wall Street crash of 1929 had settled
deep into the mood and pulse of the nation. The richest country
in the world was pockmarked with joblessness, poverty, and despair. Millions of Americans were in trouble. Breadlines in the
cities and forlorn migrants drifting along the country's highways
in search of hope badly shook America's traditional "can do"
confidence. It was evident that there were things that America
could *not* do.

One thing which most Americans, regardless of political
persuasion, wanted not to do was get embroiled again in foreign
squabbles. Those on the left wanted the United States to stay
clear because any involvement—even confined to lending material support from afar—would mean diverting public funds from
programs designed by President Franklin Roosevelt and his New

Deal to lift the country out of the depression. Those on the right maintained that involvement would shift America's limited military resources away from their prime function of guarding the security of the United States. Even many who felt strongly about European developments believed it was wrong and rarely effective to try to sort out other people's problems.

It was argued that America's experiences in the First World War demonstrated that the United States was right to remain aloof. The earlier conflict was dismissed as having been a pointless brawl in which American lives and money had been squandered on behalf of European ingrates and incompetents for nothing more than a chance to do the same again a few years down the road.

Best-selling books and magazine articles, and a high-powered Senate investigating committee, blamed the greed and unscrupulousness of arms merchants for America's having been drawn into the earlier European conflagration. Former President Herbert Hoover asserted that the squandering of American resources in Europe in the First World War was the root cause of America's economic troubles, and he warned the country against making that mistake again. So strong and widespread was isolationist sentiment that Congress passed neutrality legislation decreeing that when war broke out anywhere, Americans would be banned from selling munitions to any belligerents.

President Roosevelt, and American political leaders generally, abominated Hitler and were disgusted by Nazi perpetrations. William Dodd, the American ambassador in Berlin in the early years of Hitler's rule, had "a sense of horror when I look at the man." But a greater sense of horror was induced by the image of war and the possibility that America might again be bamboozled into taking part in one. Though suspected by many isolationists of deliberately leading the country in that direction, Roosevelt was no less appalled by the prospect.

I have seen war. I have seen war on land and sea. I have seen blood running from the wounded. I have seen men coughing out their gassed lungs. I have seen the dead in the mud. I have seen cities destroyed. I have seen two hundred limping, exhausted men come out of the line—the survivors of a regiment of one thousand that went forward forty-eight hours before. I have seen children starving. I have seen the

agony of mothers and wives. I hate war. I have passed unnumbered hours, I shall pass unnumbered hours, thinking
and planning how war may be kept from this nation.

Roosevelt would soon come to believe nevertheless that the
United States would ultimately have to meet the challenge of
Nazi Germany. Aside from a possible military threat, as Germany began digesting parts of Europe, the president was told by
trusted advisers that America's economic recovery and well-
being were at stake.

Germany does not have to conquer us in a military sense. By
enslaving her own labor and that of the conquered countries,
she can place in the markets of the world products at a price
with which we could not compete. This will destroy our standards of living and shake to its depths our moral and physical fiber, already strained to breaking point.

But Roosevelt was inhibited by prevailing popular sentiment from publicly suggesting that the United States take sides
as Europe tumbled toward war. A storm of protest was unleashed when an American bomber crashed during a test flight
in California and it was discovered that among those killed in
the crash was an official of the French Air Ministry. The administration was accused of plotting to plunge the United States into
Europe's convulsions while claiming to be horrified by the prospect.

Though most Americans were appalled by what their newspapers and radio stations reported about Nazi Germany, their
disapproval and abhorrence were dwarfed by relief that the
United States was far removed from the scene and unencum-
bered by foreign entanglements. Respected newspaper colum-
nist Walter Lippmann advised, "Let us remain untangled and
free. Let us make no alliances. Let us make no commitments."
Popular singer Kate Smith reassuringly warbled on her weekly
radio program, "While the storm clouds gather far across the
sea, let us pledge allegiance to a land that's free."

Many Americans objected to involvement in European im-
broglios for ethnic reasons. It was evident that if the United
States was drawn in, it would not be on the side of Germany.
While most Americans of German origin were repelled by Nazi

ideology, few welcomed the idea that the United States might once more join in ganging up on their ancestral homeland. They recalled the prejudice they suffered during the First World War when anti-German feeling in America grew so extreme that the popular Katzenjammer Kids newspaper comic strip, featuring a pair of lovably mischievous German-American urchins, had to change its name to the Shenanigan Kids for the duration of the conflict. And the large, articulate, and devoutly anti-British Irish-American population, not overly distressed by Britain's unfolding predicament, fumed at the prospect of the United States again rushing to the aid of their ancestral nemesis.

Some prominent Americans were impressed by Nazi achievements in giving people work and boosting national morale at a time when democratic nations were shrouded by mists of despair. Newspaper magnate William Randolph Hearst returned from a visit to Germany extolling Nazi accomplishments. Pioneer aviator, national hero, and international celebrity Charles Lindbergh was warmly received during visits to Germany and was impressed both with the striking developments in German military aviation and with the spirit of confidence and achievement which his Nazi hosts displayed. Hugh Wilson, the American ambassador in Switzerland, told Secretary of State Cordell Hull that he detected growing moderation in Hitler's thinking and urged sympathy for German national revival.

The failure of Britain to confront the Nazi challenge more vigorously hardly inspired those who believed that Hitler had to be stopped. William Allen White, the Kansas newspaper editor who was soon to found an influential nationwide pro-Allies lobbying group, was particularly scathing.

> What an avalanche of blunders Great Britain has let loose upon the democracies of the world! The old British lion looks mangy, sore-eyed. He needs worming and should have a lot of dental work. He can't even roar.

The Americans most directly concerned with European developments in the years leading up to the Second World War were the country's senior State Department officials and military officers. The navy was then the strongest and most important American defense arm. But much of the U.S. fleet was based in the Pacific Ocean to meet the threat of Japanese expansionist aspirations. The U.S. naval command was counting on the British fleet to keep the rebuilt German navy from seizing mastery in the Atlantic Ocean and thus becoming a force to be reckoned with in the Western Hemisphere.

At the same time, the State Department was worried about the danger of Nazi incursions in Latin America, which, then as now, was considered of critical strategic and economic importance to the United States. America derived cheap raw materials from the region, which it had long dominated, and it found a secure market there for its manufactured goods. But substantial colonies of German immigrants had settled in South America and many public figures there admired Hitler's style and achievements. Reports from American embassies across South America told of growing German influence in several countries. It seemed evident that developments in Europe would have an important bearing on the Western Hemisphere and therefore on American policy.

Hitler had begun his march of conquest with a fairly modest exploit. On March 7, 1936, German troops had moved into the demilitarized Rhineland, that patch of Germany which borders France on the west bank of the Rhine, from which they had been barred by the Versailles Treaty. Senior German generals had urged Hitler not to proceed with the operation. They had warned him that the French army was more than capable of annihilating the comparatively meager German forces then available for the task. At the postwar Nuremberg war crimes trials, General Alfred Jodl, who had been on the German general staff at the time, testified, "Considering the situation we were in, the French covering army could have blown us to bits."

But locked into their Maginot Line theology, the French were reluctant to act, and the official British view was summed up by veteran British diplomat Lord Lothian, who reasoned, "The Germans, after all, are only going into their own back garden." In truth, they were. But had the French, with British backing, done something about it, Hitler, his troops routed, humiliated in his first major international adventure, might well have been deposed by his generals and other senior figures in Berlin who secretly harbored serious reservations about the First World War corporal who was now their Fuehrer.

Alarmed by the Rhineland episode and continuing Nazi diatribes against Bolshevism, the Soviet Union called for an international conference to examine options for dealing with the German menace. But the British Foreign Office refused to accept that anything of consequence had happened, and the French were paralyzed by recollection of their dismal First World War experience. The United States expressed formal disapproval of Hitler's Rhineland move, but if the Europeans declined to act, it was hardly a matter for Americans to bother with. Though his armed forces were still comparatively impotent, the German dictator thus emerged triumphant from this gamble.

Two years after the Rhineland episode, Hitler was prepared to begin moving against his country's three eastern neighbors, Austria, Czechoslovakia, and Poland. On March 12, 1938, German tanks and troop-carrying trucks rolled across the Austrian border to "restore" that country to the German Reich. Britain and France ritually protested. But both countries had earlier signaled acceptance that a closer connection between Germany and Austria was likely sooner or later for historic reasons. After all, Hitler was himself Austrian by birth. If the inevitable coupling was going to happen anyway, there seemed little point in objecting overly strenuously if it took place earlier than anticipated, especially when ecstatically cheering crowds welcomed Hitler in Vienna, testifying to Austrian eagerness to be absorbed into the Third Reich.

With Austria painlessly annexed, Hitler next targeted Czechoslovakia, a much more risky operation. No one had earlier conceded his claim to territory there. But furiously denouncing the government in Prague for allegedly persecuting the German-speaking majority in the Czechoslovak province of Sudetenland, he demanded that the province immediately be granted autonomy. He did not trouble to deny that the next step after autonomy for Sudetenland would be its incorporation into the German Reich. Nor did he refrain from issuing fierce warnings that Germany would not stand quietly by if his demands were unfulfilled.

The Czechoslovaks were not about to succumb to threats. Though theirs was a much smaller country, they had a first-rate army of their own. What was more, they had friends. France was bound by treaty to come to their aid if they were attacked, and the Soviets were bound by treaty to do the same if called upon after France had begun fulfilling that treaty obligation.

*   *   *

By the time the Czechoslovak crisis began unfolding, Germans who disapproved of Hitler had been cowed into silence, driven into exile, or eliminated. But a group of high-ranking military officers, involved in or familiar with planning for the invasion of Czechoslovakia, were convinced that their country, under Hitler's stewardship, had embarked on a course of action that would ultimately lead to a war which Germany could not possibly win, and they aimed to stop him. They planned to arrest him and put him on trial for recklessly plunging Germany into a hopeless conflict for which, as in the First World War, its people and army would have to pay dearly.

Proper timing was crucial to their plot. Hitler was to be seized and placed in confinement under strong military guard, but only after he gave the order for the attack on Czechoslovakia to commence. The conspirators feared that his immense popularity among the German people would make a coup dangerously premature if it was launched before he had actually acted to plunge Germany into suicidal war. Among senior military men involved in the scheme were General Franz Halder, chief of the German General Staff; Admiral Wilhelm Canaris, chief of military intelligence; and the commanders of the Berlin military region, the nearby Potsdam garrison, and an armored division based not far from the capital which could be deployed to neutralize any SS troops that might attempt to rally to Hitler after his arrest and incarceration.

Though the coup was prepared in considerable detail, the conspirators believed that British and French cooperation was essential if they were to succeed. They were convinced that if the western democracies knuckled under to Hitler once more, his domestic position would be unassailable, their plot would be undermined, and Germany would be plunged into a losing war soon afterward. In August 1938, at great risk, they sent Ewald von Kleist, a highly respected wealthy landowner, on a secret mission to London to persuade British leaders to stand fast over Czechoslovakia.

Von Kleist was well received by Sir Robert Vansittart, chief diplomatic adviser at the Foreign Office, and Winston Churchill. But Churchill was in political eclipse at the time, and both he and Vansittart had already been struggling in vain against Chamberlain's appeasement policies. Their views were effortlessly overridden by those of Sir Nevile Henderson, the British ambassador in Berlin, who kept informing London that no matter what unseemly noises Hitler might make, he really had no intention of unleashing a war. Henderson dismissed the conspiracy against the German leader as unworthy of serious British consideration—which it might well have been in view of the conspirators' seemingly pathetic requirement that they receive foreign support before they could act at home.

The showdown for Czechoslovakia a few weeks later turned into a tragic farce. The British and French desperately sought ways to dissuade Hitler from taking action that might require them to come to Czechoslovakia's assistance. They sternly threatened him with the dangers of armed conflict, then pleaded with him to desist from military action, and ended at a top-level conference in Munich on September 29, 1938, by begging him to accept the Sudetenland province as a gift for not fulfilling his threat to go to war. American Ambassador William Bullitt in Paris told President Roosevelt that in their secret feverish consultations on how to give the German dictator what he wanted, British and French leaders were acting "like little boys doing dirty things behind the barn. . . . The prospects for Europe are so foul that the further we keep out of the mess the better."

A British chronicler of the period captured the undignified performance of the leaders of the western democracies with great vividness.

> Like frightened householders who hear a burglar below, the British and French governments discussed what preventative measures they should take, picked up a poker and then put it down again, shouted downstairs that if the burglar did not make off, they would fall upon him, or at least call the police; even considered parleying with him, perhaps proposing that if he left the fish knives, they saw no objection to his taking other cutlery in reason; at last, fell back on deriving what comfort they might from the thought that at any rate he did not know the formula for opening the safe.

But Hitler knew exactly what he wanted. In addition to the acquisition of more *Lebensraum* through the bullying methods he had perfected, he wanted further conquest and he wanted war. Armed struggle was central to his master-race

creed. And Germany—a nation with a sophisticated cultural
and economic history—required uninterrupted high-powered
momentum under the Nazis to keep superimposed Hitlerian
practices of government, economy, and social order from collapsing under the weight of their perversities. The German
economy was indeed under tremendous strain, fully stretched in
preparation for war and facing serious trouble unless conquest
provided industrial plunder and new sources of raw materials
and labor.

German propagandists prepared the next step. They
launched a campaign to undermine morale in the western democracies and terrify people there with the prospect of inevitable defeat at the hands of the German war machine. Selected
visitors to Germany were taken to military airfields and treated
to impressive displays by the Luftwaffe's new attack aircraft. Intelligence dispatches and the popular press reported—and exaggerated—the size and might of the German air force. When the
chief of the French Air Staff visited Germany, he and his entou-
rage "were taken from one airport to another. But faster than
they could travel, the arms were dismantled and then assembled
again in the next place." The impression was given that the Germans were far better armed than they actually were.

The French government was advised by its intelligence services that Paris itself might be heavily bombed the day war was
declared. The destruction of the city of Guernica by German
bombers during the Spanish Civil War was widely publicized as
an example of what might happen elsewhere. Rough calculations
by War Office officials in London indicated that hundreds of
thousands of civilians would be killed as soon as the Luftwaffe
turned loose its fleets of bombers on British cities. Horrifying
forecasts were made publicly by military experts.

> . . . in future warfare, great cities such as London will be
> attacked from the air, and a fleet of 500 aeroplanes each
> carrying 500 ten-pound bombs of, let us suppose, mustard
> gas, might cause 200,000 minor casualties and throw the
> whole city into panic within a half-an-hour of arrival. . . .
> London for several days will be one vast raving bedlam, the
> hospitals will be stormed, traffic will cease, the homeless will
> shriek for help, the city will be in pandemonium . . . the
> government will be swept away by an avalanche of terror.

Britain had already begun bracing itself for the worst. Partial mobilization of the armed forces had been ordered. Now rearmament was accelerated. Trenches were dug in London parks. Antiaircraft guns were shifted into position. Gas masks were distributed to the public. Cellars were requisitioned for air raid shelters and people were advised to arrange "refuge rooms" in their homes where they were likely to be safest when the bombs fell. Plans had been made to evacuate schoolchildren from the capital. Convinced war was imminent, some people left their homes and jobs in major cities and headed for safety to Wales and the west of England.

Hitler had no difficulty in seizing what was left of Czechoslovakia after Sudetenland had been split off from it. Abandoned by the western democracies, warned by them not to cause a fuss, demoralized, isolated, fragmented as a nation (Poland and Hungary seized the opportunity to bite off slivers of the country as well), their army effectively demobilized, the Czechoslovaks went down to defeat without a struggle. On March 15, 1939, German troops crossed their border. As they did so, two thousand German paratroopers landed at the Prague airport. By evening, Hitler was able to proclaim, "Czechoslovakia has ceased to exist!"

In view of what was to follow, a tremendous military defeat had been inflicted on the countries that would soon be forced to fight Germany, and not a shot had been fired. Before it had been betrayed and emasculated, Czechoslovakia had been able to field thirty-four trained, disciplined divisions of highly motivated troops. Hitler had only forty divisions at his disposal at the time. His mighty panzer phalanxes were still in the process of formation. General Fritz von Manstein later testified that Germany's border with France could not have been "effectively defended by us"; nor, he said, would the Czechoslovaks have been easily beaten had they resisted a German invasion.

It is true that Britain, hoping desperately for peace, had not yet been equipped for war. But despite Hitler's threats and harangues, neither had Germany been ready for a major conflict. As his generals knew, their country would not have been capable of taking on the armed forces of France and Czechoslovakia simultaneously, with the Soviet Union obliged by treaty to help, and with Britain (with its formidable Royal Navy) also compelled by reasons of national interest to join this reluctant alliance against Nazi Germany. It was a monumentally missed opportunity.

Czechoslovakia was, however, a turning point. Voices of outrage in the western democracies now drowned out those of the comparative few who still clung to the hope that appeasing Hitler would avert the devastation of war. Mournfully conceding that he had been deceived by the German dictator, Chamberlain promised unequivocally on March 31, 1938, that if Poland, which Hitler was pinpointing as his next major target, was attacked by the Germans, Britain would "at once . . . lend the Polish government all support in [its] power." The prospect of imminent, unavoidable, dreaded war now came to shroud the British consciousness like a pea-soup fog.

Foreboding was even more pervasive in France. Friendship between the French and the Poles had deep historic and cultural roots. It was buttressed by a detailed commitment by France to come to Poland's aid if it was attacked. The French government issued assurances that it would this time honor its obligations.

In Washington, the administration tried to seize upon growing popular revulsion against Hitler to undercut the strength of isolationist sentiment. President Roosevelt asked Congress to relax the provisions of the Neutrality Act so that he might respond to urgent requests from London and Paris for war supplies. But despite political arm-twisting by the White House, Congress still wanted no part of Europe's turmoil.

The Soviet Union also kept at a distance, though still not by its own choice. The French government was anxious to respond to continuing Soviet efforts to build a security alliance. British Foreign Minister Lord Halifax agreed that whatever its likely shortcomings, an arrangement between the western democracies and the Soviets might force Hitler to reconsider his expansionist aspirations. Efforts were made to pin down points of understanding and agreement with Moscow. But any possibility of a breakthrough was thwarted by Chamberlain's belief that Stalin's primary motive was to prod the capitalist powers "to tear each other to pieces."

Also standing in the way was Poland's unrelenting fear, suspicion, and hatred of the Russians. Without Poland's accord, agreement with Moscow would be pointless. If Soviet troops were barred by the Poles from crossing their land, Hitler would have nothing to fear from them. But when pressed, the Poles argued, "With the Germans we risk losing our liberty, but with the Russians we would lose our souls."

Weary of seeking to impress the British and French with their uncharacteristic displays of reasonableness and good intentions, the Soviets grew ever more convinced that the aim of the western democracies was to channel Nazi aggression in their direction. They began secretly exploring the possibility of an accommodation with Hitler. As their talks with the British and French dragged on inconclusively, their consultations with the Nazis raced toward a climax. Hitler was anxious to launch his invasion of Poland before his panzers had to cope with autumn mud, and he needed assurances that the Russians would not present problems as he went about pounding the Poles into submission. On August 23, 1939, Germany and the Soviet Union signed a nonaggression pact eliminating that danger.

Paris and London were staggered by the announcement. Word of talks between the Soviets and the Germans had filtered through. But not even the most dedicated anticommunist believed that Stalin would be capable of reaching agreement with the fascist thugs in Berlin who considered obliterating Bolshevism a primary objective and who publicly scorned Slavs as subhuman creatures. The entire political and military complexion of Europe was suddenly transformed. Hitler had no reason any longer to fear the emergence of a grand triple alliance against him. His armies were ready to roll. The Second World War was around the corner.

War

Nine days after the signing of the Nazi–Soviet nonaggression pact, on August 31, 1939, twelve inmates at a German concentration camp were made to don Polish army uniforms. They were then given fatal injections by SS doctors and their bodies were riddled with gunshot. Late that night, SS troops carried those bodies to a forest near the German side of the German-Polish border. There they arranged them to look as though they had belonged to a Polish unit which had made an armed intrusion on German territory and which had been driven back, abandoning its dead.

At about the same time, a squad of SS troops occupied the radio station in the German town of Gleiwitz, also close to the Polish border. They stayed there long enough for one of their number, a Polish-speaking German, to broadcast a speech in Polish calling for Poles to attack Germans and saying the time had come for a Polish-German showdown.

In response to these fabricated Polish incursions and provocations and the alleged mistreatment of Germans in Poland about which Hitler had been voicing outrage for months, Germany invaded Poland the following morning. At 5:00 A.M. on September 1, German aircraft bombed Polish military positions and installations near the border. An hour later, the German army rolled in strength into Poland. Forty infantry divisions and fourteen mechanized divisions quickly overran Polish border defenses and thrust forward toward the Polish heartland.

"The Polish State," Hitler explained, "refused the peaceful settlement which I desired. . . . Germans in Poland are per-

secuted with bloody terror and driven from their homes. . . . A
series of violations of the frontier, intolerable to a great power,
prove that Poland is no longer willing to respect the frontier of
the Reich."

This was the German leader's most daring gamble yet.
Once more his senior generals warned him that he was treading
a perilous path. He dismissed their fears as groundless, convinced that the usual utterings of outrage and alarm, and perhaps the mobilization of their armies, were the most that was to
be expected from the timid western democracies.

Such confidence was not shared by the German public. Like
other Europeans, most Germans personally recalled the grief of
the First World War when more than two million of their young
men had been killed and twice that number had been wounded.
Hitler's harangues and fabricated justifications could not keep
them from being deeply apprehensive about the invasion of Poland and the possibility that a new major war loomed.

An American correspondent in Berlin described ordinary
Germans as "nearer to real panic . . . than the people of any
other European country," presumably excluding the Poles that
day. Another correspondent described the jitteriness in the German capital on the first day of the war.

> At twilight the air raid siren went off—a long, wailing
> sound, invented especially for the end of the world. Every-
> one ran for cover like ants whose anthill has been carelessly
> kicked. Buses and cars froze to curbs. Ten minutes later,
> another siren released 4,000,000 people to walk and talk and
> hurry home to argue throughout the night whether it was
> practice or the real thing.

William Shirer, stationed in Berlin for CBS News, noted in
his diary, "The people cannot realize yet that Hitler has led
them into a world war. . . . On the faces of the people astonishment, depression. [There is] no excitement, no hurrahs, no
cheering, no throwing of flowers. . . ."

At first it seemed that Hitler would be proved right about
the timidity of the western democracies. Shilly-shallying was the
almost reflexive response of the British and French governments. They remained terrified that within hours of their finally
taking steps to stop Hitler, the Luftwaffe would reduce parts of

London and Paris to rubble. They had to consult together on what to do. The crisis had been escalating for months but they had neglected to draw up joint contingency plans. As German tanks rumbled across the Polish plain, French Foreign Minister Georges Bonnet toyed with the idea of a peace conference— another Munich, another betrayal of an ally.

In London, Chamberlain declared, "It now only remains for us to set our teeth and to enter upon this struggle." But frustration in the House of Commons at his failure to do more than only threaten Germany with war cut across rigid party loyalties which were, as they are today, usually enough to block collaboration between Conservatives and the opposition Labourites. When, on the day after the invasion, acting Labour Party leader Arthur Greenwood, not normally a favorite of the Conservatives, rose in the Commons to respond to a limp presentation by Chamberlain of the British view of the situation, a prominent Conservative called out to him, "Speak for England, Arthur." It was proof that a great many in Parliament were convinced that the prime minister no longer did so.

By the night of September 2, two days into the German invasion, pressure on the British government to stop hesitating became irresistible. So angry was the mood of the House of Commons that it seemed likely that Chamberlain would not survive in office another day unless action was finally taken against Hitler. The Royal Navy was anxious to make important dispositions it could make only if war was declared. Even the BBC had suspended its usual courtesies in reporting on Germany. It had stopped referring to the Fuehrer as Herr Hitler. As an expression of outrage, it was now calling him simply Hitler.

The mood in Britain tolerated no further delay. At 9:00 A.M. on September 3, the British ambassador in Berlin handed the Germans an ultimatum. Unless, by 11:00 A.M. that day, Germany gave satisfactory assurances that its troops would be promptly withdrawn from Poland, a state of war would exist between Britain and Germany.

No such assurances were received by the time the deadline expired, and Chamberlain, looking "crumpled, despondent and old," went on the BBC to mournfully tell the people of Britain that they were at war again. Having finally also issued its ultimatum to Hitler, France declared war on Germany six hours later. By that time, London had been subject to its first wartime air raid alarm. Sirens sounded, cars and buses stopped dead in the streets, and steel-helmeted wardens and police shepherded worried, frightened people to air raid shelters. Emergency squads hurriedly gathered to rush to where they might be needed. Antiaircraft balloons designed to foil enemy planes rose into the air over the capital. It was a false alarm, triggered by the air attaché at the French embassy heading home across the English Channel in a light aircraft without seeking permission from or notifying the appropriate authorities.

Convinced that the British and French would not fight for Poland no matter what gestures they made, Hitler was nevertheless badly shaken when they actually declared war. The bulk of his forces was tied down in Poland, his generals had warned him of the great risk he was incurring, and he was ceaselessly tormented by suspicions of treachery at home; he was stunned by the possibility that his thousand-year Reich might be shattered even before it had been properly established. The following days were to be an ordeal for him as he waited to see whether the Allies would confine their response to the invasion of Poland to hollow pronouncements.

It was the middle of the night Washington time when the news of the invasion of Poland reached the White House. President Roosevelt was awakened to be told what had happened. He had his senior aides awakened as well to discuss the situation. Before dawn, he approved messages to be sent to the governments of the western Allies, Poland, Germany, and Italy urging all concerned to refrain from air attacks on civilian centers. By then, Warsaw had already been bombed by the Luftwaffe.

Condemnation of the latest act of German aggression was virtually unanimous across the United States. Most isolationists were as outraged as interventionists and feared it would strengthen the hand of those urging the dispatch of badly needed supplies to the Allies. They intensified their insistence that the United States had to steer clear of Europe's infectious convulsions. Their view was spelled out by the *New York World Telegram*.

Here is one war about which we predict that historians will never dispute where blame lies. But we, who are so fortunate as to live on this side of the Atlantic—it is not for us at this time to assess the responsibility for the tragedy that has overtaken Europe. Rather should all our energies and all our resolutions turn to efforts to prevent our own involvement.

Undersecretary of State Sumner Welles said that "except in one or two sections," the country had "reached another climax of out-and-out isolationism. Popular feeling demanded that this government refrain from any action, and even from any gesture, which might conceivably involve the U.S. with the warring powers."

Roosevelt told a press conference that he hoped and believed the United States could stay out of the war and that "every effort will be made by the administration so to do." On September 3, the day Britain and France declared war on Germany, the president went on radio to tell the American people in one of his famous fireside radio chats that the war in Europe would inevitably have an effect on the United States. But that was as far as popular sentiment permitted him to go. He promised, "As long as it remains within my power to prevent, there will be no blackout of peace in the United States." Meantime, American tourists were besieging American embassies in London and Paris, seeking help to get home from places where "blackout" was not merely a metaphor and where bombs might soon be falling from the skies.

Within hours of declaring war, Britain took military action. The RAF bombed German naval vessels which had been spotted setting off from the port of Wilhelmshaven. It was not an overly successful raid, but because of persisting fear of Luftwaffe reprisals against British cities, not only was RAF Bomber Command ordered to refrain from following it with attacks on Germany itself, but France was urged by the British not to take "precipitate action" which might involve inflicting casualties on German civilians.

Concern in London about possible French "precipitate action" was misplaced. The French High Command displayed not the slightest intention of behaving boldly or hastily. Air Chief Marshal Sir Cyril Newall, the chief of the British Air Staff, told the War Cabinet he did not intend to look kindly on a request from Paris for the RAF's Air Striking Force to operate in close cooperation with the French army until the French began active operations of their own—and they showed no sign of doing so.

RAF bombers did make two minor bombing raids on German territory in the first days of the war. But they otherwise were limited to dropping propaganda leaflets, "to arouse the Germans to a higher morality," as Winston Churchill later noted dryly. With the Wehrmacht streaking across Poland and no significant response elicited from Poland's allies, those leaflets seemed unlikely to have much impact on either German morale or standards of morality. When it was suggested to Secretary of State for Air Kingsley Wood that incendiary bombs be dropped on the Black Forest, where the Germans were believed to have stored large amounts of munitions and arms, he huffishly demanded, "Are you aware it is private property?"

So carefully did the RAF steer clear of targets which might have been considered nonmilitary that it avoided dropping bombs on German railway yards through which troops and equipment were flowing. A squadron of bombers made a reconnaissance sweep over the north German port of Kiel and came under such heavy antiaircraft fire that it lost five of its planes, but it refrained from dropping its bombs on the warships in the harbor for fear of damaging privately owned port installations or injuring civilians working there.

However, Churchill, who had been among the most outspoken critics of appeasement, was brought into the War Cabinet as First Lord of the Admiralty and immediately began pressing for the Allies to seize the military initiative. His presence in Chamberlain's government lent it a pugnacity and determination which Chamberlain and his closest advisers could not generate, even after they had turned away from appeasing Hitler. Upon hearing that he had been appointed to the British government, Luftwaffe commander and Hitler crony Hermann Goering wearily conceded, "That means the war is really on."

Churchill urged that the RAF and the French army immediately begin coordinated operations against the Siegfried Line, Germany's West Wall, to relieve pressure on Poland. His proposal won general agreement from his cabinet colleagues, but Chamberlain still trod cautiously. Action which might at that stage have had meaningful consequences was limited instead to a request to Paris for consultations on the roles British and French forces would play in such operations.

However, a start was made in dispatching a British Expeditionary Force to be deployed in France. Infantry and support units were shipped across—two divisions in the first days of September, to be built up to ten divisions during the autumn and winter. Some reservists who had gone off to camp for their annual training sessions in August were sent over directly, without having a chance to return home to organize their affairs and take leave of their families. Many would never return.

In France, they were warmly received by the populace as their trains and trucks carried them across the country. In Paris, restaurants served up such specialties as Trout Chamberlain and bars hung out signs saying "English Beer Sold Here" and "Welcome Tommy," though few Tommies were able to get anywhere near the French capital. Most were shunted immediately into position in northern France near the Belgian border through which a German attack, if one was forthcoming against the French, was thought likely to materialize.

Back in Britain, the climate of foreboding had thickened perceptibly. Examining how the country had reacted to the declaration of war, an American diplomat reported to Washington, "In London, the universe had suddenly become fixed in rigid suspense."

Gone are the carefree days! Bayonets flash throughout England. Every important rail junction—every large station—bridges—tunnels—factories—all girded by cold steel. Little encampments and huts springing up along the railroads, housing the home guard army. . . . Soldiers, sailors and airmen, in uniform, walking in small parties here and there. . . . Public houses rather noisy and gay. John Bull is not yet beyond drowning his worries in a bit of the stuff. . . . A population grim, anxious, unhappy—but determined. . . . The bobbies are very strict about the black-out. Here or there a careless window flashes out, and the occupants hear about it promptly. A serious business this. . . . Sand bags are going in by the thousands. . . . Every cellar being examined for use as a shelter. . . . Evacuation. The children are gone [from London]. Many families are on the way. . . . Where are the idle rich? . . . In the Commons debate, a Labour spokesman remarked somewhat grimly that the rich are evacuating London while the laboring man and the poor must hang on. It is not entirely true. But I imagine there must be something in it.

The blackout was decreed from sunset to sunrise, a period that would grow increasingly long as autumn came on and moved toward winter. People were required to make arrangements for the lights of their motor vehicles to be dimmed. A ban was placed on the sounding of factory sirens and other similar signals, except to give warning of air raids. Poisonous snakes were killed at London's zoo to prevent their escape in case of air raid damage. Theaters and cinemas were ordered closed until further notice, including one movie house which had appropriately been showing the gunfight western *Dodge City*. But suggestions that they remain shut for the duration were rejected because of the adverse affect it might have on public morale.

Air raid precautions were tightened in Paris as well, and a crackdown was launched against possible fifth columnists. Blank spaces began appearing in France's censored press as the government sought to screen from the public anything that might undermine morale. But performances in Paris of the operetta *Rose Marie* had to be canceled because the male chorus line had been called to the colors.

The failure of Britain and France to go on the attack in earnest in response to Hitler's invasion of Poland was to prove to be a prodigious blunder. At the time, French forces alone far outnumbered German defenders on the Siegfried Line. The bulk of the German army and virtually all of the Luftwaffe were committed to the conquest of Poland. Along their border with France, the Germans fielded only eleven regular divisions backed up by twenty-three reserve divisions, not a company or battery of which had ever practiced with live ammunition. Against them, the French forces could deploy eighty-five divisions armed with twenty-five hundred tanks and ten thousand guns. Germany's West Wall was hardly an impregnable line of defense. In places it didn't even exist. German General Siegfried Westphal was amazed at the failure of France, having declared war, to take action.

During September there was not a single tank on the German Western front. The stock of ammunition would have lasted for three days in battle. We had no serviceable reserve in the rear. All the flying units of the Luftwaffe were in service in Poland, leaving only a few reconnaissance planes and obsolescent fighters available for the West. Every expert serving at the time in the Western army felt his hair stand on end when he considered the possibility of an immediate French attack. It was incomprehensible that no such attack should take place, that the appalling weakness of the German defense should be unknown to the French leaders.

It is true that General André-Gaston Pretelat, commander of the French Second Army Group, was instructed to begin operations across the French-German border. But he was told to confine those operations to reconnaissance and "minor attacks." He was informed by General Gamelin, "Our duty as an ally imposes on us the need to begin our operations beyond the frontier." That was hardly a ringing declaration of loyalty to Poland. The French still wished the war would go away.

That wasn't the way British newspaper readers were led to see things. A London *Daily Mail* correspondent reported from France, "There is not a village or a town throughout this fair land of sweeping cornfields, vineyards and pastures which does not show signs of great and disciplined military effort which has brought some 6,000,000 of her sons under arms. . . . I . . . have seen the rising of a nation in might and confidence." Headlines in London told of "FRENCH ARMY POURING OVER GERMAN BORDER."

That was a far from accurate account of what the army touted as the most powerful in the world was actually up to. French forces moved into the twelve-mile-wide no-man's-land between the Maginot Line and the Siegfried Line, an area which the Germans never intended to defend and where the opposition the French forces encountered consisted mostly of a few booby traps and minefields. By the time Warsaw fell to the Germans less than a month later, they had advanced no more than five miles beyond the French border, and they were pulled back into France soon after, because, it was explained, they were unlikely anymore to influence events in Poland.

A few days before the Poles surrendered, the High Command in Paris had finally reported that mobilization of the French army was sufficiently complete for France to be ready for the war the country had been nervously expecting for years. General Gamelin declared, "Soldiers of France, at any moment now a great battle may begin on which will depend once again the future of the country." But by then, not a few of his citizen-soldiers wondered what the point of it all was.

The failure of the Allies to disrupt the German blitzkrieg against Poland or make any other major military move against Hitler influenced the mood in Britain as well. Alfred Duff Cooper, soon to be minister of information, later recalled, ". . . people began to say that they were sorry for the Poles, but that there was nothing more to be done about it, and why should we go on fighting?"

American Ambassador Joseph Kennedy reported home from London that former Foreign Secretary Sir Samuel Hoare, who was known to be close to Chamberlain, seemed not at all disturbed by the possibility that after Hitler had finished with Poland, the German leader would seek an amicable way out of confrontation with Britain and France. Kennedy was convinced that Britain would be defeated in an all-out war and believed all responsible British leaders felt the same way, even if they pretended otherwise. Reporting to Washington on September 18, on a conversation with Chamberlain, Kennedy made his own view of the situation clear.

> After listening to it all, I came away with this one impression based on my experience: when I was in the [movie] picture business whenever a new picture was being shown for the first time in the projection room a few of the top side executives would go in to look at it before it was shown to anybody on the premises and when we came out the crowd would be gathered around to see what we thought of it and in my 4 years I have never seen any executive come out that did not say the picture was "great," and in all that time I have never seen the group that waited outside for the judgment ever wrong in deciding that the tone of the executives "great" meant it was really lousy; so while the word was always the same the real impression was gathered accurately. I draw a parallel from my picture experience to this conversation today. While Chamberlain did not say everything was great, he certainly did not want to give me the impression that everything was lousy, but nevertheless that is what I think it is.

Both the White House and the State Department were suspicious of Kennedy's analysis of the situation. Unlike his ambassador in London, Roosevelt did not see a hastily arranged armistice in Europe as a prize devoutly to be wished. He feared that the war might end "in a patched-up temporizing peace which would blow up in our faces in a year or two." Kennedy's pro-appeasement inclinations also conflicted with the strong anti-Nazi sentiments of both the president and Secretary of State Cordell Hull. Roosevelt told Henry Morgenthau, his secretary of the Treasury, "Joe always has been an appeaser and always will be an appeaser. If Germany . . . [made] a good peace offer tomorrow, Joe would start working on the King and his friend, the Queen, and from there on down, to get everybody to accept. He's just a pain in the neck to me."

It was partly because Kennedy had become "a pain" to Roosevelt that contrary to protocol, the president opened a personal correspondence with Churchill, over the heads of Prime Minister Chamberlain and Foreign Secretary Halifax. He wanted a clearer understanding of developments in the war as seen in London than either Chamberlain's ambassador in Washington or his own envoy in London could provide.

On September 17, in accordance with secret Soviet-Nazi arrangements, while Polish troops battled with Germans invading from the west, Soviet troops invaded Poland from the east. Resistance to them was quickly crushed, setting the stage for the country to be partitioned between the two invading powers. The failure of the British and French to mount a forceful response to the German invasion of the country at the beginning of the month had come as no surprise to Stalin. It confirmed his belief that the Allied powers had been counting on a German move against the Soviet Union rather than against themselves. If Britain and France tried to negotiate an armistice with the Germans, the Soviet Union was now certain to be a party to whatever share-out emerged from such dealings. The partition of Poland was also confirmation—if proof was still needed—that the western democracies could expect no help from the Soviet Union if they finally did join in all-out battle with the forces of Germany.

Rumors of an imminent German assault westward circulated with increasingly tiresome frequency during the months following the fall of Poland. Allied troops were repeatedly put on the alert and just as often stood down again. However, Lord

Gort, the British Expeditionary Force commander, was certain that the Germans were not about to launch their attack before the spring; unfavorable ground and cloud conditions during the late autumn and winter would hamper the operations of their tanks and aircraft.

Lord Gort (John Standish Surtees Prendergast Vereker before he succeeded to his father's title) had been appointed to command the BEF the day war was declared. There was much grumbling about the appointment. His personal valor in combat during the First World War, when he had won the Victoria Cross for leading his men in battle after being seriously wounded, was unquestioned. But several senior figures doubted his leadership abilities. His appointment, over the heads of a number of generals senior to him in rank and experience, sparked considerable resentment. General Sir Edmund Ironside, the senior officer on active service, a dynamic, vastly experienced, but aging soldier, had expected to get the BEF command and was deeply disappointed when made to settle instead for becoming Gort's successor as Chief of the Imperial General Staff, which he considered little more than a glorified desk job. Ironside was convinced that Gort didn't "even begin to know how to run the bigger things."

Major General Sir Edward Spears, soon to be sent to Paris to be Churchill's personal representative there, thought Gort to be a trustworthy, steadfast, and courageous but "not very clever man." General Alan Brooke, one of Gort's three BEF corps commanders, was deeply jealous of Gort and "had no confidence in his leadership." Brooke did not consider Gort capable of exercising sufficient independent initiative. The question of independent initiative was to be a matter of critical importance in view of the fact that Gort and the BEF had, to Brooke's horror, been put under French command because of the comparatively small British ground force contribution to the Allied cause—one-tenth the size of that of France. He was to take his orders from General Gaston Billotte, commander of the French First Army Group, who was in turn subordinate to General Alphonse Georges, commander of Allied forces in the northeast of France, who was himself subordinate to the supreme Allied commander, General Gamelin.

With the Maginot Line fortifications blocking the Germans off from direct access to France, it was Gamelin's firm belief that the attack on his country would come by way of Belgium, along substantially the same route Kaiser Wilhelm's armies had taken in the First World War. He would foil this assault by swiveling the forces he had poised along the French-Belgian border—including the BEF—into Belgium when the Germans launched their offensive. They would be stopped cold there before they could reach French soil.

The Belgians were understandably anxious to know Allied plans. But striving desperately to maintain their neutrality and fearing to provoke Hitler's displeasure, they refused to countenance the precautionary positioning of Allied troops on their territory. They even refused to let Allied officers reconnoiter the terrain in which they would have to fight if the Germans did invade their country, as intelligence reports said Hitler intended soon to do. Cursory inspection of landscape by a few officers in civilian clothes pretending to be tourists was all that was permitted. The Belgians even refused to agree to staff consultations between their own and Allied officers. With contingency planning for combat fashioned from afar and with limited knowledge of geographic factors, Allied tactical calculations were patchy at best and, to the dismay of some staff officers, sheer guesswork in some places.

By mid-September, when his victory over Poland appeared to be beyond doubt, Hitler had begun shunting troops and equipment to the western front to prepare to attack westward. He did not intend to wait for the French and British to seize the initiative. Once more, his generals were thrown into despair. An autumn attack, they maintained, would be folly. The days were too short. Despite the transfer westward of forces no longer needed in Poland, the Allied powers were, on paper at least, still stronger than the Germans. They would now be able to field 114 divisions to 98 for the Germans. Fog would inhibit the use of attack aircraft. The weather would make ground conditions unsuitable for tank operations. Though Poland had been quickly defeated, potentially disastrous mistakes had been made during the conquest. Ammunition for advancing troops and replacement parts for the panzers had been in short supply. In crushing a small nation, it was possible to make good such shortcomings. It would be a different matter when taking on the mighty French army and its British allies.

General Halder recorded in his diary that none of the "higher headquarters" believed the offensive had "any prospect of success," and even the trusted Goering favored delay. He hoped that peace feelers he had put out to Britain and France through neutral intermediaries might permit Germany to consolidate its latest gains before undertaking further action. But Hitler was intoxicated by his triumph in the east. Enraged by the timidity of his generals—some of them again plotted to depose him and again failed to execute that plot—he insisted that the attack westward be launched as soon as possible. At the same time, he attempted to lull the Allies into complacency by publicly issuing an appeal for peace.

> My chief endeavor has been to rid our relations with France of all trace of ill will. . . . I have always expressed to France my desire to bury forever our ancient enmity and bring together these two nations, both of which have such glorious pasts. . . . I have devoted no less effort to the achievement of Anglo-German understanding, nay, more than that, of an Anglo-German friendship. . . . I believe even today that there can only be real peace in Europe and throughout the world if Germany and England come to an understanding.

A rumor broadcast by German radio that a new British government was taking office in London and would be prepared to come to terms with Hitler, and that an armistice between Germany and the Allies was in fact in the making, touched off a spasm of relief and elation among the German people. It was short-lived. The story was without substance. Recalling Hitler's earlier empty assurances, Chamberlain told Parliament that the German leader could not and would not be trusted. French Premier Daladier felt the same way.

This time the judgment of the French and British leaders was not mistaken. On October 10, even before their rebuffs to his peace appeal had been formally delivered to Berlin, Hitler had commanded his generals to make detailed preparations "for an attacking operation" against France.

> This attack must be carried out . . . at as early a date as possible. . . . The purpose will be to defeat as strong a part of the French operational army as possible, as well as allies

fighting by its side, and at the same time to gain as large an area as possible in Holland, Belgium and northern France as a base for conducting a promising air and sea war against England.

The attack was scheduled for November 12. The Allies were informed as much. Colonel Hans Oster of German army intelligence, a dedicated anti-Nazi bitter at the failure of his superiors to carry out their planned conspiracy against Hitler, passed a warning of it to Dutch and Belgian contacts. But it proved to be a false alarm. Hitler was overruled—not by his generals but by the weather. Forecasts by the German meteorological service persuaded him to delay the big offensive. He ordered that his troops be kept on the alert "to exploit favorable weather conditions immediately." But to his increasing exasperation, favorable weather conditions remained elusive. He was obliged to put off the offensive right through the autumn and winter, a total of eleven times!

It was a savage winter, the coldest in years. Rivers iced over. Troops shivered in their forward bivouacs. All the Allied forces could do was dig in where the frozen ground permitted and await Hitler's next move. Such inaction was out of character for Churchill. From the moment he had joined Chamberlain's War Cabinet, he had been its most assertive and dynamic member, repeatedly urging greater effort in the prosecution of the war. He sparkled with ideas, proposals, and schemes for beating the Germans. To the irritation of some of his cabinet colleagues, he did not confine his attentions to his official realm at the Admiralty but explored all areas of possible military and diplomatic advantage in the war. He was a stirring speaker and phrasemaker, and his oratorical flourishes in Parliament and on public occasions aroused much admiration. He appeared to be the only member of the cabinet capable of delivering a truly fighting speech. With Chamberlain appearing increasingly despondent and worn out, there was talk that he would take over as prime minister before much longer.

That prospect attracted less than unanimous acclaim in the Conservative Party, many of whose senior figures took exception to Churchill's past performance as a maverick who had switched political parties to suit the moment. They also objected to the flamboyant manner in which he now upstaged Chamberlain and other War Cabinet members. Presented with the suggestion that Churchill might indeed become prime minister, a prominent Tory went so far as to pray "that such a catastrophe will be averted." Hearing one of his inspiring radio orations, a junior member of Chamberlain's staff was led to conclude that Churchill would become prime minister before the war was over, but he feared that "judging from his record of untrustworthiness and instability, he may in that case lead us into the most dangerous paths."

As autumn had given way to winter, Hitler had grown worried that the pace of events was slipping from his control. He feared the Allies might seize the initiative by launching an offensive to capture Germany's Ruhr industrial basin. If they did attack, it would completely upset his calculations, and if they succeeded in seizing the Ruhr, his war machine would soon stagger to a halt.

Exasperated, anxious, suspicious of advice to the contrary, fed up with delays, Hitler decided he would wait no longer. He commanded that the planned combined land and air attack on the Allies be launched through Belgium and Holland on January 17, 1940. Detailed preparations were made, and the attack would have taken place, and perhaps resulted in disaster for the German army and Hitler, if an accident had not forced another delay.

On January 10, as the forces which were to invade the Low Countries were about to move into attack position, a German military plane on a domestic flight lost its way in the clouds and made a forced landing across the border in Belgium. The pilot was Major Erich Hoenmanns, a reserve Luftwaffe officer on active duty, who had been trying to find an excuse to get to Cologne to see his wife there. His passenger, who gave him that excuse, was Major Helmut Reinberger, a staff officer of the German 7th Airborne Division. Reinberger was bound for Cologne on urgent duty but had been prevented by rail congestion from getting there by surface transport. Documents he was carrying included top-secret Luftwaffe operational instructions for the coming invasion.

Stepping out of the plane and realizing that it had touched down in Belgium rather than across the border in Germany,

Reinberger immediately tried to set fire to those documents. Belgian soldiers who rushed to the plane when it landed quickly extinguished the blaze. When the two Germans were taken to the local military headquarters for interrogation, Reinberger seized the charred documents, which had been put on a table, and thrust them into a stove. Again he was foiled, this time by a quick-acting Belgian officer who, despite burns to his hand, managed to salvage enough of the papers to reveal that they were plans, replete with maps, for the German assault on Belgium and Holland. They were immediately passed on to senior Belgian officers.

The Belgians were at that stage so jittery about the possibility of a German attack that their initial conclusion was that it was a setup, a plant, possibly to trick them into inviting Allied forces into Belgium and thereby provide Hitler with an excuse to launch his invasion of their country. However, the documents seemed to confirm intelligence reports from other quarters, including well-placed anti-Nazi military officers in Berlin, which told of an imminent German attack. Besides, a close examination of both the circumstances and the way the two captured Germans behaved seemed to indicate that this was no attempted deception. The two officers appeared genuinely troubled by the situation in which they found themselves, with good reason. Hoenmanns had been making an unauthorized flight and Reinberger knew that he should not have been carrying those plans on the trip.

The German air attaché in Belgium was very anxious to speak to the two men as soon as he could gain permission from the Belgian authorities. When he did, in a room that was bugged by the Belgians, the first question he asked was whether the documents had been destroyed. Reinberger, fearing for his military career and probably his life, assured him that they had.

The German High Command was, however, not convinced that this was true. Sudden Belgian troop movements led it to conclude that the plans Reinberger had been carrying had been recovered intact and that they had very likely been passed on to the British and French. Although Goering consulted a fortune-teller who assured him that this had not happened, Hitler was furious and reluctantly accepted that there was no alternative but to delay further the assault on the west so that strategy for the operation could be reviewed. (Reinberger and Hoenmanns were fortunate not to be handed back to Germany. They were soon to be sent to Canada as prisoners of war and stayed there for the duration.)

The Belgians had indeed passed details of the captured documents on to the Allied senior commanders, who immediately put their forces on the alert. They were, however, still barred by the Belgians from taking up defensive positions within Belgium. The French government pleaded with them to be realistic. Allied troops, vehicles, and horses were ready to move; they could not be kept on the alert indefinitely. But the Belgians still hoped that Hitler would refrain from attacking them if they clung faithfully to their neutral status. The Belgian High Command even renewed orders that *any* foreign forces trying to enter Belgium were to be resisted, regardless of their purpose, leading to the absurd possibility that rather than fighting the Germans, Belgian troops would find themselves doing battle with the French and British who were poised to rush to the defense of their country.

The Allied ground forces deployed in France to meet the expected German attack were organized in three army groups. Elements of the French Second and Third army groups were positioned to guard the German-French border, with some of the most elite French forces deployed in or behind the Maginot Line, where, because of the fortifications, they were least needed. Barred from Belgium, the First Army Group, including nine divisions of the British Expeditionary Force (one of the BEF's divisions was shifted south to help man French defenses near the German border), was deployed along the "Little Maginot Line," from the end of the Maginot fortifications along the French-Belgian border to the sea. These were the troops who were braced to swivel swiftly into Belgium to block a German breakthrough once Hitler had launched his main attack there.

With the approach of spring, all concerned realized that the quiet months of watchful waiting would soon come to an explosive conclusion. As the German general staff prepared for its western offensive, Allied attention focused on Scandinavia and particularly on Swedish iron ore shipments to Germany—by rail from the mines at Gällivare in Sweden to the port of Narvik in Norway and then by ship through Norwegian territorial waters to north German ports. Without that ore, the German war effort would collapse. Churchill had been pressing Chamberlain to let the Royal Navy mine Norwegian waters to block the passage of the German ore freighters. British control of the Norwegian coastline was, he said, a strategic objective of crucial importance. The French felt the same way and were also anxious for the Allies to turn Germany's northern flank in the hope of keeping the war from reaching France.

The conquest of Norway was not high on Hitler's list of priorities. He was preoccupied with preparations for his long-delayed westward offensive. Nor did his racial fantasies incline him to rush into subjugating Teutonic peoples in the north before he had imposed his will on lesser species elsewhere. But he realized that if the Allies gained a foothold in Norway, which German intelligence reported they were contemplating, it would present Germany with serious problems. "The enemy," Hitler said, "would [then] find himself in a position to advance on Berlin and break the backbone of our two fronts." Both the Allies and the Germans therefore drew up plans to secure a strategic advantage in Norway. Denmark was included in the German plans so that the Luftwaffe could acquire forward fighter bases there.

On April 8, Chamberlain finally acquiesced to Churchill's persistent urgings that the Norwegian territorial waters be mined. It was expected that the Germans would respond by trying to seize key Norwegian ports, a move the Allies intended to preempt by dispatching forces of their own to occupy those ports before the Germans could get there. All of this was to take place within the next few days. British troops to be landed in Norway were already boarding at Rosyth in Scotland on vessels that were to carry them there.

But Hitler moved first. At 4:30 in the morning on April 9, his emissaries in Oslo and Copenhagen roused the foreign ministers of Norway and Denmark from their respective beds to offer their countries "the protection of the Reich." They were informed that "any resistance would have to be, and would be broken by all possible means." German invading forces were already on their way.

Denmark, whose people had managed to avoid being caught up in war for almost a century and who prided themselves on maintaining virtually no army to speak of, capitulated without a struggle. It was a small, flat country, the largest part of which bordered on northern Germany and was therefore vulnerable to lightning land attack. Less vulnerable to immediate conquest in their much larger, mountainous homeland, the Norwegians refused to succumb. The resistance of their armed forces was aided by a brigade of British troops. But superior German tactics implemented earlier, relentless Luftwaffe bombing and strafing attacks, and the first use of paratroops in the war gave Hitler's forces advantages in Norway that could not be overcome. The Allies managed to seize the strategically located port of Narvik from the Germans, but only temporarily. After a series of setbacks, they were soon to be compelled to evacuate their forces from Norway and the country was forced to endure the affliction of Nazi occupation till the end of the war.

France had been in political turmoil right through the autumn and winter. The failure of the French armed forces to respond convincingly to the invasion of Poland was widely seen as reflecting the spinelessness of the government in Paris. Politicians seized upon the smoldering war crisis to blame each other for France's predicament. Ministers intrigued against each other. Efforts were made to lure eighty-three-year-old Marshal Henri Philippe Pétain, the First World War hero serving as ambassador to Spain, into the government, to lend it stature. Pétain insultingly rejected the suggestion, dismissing the government he was being urged to join as unworthy of holding office.

The "Winter War" which had just ended, in which the Soviet Union attacked and defeated Finland, had aroused strong passions in France. A small, self-reliant democracy, Finland had refused to make territorial concessions demanded by the Soviets and had fought against its giant neighbor with spirit and obstinacy before being overwhelmed. The failure of the Allies to come to the aid of the Finns, despite solemn pronouncements that they would do so, provoked particular bitterness in France. Premier Daladier was forced to resign on March 20 because of it. Diminutive, dapper, sharp-tongued Paul Reynaud who had been Daladier's minister of finance, emerged in his place as French leader, determined to block the efforts of defeatists in Paris to undermine the country's morale and fortitude and to lead it to victory over Hitler.

Relieved that a man unlikely to be cowed by the German dictator was in charge, Reynaud's supporters were, however, startled by some of the new premier's eccentricities. Soon after he took office, he was stricken with pulmonary congestion and was ordered to bed by his doctor. Despite the gravity of the situation, to the astonishment of some and the dismay of others, he permitted his mistress, the overbearing, high-strung Countess Hélène de Portes, to act in his place while he was indisposed. She did not make a serious impact on the situation but it is conceivable that she might have. France was at war, but a visitor found this diplomatically inexperienced, totally unqualified political dabbler behind Reynaud's desk, attended by generals, members of the Chamber of Deputies, and senior officials, she doing most of the talking, "advising and giving orders." Countess de Portes and Daladier's mistress, Marquise Jeanne de Crussol, detested each other for personal and political reasons, and both, hungry for power and position, fueled the bitter rivalry between Reynaud and Daladier, who had now become minister of war.

Reynaud hadn't been premier long when he had to face up to what was turning into the Allied too-little-too-late blundering in Norway. He was sharply critical of the way the British, who had masterminded the operation, were handling it, without proper preparation, without speed, and without an understanding of how to see it through. Unlike most members of his cabinet, the new French premier was fundamentally an Anglophile, but he feared that the failure to commit the necessary forces at the right time reflected a "lack of brains in the British government and British High Command."

In London, the miscarriage of the Norway operation also aroused anger and resentment. Men and ships were being lost there, and the bid to seize the initiative from Hitler was turning into a fiasco. Chamberlain's government was held responsible. But the criticism quickly extended to beyond the costly, humiliating setback in Norway. So widely acclaimed when he returned from Munich after giving Hitler carte blanche in Czechoslovakia, Chamberlain was now as resoundingly denounced for Britain's failure to prepare adequately for Hitler's onslaught in Europe, for the gloom and foreboding which was shrouding his country, and for the inability of his government to provide dynamic leadership at a time when the Germans were expected momentarily to launch their offensive on the western front.

As a member of Chamberlain's cabinet, Churchill was as

responsible as anyone and more responsible than most for mistakes in the Norwegian operation. But because of the unwavering stand he had taken against Hitler all along and his efforts to inspire a defiant we-will-win spirit among his countrymen, he managed to avoid being tarred with the same brush as the prime minister.

Chamberlain's continuing inability to transform himself into a rousing leader of a nation at war, combined with his early record of catering to Hitler, tried the patience of the House of Commons. His position became untenable. Despite the solid majority enjoyed by his Tory Party in Parliament, he could no longer rally enough support there to control the situation. On May 7, 1940, as German armies were deploying for their repeatedly postponed western front offensive, Leopold Amery, a prominent Tory and a privy councillor, rose in the Commons during a debate on the Norwegian campaign and, invoking an almost biblical denunciation borrowed from Oliver Cromwell, mercilessly told Chamberlain: "You have sat too long here for any good you have been doing. Depart, I say, and let us have done with you. In the name of God, go!"

When such scorn and rejection could be uttered by a distinguished member of the prime minister's own party, there could no longer be any doubt that he would have to step down. Chamberlain recognized as much and prepared to resign. Churchill remained a strong candidate to succeed him. More than any other figure in Britain, he had assumed the stance of a wartime leader, someone who could inspire people with martial ardor. But Lord Halifax, not as burdened as Chamberlain by the image of futile appeasement of Hitler, was widely considered the prime minister's natural successor. A much-respected figure with a reputation for considerable intellect, firmness of spirit, and wide experience in international affairs, Halifax had strong support among the Tories in Parliament. Several leading Labourites also preferred Halifax to Churchill, the only other likely candidate for the job. Churchill had often offended them with his barbed ridicule of the Labour Party and its policies. As Chamberlain prepared to step down, it was not clear whether Halifax or Churchill would take over from him as the man in command of Britain's fate in the war.

While the British parliamentary crisis was being brought to a boil, France was once more also undergoing a political convulsion. On May 9, ignoring still another intelligence report of an imminent German attack, Premier Reynaud had delivered an angry diatribe against the military High Command of his country. He had long believed that the French army needed a more forceful, more astute commander in chief than Gamelin. Reynaud had earlier decided to put Gamelin out to pasture. Now he demanded the general's immediate removal, citing partial French responsibility for the Allied fiasco in Norway as last-straw justification. Reynaud declared that if France continued to be subjected to the kind of military leadership Gamelin had provided, Hitler was certain to win the war.

This vilification of the French commander was immediately challenged by Minister of War and former Premier Daladier. Daladier called Gamelin an excellent military chief and denounced Reynaud for not giving the general an opportunity to defend himself against the abuse to which he was being subjected. He insisted Gamelin could not be blamed for the Norwegian debacle. That, he maintained, had been the exclusive responsibility of the British.

Unable to gain support for his position from other members of his cabinet, Reynaud dissolved the government to make way for the appointment of a new cabinet over which he would be able to exercise greater control. But Gamelin did not intend to wait for that to happen and to be formally fired and disgraced. He immediately composed an anguished letter of resignation. It was impossible for him to serve any longer under a head of government who thought so little of him.

As the commander of Allied forces in France wallowed in an agony of resentment and humiliation and as the premier of France retreated into seclusion convinced he had his political enemies on the run, German commanders on the western front made ready to make their squabbles look very petty indeed within a matter of hours.

Breakthrough

On the morning of May 10, 1940, Belgian troops manning Fort Eben Emael near the Belgian-German border were braced for trouble. Intelligence reports the night before had alerted their officers to an imminent German assault. They were confident they could deal with it.

The huge fort, towering over the Albert Canal near its confluence with the Meuse River, was the most up-to-date fixed fortification in the world. Measuring 770 by 900 yards and completed only five years earlier, it bristled with modern defense refinements. Constructed of steel and concrete, it was manned by a battalion of specially trained troops and turreted for artillery, antitank guns, light cannon, and machine guns. It was equipped with electrical generators that made it independent of external power supply. It housed vast ammunition storage compartments, elevators to deliver ammunition to gun positions, a communications center, and a hospital. The doors to its various compartments and sections could be quickly bolted with steel beams to prevent them being forced. Its walls were encircled by barbed wire and, where it did not front on the Albert Canal, by antitank obstacles and minefields as well.

So formidably constructed and powerfully armed, Eben Emael—named after a nearby village—was believed by all who had inspected its features to be capable of keeping an enemy at bay no matter how fierce his attack. What was more, the fort's commander was confident he could retain command of the adjoining border area too; his guns could knock out nearby bridges if they were in danger of being seized by the enemy. It seemed as though all possible contingencies had been taken into account. What was not expected was the unique form the assault on the fort would take and the direction from which it would come.

As dawn broke, troop-carrying gliders which had been lifted off from an airfield at Ostheim across the border in Germany silently swept out of the sky, and with amazing precision, nine of them landed right on top of the fort. The seventy-eight German shock troops they carried were led by Sergeant Helmut Wenzel; the glider carrying Lieutenant Rudolf Witzig, commanding the operation, had broken its tow rope and landed elsewhere. The airborne invaders leaped from their gliders and immediately proceeded with the exercise for which they had been in rigorous training for more than six months in Germany and on previously seized Czechoslovak fortifications. Confounding the defenders within the fort by their surprise arrival, using flamethrowers and newly developed powerful hollow-charge explosives, they effectively immobilized Eben Emael in less than an hour. It was a bold, imaginative exploit carried out with great resourcefulness and daring. Belgian troops deployed nearby rushed to dislodge this comparative handful of invaders but were foiled first by Stuka dive-bombing attacks and then by the arrival of German paratroop reinforcements.

Meantime, other German troop-filled gliders also came to ground as planned in Belgium west of the Albert Canal. The troops they disgorged weren't quick enough to prevent Belgian guards from blowing up a bridge across the canal. But they seized two others spanning the waterway and quickly went about making good their control of the border region. The incapacitated, beleaguered defenders of Eben Emael formally surrendered on the morning of May 11. Within thirty-six hours, the German invaders were able to overcome border obstructions that had been expected to hold them back for at least a week until Allied reinforcements could dig in at strong defensive positions farther back.

While Belgium's border defenses were being overrun, Holland, which had also attempted to preserve its neutrality, was reeling from a German assault as well. In an operation timed to synchronize with the invasion of Belgium, Hitler's bombers launched surprise attacks on installations at the three major Dutch airfields—sparing the runways so that they might be put to immediate use by the Luftwaffe after capture. Airborne troops were then quickly glided or parachuted down to take control of those airfields and seize other strategic points in the country. The intention was to leapfrog defensive positions at the canals which crisscrossed Holland, the natural barriers which, like the Albert Canal near the Belgian-German border, could obstruct the advance of an invading force.

Having launched this fierce attack on the Dutch, the Germans explained that, as with Belgium, theirs was a preventive strike, undertaken to block planned British and French aggression. They demanded that the Dutch immediately cease all resistance. Fighter planes were dispatched to strafe the streets of The Hague to demonstrate to Dutch leaders that Hitler was determined to have his way.

French and British installations in northern France had come under aerial attack as well. Awakened at dawn by the crump of falling bombs, troops for whom the war till then had seemed a charade hurriedly crammed themselves into their uniforms and rushed to seek shelter. At installations which were spared initial bombing, troops were roused early as well as soon as word of the bombing spread. They were quickly formed up to await orders. The variously named long wait—the Phony War, Bore War, *drôle de guerre, Sitzkrieg*—was over. Almost as if he believed the play-acting might have gone on forever, a British officer stationed near Lille just south of the Belgian border noted in his journal, "So there's to be a real war after all." It would prove more agonizingly real than he or anyone else imagined.

This, finally, was the dreaded commencement of the replay, magnified a dozen times over, of the Great War, the memory of which remained alive in the hearts and memories of countless people across Europe and elsewhere. That morning's orchestrated German onslaught was the overture to a struggle that would convulse virtually all of Europe for the next five years, devastate other parts of the world as well, claim tens of millions of lives, leave hundreds of millions grieving, and end European world dominance by bringing new superpowers center stage in global affairs.

"The battle which begins today," Hitler proclaimed on the morning of his westward march of conquest, "will decide the fate of the German nation for the next thousand years." As the first heady reports of the day's operations came in, the German Fuehrer, though jittery as always, had reason to believe the Nazi millennium he had forecast had in fact begun. His armed forces reported no initial setbacks, no serious bungling, no resistance that had not been overcome. They appeared well on their way to achieving their immediate objectives. They had not yet engaged in any major clashes with the mighty French or the British, but, added to Hitler's unbroken chain of previous triumphs, first impressions of how the battle was going fortified German troop morale and confidence. In a quick note to his wife the next day, General Erwin Rommel, commander of the 7th Armored Division, was able to boast, "Everything wonderful so far." General Halder, the German army's chief of staff and former anti-Hitler conspirator, noted in his diary that "reports on the whole corroborate satisfactory picture developing. . . ."

Meantime, the Allies were no longer barred from deploying their forces on Belgian territory. Having been thrust unwillingly into Allied ranks and aware of how feeble were its own military resources, Belgium had been calling desperately since dawn of May 10 for help from France and Britain. The Allied High Command had been receiving word of ominous German troop movements right through the previous night and, despite the succession of earlier false alarms, was able to respond quickly. At six o'clock in the morning, the First Army Group—composed of three French armies and the British Expeditionary Force—received orders to swivel into Belgium from the positions they had held along the French-Belgian border. These forces were to deploy as planned along the Dyle-Meuse River line in Belgium to stop the main enemy thrust dead in its tracks, wear the Germans down, and then drive them back. It was sound textbook soldiering.

In London and Paris, senior military and civil defense councils gathered in emergency session. Plans had to be made for increasing war production, accelerating mobilization, and intensifying military training programs. Civil defense had urgent priority. In Britain, people were reminded by the BBC that air raid warnings were given "by means of sirens and hooters sounding a warbling note in some places and short intermittent blasts in others." They were instructed that if caught in the open during a raid and unable to reach a shelter, they should lie on the ground and cover their heads with their arms. They were to have buckets of water ready at home and at work to deal with incendiaries.

In France, Premier Reynaud broadcast to the French people a call to arms: "It is now France's turn to show the way with her troops and planes. . . . France has drawn the sword." Meantime, French people were warned to be vigilant against fifth columnists and to beware, in case of air raids, of certain kinds of German bombs that did not explode until an hour or more after being dropped.

During the first day of the German offensive, and for several days afterward, the full significance of what was happening on the battlefield was not fully grasped in either London or Paris. Close attention was of course paid to reports from the front as they came in. But despite the extreme perils of the moment, attention in both Britain and France was not undivided. Leaders and officials in both countries were distracted by the political crises paralyzing their senior commands. Until those were resolved, neither government could concentrate fully on dealing with the German onslaught.

In London that morning, Prime Minister Chamberlain, having previously reluctantly agreed that he would have to resign, changed his mind. With the war escalating dangerously, he decided that as a matter of honor it would be wrong for him to leave his post. The emergency, he thought, would neutralize the clamor for his resignation. He was wrong. The latest developments made it important to guarantee national unity by forming a government that would include senior representatives of the opposition parties, and that was something Chamberlain could not do. The Labour Party wanted no part of him and told him so. To his surprise and humiliation, several prominent Tories also made it plain that because of the German offensive, it was essential that he resign quickly and without fuss. Abandoned and repudiated by people whose support he needed, he was left with no choice but to have his car summoned and to make the journey up Whitehall and along the Mall to Buckingham Palace to inform King George VI that he was stepping down.

Halifax and Churchill remained the favored, indeed the only, prime ministerial candidates. But Halifax had strong doubts about taking the job. He believed that, though not impossible, it would be difficult for him to perform the duties of prime minister from his perch in the House of Lords. As a peer of the realm, he was constitutionally barred from even stepping onto the floor of the House of Commons, where the main business of government was transacted. He would have to function in the Commons through ministerial subordinates. He felt that he would "speedily become more or less honorary Prime Minister, living just outside the things that really mattered."

Halifax might nevertheless have considered the job if there had been some way to keep the grandiloquent, opinionated Churchill, the irrepressible gadfly with a million ideas and ceaseless proposals, the most energetic symbol of British defiance, out of his cabinet, where he might overshadow the prime minister and complicate his control of the situation. According to Maurice Cowling, a Cambridge University chronicler of the period, "It was only the realization that Churchill would make a great deal of trouble if he [became prime minister] that made [Halifax] insist on Churchill grasping the nettle."

Though he had his dedicated supporters, Churchill remained an object of suspicion and even dislike to many Tories in the House of Commons who found his theatrical declamatory flourishes unseemly and could not forgive his earlier cavalier attitude toward party loyalty. Nevertheless, he was the preferred choice of several senior parliamentary figures. He had been a government minister during the First World War, and people with wartime ministerial experience were in short supply. When, to Chamberlain's regret, Halifax disqualified himself as a candidate, Churchill became the only one likely to command the support of a majority in Parliament and therefore the only possible choice to take over as prime minister.

Chamberlain informed King George as much. The king was not pleased. Nevertheless, that evening, as the first day of the fighting war in the west drew toward a close, Churchill was duly summoned to the palace to receive the king's commission. The following day the king wrote in his diary, "I cannot yet think of Winston as PM. . . . I met Halifax in the garden [of Buckingham Palace] & I told him I was sorry not to have him as PM."

Had it not happened the way it did, had Halifax agreed to become prime minister, the course the war was to take and the fate of Britain, Europe, and the world might have been very

different, as will be seen. As it was, when congratulated on his
appointment by his bodyguard, Detective W. H. Thompson,
while returning from the palace, Churchill replied, "I hope it is
not too late. I am very much afraid that it is."

There would be other moments in the months that followed
when he would drop his guard of flamboyant confidence and reveal the anxiety he felt about German military successes. But in
characteristic fashion, Churchill, sixty-five years old when he
took office, set energetically to work immediately after returning
from the palace as prime minister. Before that first day was
out—it ended at 3:00 the next morning for him—he had laid the
groundwork for a government of national unity and was well
into the formation of his cabinet.

The pressures Churchill came under in taking command of
his country at one of the most perilous moments in its history
were compounded by the undisguised resentment he faced from
those in his own Conservative Party who considered him a mischievous adventurer, incapable of responsible leadership. Lord
Davidson wrote to former Prime Minister Stanley Baldwin,
". . . the Tories don't trust Winston. . . . After the first clash of
war is over it may well be that a sounder Government may
emerge."

Suspicions about Churchill's abilities and staying power
were shared by many holding government and military office.
Sir Alexander Cadogan, permanent under secretary at the Foreign Office, described him as "useless" in his diary. General
Ironside believed Churchill "has not got the stability necessary
for guiding the others." Ian Jacob, military assistant secretary to
the War Cabinet, said, "We had known of Churchill . . . above
all as a cantankerous, headstrong, and redoubtable controver-
sialist. . . . We worried how this difficult and seemingly erratic
character would get on as leader of a team in a situation of such
grave urgency." John Colville, then a junior member of the
prime ministerial staff and later also a devoted, valued Churchill
aide, observed:

> . . . the mere thought of Churchill as Prime Minister sent a
> cold chill down the spines of the staff at 10 Downing
> Street. . . . Churchill's impetuosity had, we thought, contrib-
> uted to the Norwegian fiasco, and General Ismay [secretary
> of the Committee of Imperial Defense] had told us in de-

spairing tones of the confusion caused by his enthusiastic ir-
ruptions into the peaceful and orderly deliberations of the
Military Coordination Committee and the Chiefs of Staff.
His verbosity and restlessness made unnecessary work, prevented real planning and caused friction. . . . Our feelings
. . . were widely shared in the Cabinet offices, the Treasury
and throughout Whitehall.

With Churchill in office, many in Whitehall and in the Conservative Party were convinced that "the country had fallen into
the hands of an adventurer, brilliant no doubt and an inspiring
orator, but a man whose friends and supporters were unfit to be
trusted with the conduct of affairs in a state of supreme emergency."

Some Conservatives made little effort to conceal their
thoughts and feelings about the new British leader. In the days
that followed Churchill's appointment, Chamberlain, who was
kept on in the cabinet by him as lord president of the council,
raised cheers from the Conservative benches of the House of
Commons when he entered the chamber, while Churchill was
often received in silence, a deliberate snub.

Despite the strong support and best wishes expressed by his
friends and admirers, Churchill must have felt humiliated. But
he gave no sign of recognizing the awkwardness of a situation in
which the opposition members of the Commons appeared to be
offering him more enthusiastic backing than a good portion of
his own side of the House. He knew the importance of appear-
ances and wasted no time in launching a campaign to dispel the
feeling in Britain that the country was inadequately led or impotent in the face of the German onslaught. "You ask," he told
Parliament on May 13, "what is our policy? I will say it is to
wage war, by sea, land, and air, with all our might. . . . You
ask, what is our aim? I can answer in one word: Victory—victory at all costs, victory in spite of all terror, victory, however
long and hard the road may be. . . ."

That pronouncement was loudly cheered. But some Tories
were little impressed with emotional outpourings or stirring oratory. Nor were all of his chief associates happy with his practice
of holding cabinet meetings which began late at night—he was a
strong believer in long midday naps—and which sometimes continued into the early-morning hours. When one such session did

not begin until 10:30 P.M., Lord Halifax, whom Churchill had
asked to stay on in the cabinet as foreign secretary, thought it
was "Quite intolerable. . . . One must acquiesce during these
two or three days. After that I shall tell him that if he wants
midnight meetings, he can have them without me." Colville was
moved to note in his diary, "There seems to be some inclination
in Whitehall to believe that Winston will be a complete failure
and that Neville [Chamberlain] will return."

As for the French, their political crisis on the day the German onslaught began was not only badly timed; it was grotesque. It was the kind of spring day—warm, bright, and
sunny—people in ordinary times wrote songs about. Parisians
strolled through the Bois de Boulogne, lounged over coffee and
croissants at outdoor cafés on the Boulevard St. Michel, and
watched street artists at work in Montparnasse. But these engaging scenes were no more than a charming facade. The grim reality was that despite the signs of normalcy in the streets of Paris,
France was once more in grave danger and its leadership was in
disarray. When Hitler's forces began blasting their way westward in the early hours of May 10, the country was without a
government and its political and military command was a steam-
ing caldron of distrust, resentment, and hatred.

Realizing the dangerous absurdity of such turmoil at the top
when the nation was under threat, Reynaud immediately withdrew his resignation as premier and canceled his plans to ap-
point a new government. Fearing that confusion might result
from a change in the military High Command at that critical
moment, he also felt he had no choice but to keep Gamelin on
as military commander and to patch things up with him. "The
battle is joined," he wrote to the general. "The only thing that
matters is to win it. We shall work together to do so." The army
commander replied in a similar spirit. Privately Reynaud indicated to Paul Baudouin, secretary to the government's War
Council, that this exchange did not make him any more confident of the general's talents or abilities. "We shall see," he
said, "what Gamelin is worth."

Whatever the premier's persisting doubts about him, the
French army commander displayed no lack of self-assurance.
Though normally undemonstrative, he strode up and down the
corridor at his Vincennes fortress headquarters outside Paris

that morning, humming contentedly to himself. It may have been that he believed the German attack had finally handed him the battlefield opportunity for which he had been preparing for years. But the enemy had just rescued him from forced retirement and disgrace. That may also have contributed to this uncharacteristic public display of satisfaction.

As the Allies went about sorting out their political predicaments and military dispositions, the Germans relentlessly proceeded with their offensive. By midmorning of May 11, their lightning tactics had effectively shattered the Belgian army's first line of resistance, which had been expected to bog them down for a few days at least, and their forces were preparing to press confidently forward across the country to confront the Allied troops moving into backup positions on the Dyle-Meuse line in Belgium.

The Dutch were taking a beating as well but were proving far more stubborn than the Germans had anticipated. Where they had not yet been completely overwhelmed, they fought back vigorously. The three airfields the invading airborne troops had seized at the start of the attack were recaptured after heavy fighting, and German forces trying to take The Hague were beaten off.

Deeply committed elsewhere on the front, the Germans had deployed only a limited force, inferior in size to the small Dutch army, for the conquest of Holland. But the Dutch had been too fully stretched guarding a frontier more than two hundred miles long to be able to concentrate defenses adequately at key vulnerable locations. The Dutch air force, small and obsolete, had been virtually demolished by the enemy at the very start of the attack. Holland's venerable tanks, comparatively few in number, could not long cope with German attackers battle-hardened in Poland. Organized Dutch resistance was also undermined by a farrago of rumors that told of a host of enemy saboteurs and fifth columnists and of German troops disguised as Dutch soldiers, policemen, priests, and even nuns. These stories were virtually all baseless, but they had their impact, and in places the defenders weren't sure whom to trust and whom to fight.

Once German airborne troops had successfully landed behind Dutch lines to seize strategically located canal-spanning bridges, Holland was effectively beaten. However, the Dutch obstinately refused to submit. At 5:00 in the morning on May 13, three days after the launching of the German assault, King George was awakened in London by a phone call from Queen Wilhelmina of Holland, who pleaded with him to dispatch military aid for her beleaguered troops. The king passed word along to the competent military authorities and noted in his diary, "It is not often one is rung up at that hour, and especially by a Queen."

In fact, the British had already sent a battalion of troops to help the Dutch, but in the prevailing confused circumstances, it failed to make contact with the enemy, and, as Holland appeared doomed to defeat, it was hastily withdrawn. Acting in accordance with previously arranged plans, the French Seventh Army had rushed into Holland to bolster Dutch defenses, but also did not stay long. Under concentrated German dive-bombing attack, running short of ammunition and aware of the imminence of the Dutch collapse, it withdrew. In advancing, it had performed with immaculate precision but had neglected to take account of a key factor—the capabilities of the enemy.

Such were those capabilities and so ruthless were the terror tactics of the invaders, whose bombers flattened the heart of the city of Rotterdam to show the Dutch how futile was their resistance, that a mere five days after the invasion was launched, Holland was forced to surrender.

The Allied High Command had not at first been discouraged by developments. War was war, and some setbacks were to be expected when the enemy was permitted to choose the time and place to strike. The true impact of the invasion was yet to be felt. Reducing the situation to what he then thought were its basics, Churchill observed on the morning the offensive was launched, ". . . the German hordes are pouring into the Low Countries, but the British and French armies are advancing to meet them, and in a day or two there will be a head-on collision." Reports that the Germans might have used a secret weapon to make short work of Belgian resistance at Fort Eben Emael triggered rumors that they had developed nerve gas or some such terrifying instrument of conquest. Extensive German use of tracer bullets led to reports from inexperienced troops that the enemy was shooting balls of fire at them, another

frightening innovation. But British and French commanders refused to be panicked. It was the kind of thing they left to civilians who had no idea what war was about. Gort's chief of staff,
Lieutenant General Henry Pownall, wrote in his diary, "So far
so good."

They were much encouraged by how smoothly their forces
were swiveling into their assigned positions along the Dyle-
Meuse line—the French Ninth Army from Namur to Mézières,
the French First Army between Wavre and Namur, and the British Expeditionary Force between Louvain and Wavre. Belgian
forces would cover the remaining gap between Antwerp and
Louvain. This unbroken defense line, assigned the task of ab-
sorbing the German thrust and throwing it back, was well on its
way to being set firmly in place. It was a complicated operation
but had been meticulously planned and, with a few minor
hitches, was completed in less than forty-eight hours.

As they moved into position, welcomed by the cheering,
waving, flower-throwing Belgian civilians through whose towns
and villages they rolled, the Allied forces came under surprisingly light enemy air attack, although their commanders had
risked deployment by daylight because of the emergency. Some
astute observers wondered where the much-touted Luftwaffe
was and whether the Germans, who were bombing and strafing
helter-skelter elsewhere, were deliberately refraining from air
attacks. Colonel Marie-Joseph-Victor de Villelume, Reynaud's
military adviser, perspicaciously wondered, "Are they letting us
walk into a trap?"

But a British defense expert, Lieutenant Colonel T. A.
Lowe, wrote reassuringly in the London *Daily Mail,* "An offensive on the scale the Germans have launched is an alarming
thing in the beginning. The weight is such that it is bound to
succeed at first. . . . But . . . we are ready for whatever may
come and we have the means ready to counter it. Our fighters
will swarm against the German bombers; our antiaircraft guns
will keep them high. . . . On land, tank will meet tank." It was
an illusion.

Taking up their new positions in Belgium, the British and
French were appalled to find little evidence of the defensive fortifications the Belgians were supposed to have erected along the
line they were to hold. At the strategic Gembloux Gap, high
ground which his troops were supposed to defend, a French

commander found, "no defense works [though this was] one of the key-points in the defense line, no decent trenches, no barbed wire . . . practically nothing at all." Having no previous familiarity with the terrain, the British were painfully surprised to find that the River Dyle, along which they were to make a stand, was in places an easily forded narrow stream rather than the substantial natural barrier they had assumed it to be. In one place British forces advancing to their assigned positions were fired upon not by the enemy but by jittery Belgian troops who believed they were German paratroopers. Units of Major General Bernard Montgomery's 3rd Division ran into trouble on the French-Belgian border when a customs official, having received no special instructions, refused to let them pass because they had no "permit" to enter the country. When argument failed, a heavy truck driven at speed through the border barrier proved to be permit enough.

There were other confusions, complications, and muddles and some friction between Allied officers as to who was to be where, a difficulty inevitable because there had been no earlier consultations between Allied staff officers and the previously neutral Belgians. But for the most part the movement into Belgium proceeded promisingly. British Chief of Staff Lord Ironside was convinced that once in place, the Allies would block the main route to the west that he, like Gamelin, had no doubt the Germans intended to take, and that it would be a war of attrition in which the Germans would finally exhaust themselves battering against solid Allied defenses. He noted in his diary, "A long battle is going to ensue. . . . On the whole the advantage is with us."

It was a total misreading of the situation. As the Allies would soon discover, their shift into Belgium, so masterfully executed, fitted so neatly into German plans that it might have been programmed by Hitler himself. The fact was that when the assaults of Belgium and Holland were launched on May 10, the biggest, most important component of the German operation was shaping up elsewhere. The much-respected military correspondent of the London *Times,* who confidently asserted the following day, "This time at least there has been no strategic surprise," was about to be proved profoundly mistaken.

Though he had been anxious to launch the offensive much sooner, and though he was infuriated by the repeated delays,

Hitler had agreed that attack strategy would have to be reviewed after the crash-landed plane incident in November which gave the Belgians details of his invasion plans. It had meant further delay but it had given Lieutenant General Erich von Manstein an opportunity to outline a comprehensive alternative strategy to the Fuehrer. Manstein proposed that the drive into Belgium, originally conceived as the major thrust against the Allies, be downgraded to the status of merely a diversion in strength. It would be powerful enough to tie down the repositioned Allied armies, the shift of which from northern France into Belgium was obvious and expected, and prevent them from disengaging to challenge the main German thrust farther south. That was where Manstein proposed that the armored divisions spearheading the German offensive should strike, plunging through the Ardennes Forest and into France.

Most of Hitler's generals at first pooh-poohed the idea, for the same reason the French did. They believed an armored romp through the Ardennes would be doomed to failure. They said the forest was totally unsuitable tank terrain. They said it would take many days, perhaps as long as two weeks, for the armored divisions to negotiate passage in strength through such countryside, by which time the element of surprise on which the maneuver depended would long have been forfeited. Arguments raged as to whether this was true or not, and the generals were finally persuaded that the drive through the Ardennes need not actually take so long. More important, Hitler, who had been growing disenchanted with the thrust-through-Belgium plan and who had also been wondering about the possibility of a drive through the Ardennes instead, was won over. Modified in a number of details, it became official German strategy and the formula for one of the most remarkable military routs in history.

Army Group B, under the command of Colonel General Feodor von Bock, which was to invade Belgium and Holland in accordance with the original plan, was downgraded from thirty-seven to twenty-eight divisions, including three rather than eight armored divisions, while Army Group A, under the command of Colonel General Gerd von Rundstedt, which was to rush through the Ardennes, was upgraded from twenty-seven to forty-four divisions, including seven rather than one armored division.

By May 9, von Rundstedt's forces, spearheaded by the most concentrated array of armor ever assembled, a vast throng of tanks and armored vehicles, more than twelve hundred of them, had been drawn up in three columns stretching a hundred miles back into Germany from the border of Luxembourg. By nightfall they had begun moving off, and by dawn, with nary a challenge, they had crossed the border of tiny Luxembourg— population three hundred thousand, army five hundred men strong—and plunged into the "impenetrable" Ardennes. The panzers were accompanied by motorized infantry and self-propelled artillery and escorted by an aerial cover of Messerschmitt 109 fighters. Their mission was to roll through Luxembourg and the knob of southern Belgium that protruded into the forest and then blast through into France.

The region was a bucolic wonderland, much of it an undulating countryside of thickly wooded landscape punctuated with colorful forest villages and laced with narrow, sometimes steep winding roads. Though some of it was unobstructed pastureland, for the most part the Ardennes seemed as unlikely a route for an army of tanks as could be imagined. Accordingly, the weakest of France's armies, the Second and the Ninth, were assigned the task of guarding access to France from the forest.

More than half of the Ninth Army consisted of reserve divisions. It was poorly equipped and officered largely by inadequately trained men with no combat experience. Its commanding general was André-Georges Corap, who not only had no experience whatever of mechanized warfare but was so fat and physically out of shape that he had trouble getting into his car. It was expected that the forces under Corap's command would be required to do little more than fend off minor enemy probes. The same was true of the Second Army under the command of General Charles Huntziger, who had never held an operational command before, having spent most of his army career in staff or diplomatic posts. His divisions were also partly manned by ill-prepared, underequipped reserves who, despite intelligence warnings that an enemy assault was imminent, were in the process of being redeployed. Several of its most senior officers and thousands of its junior officers and men were on leave. These were the forces positioned just past the farthest reach of the Maginot Line fortification, on the hinge on which the Allied armies were swiveling into Belgium to stop the diversionary enemy advance there.

Though the French command had not expected anything like the long columns of enemy armor rumbling through the Ardennes, they had been immediately alerted to the advance of the German forces through the forest. A clash was both inevitable and imminent. Huntziger called on the mayor of the Ardennes resort town of Bouillon to ask that one of the town's hotels be turned into a field hospital. The mayor turned him down, explaining, "Bouillon is a summer resort; our hotels are reserved for tourists."

But the tourists wouldn't be coming that summer. Elements of General Heinz Guderian's XIX Armored Corps showed up in Bouillon a day later, but they weren't staying long enough to do justice to the town's amenities. They rolled relentlessly on toward France. As they advanced through the forest, the armored columns were extremely vulnerable. Unable to spread out over open territory, they could not travel at maximum speed. Bunched up, they rumbled one behind the other along the narrow forest roads. Any breakdown or damage could halt an entire column and keep it halted until the stricken machine was repaired or shoved aside. Those that did break down or stall were immediately pushed off the road. Snarls and tie-ups did occur but were quickly remedied.

Attacks from the air could have blocked the roads with wrecks of steel and brought all three columns to a halt. But Allied aircraft sent out against the tanks as they plowed through the forest were at first instructed to restrict their operations to reconnaissance and then ordered to "avoid bombing built-up areas," which meant that though their accuracy in targeting left much to be desired, they were prohibited from attacking the German columns when they made the clearest targets—while passing through the villages and towns which dotted that densely wooded region.

The consequences of that restraint were soon realized and the prohibition was withdrawn. It made little difference. Allied bombers which attacked the armored columns did not fare well. German developments in antiaircraft weaponry and fighter plane technology had made the bombers available to the Allied command at the Ardennes front obsolescent even before the war began. Of thirty-two RAF Fairey Battle light bombers sent to attack the panzer columns on May 10, thirteen were shot down and all the rest were damaged before they could inflict much punishment on the invaders.

With most of their troops either hunkered down behind the

Maginot Line farther south or shifting north into the prear-
ranged defensive positions in Belgium, the French had few
forces available to confront the attackers while they were still
east of the Meuse River. Defenders, some on horseback, sent to
tangle with the advancing German columns put up a spirited display but were easily outmatched and soon forced to pull back.
Some withdrew across the River Meuse so quickly that now it
was the turn of the Germans to wonder whether they were being
lured into a trap.

Nevertheless, they rolled inexorably on through Luxembourg, across the southern tip of Belgium, into France, and toward the Meuse, the main natural obstacle between them and
the English Channel. The German vanguard reached the east
bank of the river on the evening of May 12. Hitler's panzers had
been rolling through the Ardennes for two days, but the Allied
command still had no firm idea what was happening. In London,
Sir Alexander Cadogan, under secretary of state at the Foreign
Office, believed that though news from the continent was un-
clear, the "main thing is our and French troops seem to be getting on to their positions [in Belgium] without much loss."
However, in Paris that evening, French War Council secretary
Paul Baudouin noted in his diary that three attempts had been
made that day "to get accurate information from GHQ, but in
vain. We know nothing, or rather all we know is that the Dutch
and Belgian resistance is crumbling."

The day did not end as triumphantly for the Germans as
they might have hoped. The French had succeeded in destroying
the bridges across the Meuse before their advance guard
reached the river. One of General Erwin Rommel's motorcycle
battalions found a weir which had not been blown up and scam-
pered across to establish a foothold on the other side, and German infantrymen crossed the Meuse in rubber dinghies to
establish small bridgeheads elsewhere on the west bank during
the night. But at this stage, they were unable to exploit those
incursions to any serious advantage. The tanks were the key to
German plans and hopes, and they were stranded east of the
river.

At that point, the main thrust of the German offensive was
in danger of collapsing even before it had gathered momentum.
With no viable vehicle crossings, the columns of panzers were
backed up for tens of miles practically track to track. But com-

munications difficulties, failure to assimilate intelligence reports, and administrative confusion prevented the dispatch of enough Allied aircraft to cause the Germans serious problems. The massive clog of armor was, however, an inviting target for French artillery on the west bank of the Meuse, and, indeed, some of the panzers were put out of action by artillery fire. But secure in their belief that the Germans would not be able to get their tanks across, French commanders restricted the firing of their guns to economize on ammunition—enormous quantities of which were later to be captured by advancing German units.

The Germans were not so sparing with their ammunition. On May 13, the Luftwaffe was called up to begin a massive assault on the French positions west of the river. "Almost the whole of the German air force will support this operation," the 1st Panzer Division, stopped in its tracks on the east bank, was assured. "By means of uninterrupted attacks lasting for eight hours the French defenses along the Meuse will be smashed."

Most effective were wave after wave of Stukas—up to forty of them in each wave, each plane carrying two five-hundred-pound bombs—which swooped down on the guns and on the concrete pillboxes in which troops took shelter. For men who had neither experience nor expectation of such awesome and sustained assaults, and particularly for civilians past the usual age of military service who had been rushed into uniform, the effect of these *Sturzkampfflugzeuge* was devastating. Men who were not killed, wounded, concussed, or thrown into shock by the bomb explosions were terrified by the high-pitched screech of the sirens built into the plane to produce that effect. They threw themselves to the ground even when the bombs exploded well away from them. According to General Edmond Ruby, the air attacks were petrifying:

> The gunners stopped firing and went to ground. The infantry cowered in their trenches, dazed by the crash of bombs and the shriek of the dive bombers; they had not developed the instinctive reaction of running to their anti-aircraft guns and firing back. Their only concern was to keep their heads well down. Five hours of this torture was enough to shatter their nerves.

Requests for fighter planes to drive off the enemy aircraft turned into desperate pleas for aerial cover, to no avail. At a time when his troops were being bombed, bombarded, battered, and dispersed, General Huntziger, incapable of understanding what was happening, replied, "If I am obliged to engage [my fighters] every time some threat arises they will be rapidly used up."

Artillery took over when the bombing attacks let up. The Germans had brought their cannon, antitank and antiaircraft guns, and medium tanks right up to the Meuse barrier. Firing almost point-blank, they unleashed sustained fusillades against the defenders. French troops still sheltering in riverside bunkers which had survived the Stuka attacks were little more secure than those out in the open; protective armor for those bunkers had not been yet installed and they shattered when hit.

Under cover of such a bombardment, German infantry lowered inflated rubber dinghies into the river—more than two hundred feet wide along most of this stretch—and began their crossing. They came under heavy fire from defenders who had not been put out of action or driven off in panic. But those on the attack were elite combat troops not easily repelled. The ones who were not cut down before completing the crossing scrambled ashore, rushed to overwhelm defending positions, and quickly began digging in. Within a few hours, the Germans had established a series of footholds at several points on the west bank of the Meuse. But German armor was still stuck on the far side of the river, and despite the horrifying bombardments to which they had been exposed and for which they had been totally unprepared, some French troops had stood their ground and succeeded in driving off several German attempts to convert those footholds into major bridgeheads.

The Germans were still dangerously exposed. French forces which had been driven from the river by the bombing and shelling were still largely intact, as were reserve units farther back. If properly led, they had the capacity to obliterate the enemy footholds before they could be exploited to get the panzers across the river. But for counterattacks to succeed, they had to be launched immediately, before the Germans could consolidate those footholds. However, such action required coordination, and French communications at the front, not overly reliable to begin with, had been virtually obliterated in the onslaught.

Not only were French officers unable to learn anything

about German strengths and positions, they were left with limited knowledge of the condition and positions of their own forces. The most ambitious plan was for a concerted drive to be launched on the morning of May 14 to push the Germans back across the river. But by midnight of May 13, German engineer troops were well on their way to patching up the destroyed bridge across the Meuse at Sedan so that it would be capable once more of carrying the weight of heavy armor. At first light, tanks rumbled across.

Army Group Commander General Billotte issued an urgent call for the bridge to be bombed. It "means victory or defeat for us," he declared. Right through the day, British and French bombers—170 in all—soared in through thick barrages of anti-aircraft fire to knock the span out once more. They did not succeed and eighty-five Allied planes were shot down.

By midmorning of May 14, the belated French counterblow on the ground had been beaten off. By midday, German engineer troops had thrown other bridges across the Meuse and German armor was pouring across the river in three places. France had been penetrated in force by the enemy. The much-trumpeted strategy for saving the country from ever again experiencing such a catastrophe was proved to have been built on dreams.

For French commanders who had believed such things simply could not happen, the situation was agonizingly incredible. Their "impregnable" borders had been cracked in less than four days. Their famous Maginot Line, upon which enormous expense, energy, and hope had been expended, had turned out to be irrelevant and a mocking waste of all three. When the news of what was happening at the Meuse was reported to General Georges, the commander of Allied troops in the northeast was devastated. An officer present at Georges's headquarters at the time said, "The atmosphere was that of a family in which there had just been a death. Georges . . . was terribly pale. 'Our front has been broken at Sedan. There has been a collapse.' He flung himself into a chair and burst into tears."

Word reaching senior Allied commanders elsewhere left them in ignorance. It told of some sort of unspecified trouble at Sedan. Gamelin and Ironside were totally unaware how serious a setback the Allies had suffered. Both remained blissfully convinced that the main German assault was building up, as expected, in Belgium.

*   *   *

Superior German airpower was proving decisive. Senior French commanders subsequently did not appear to know exactly how many planes had been at their disposal when the Germans attacked. Though more planes were continually rolling out of France's aircraft factories, comparatively few of the available French fighters—little more than five hundred—were committed to close cover for ground forces once the battle began. When later pressed to answer why so many had been held in reserve when the need for them at the front was so great, Gamelin replied, "I confess . . . that I don't know."

The commander of the French air force, General Joseph Vuillemin, conceded that despite losses, France ended up at the time of its capitulation a month later with more planes than it had at the beginning of the war. Nevertheless, General d'Astier de la Vigerie, commander of the French air force in the battle zone, later voiced frustration at the failure to use them when they were needed.

> Almost every evening I had to lift up my telephone and take the initiative to inform the commanders of the army and of the group of armies that I had, for the following day, a certain number of formations without missions, adding, "Have you any to give them?" Their reply was invariably the same: "We thank you very much but we do not have use for them."

Of Britain's 1,873 RAF combat aircraft, 416 were based in France when the German offensive was launched. They were divided into two distinct units with different roles to play. The job of the Advanced Air Striking Force, composed of ten squadrons of bombers (Fairey Battles and Blenheims), was to inflict as much damage as possible on the German forces. They faced two major problems: though communications left much to be desired, their operations were at times effectively controlled from either England or French command headquarters; and they were suited only to daylight raiding, which made them extremely vulnerable to German fighters and highly developed German antiaircraft defenses.

The Air Component of the British Expeditionary Force operated as a separate entity. The task of its four squadrons of

Hurricane fighters, soon increased to ten squadrons, was to provide aerial cover for the troops and to escort British bombers on their missions. The Air Component's four squadrons of Blenheims and five squadrons of Lysanders were meant for reconnaissance. But, as one Hurricane pilot recalled, for the RAF the air war over France and Belgium was a shambles. "There was no intelligence. Communications were poor. Everything appeared to be ad hoc."

Air commanders often didn't know where their Hurricanes should be sent to tangle with the enemy. The speed of the German advance meant that when specific instructions were given, bombers often arrived at designated target areas to find that the enemy had already moved on. Sometimes fighters sent to rendezvous with bombers they were assigned to escort arrived too soon or too late; sometimes they or the bombers didn't arrive at all. And the fighters, so badly needed for other purposes, had to squander some of their energies patrolling their own bases to guard against possible German bombing raids there.

There had been aerial encounters with the Germans, losses and wins, during the Phony War. But the hopeless position of the Allied air forces in France did not become fully apparent until the start of the German offensive. Five of six Blenheim fighter bombers sent to attack a German position in Holland were shot down. German Dornier bombers swept in low over the airfield at Condé-Vraux in northern France, caught the squadron of Blenheims based there neatly lined up on the ground, destroyed six of them, and rendered all the others unserviceable. By the end of four days of the German offensive, the RAF had lost almost half of its 135 combat-ready bombers in France.

British fighters going up in sections of three kept running into dozens of German planes, and sometimes formations of more than one hundred, the enemy bombers almost invariably escorted by great numbers of fighters. The Hurricanes took a heavy toll of German aircraft but were so vastly outnumbered that their own losses, in planes and pilots, also rapidly mounted. Replacements for both came, and those were soon lost as well. Squadrons were soon so decimated that RAF pilots assigned merely to ferry replacement Hurricanes to France and then return to their bases in England were ordered by squadron leaders to whom they reported at French air bases to stay on and join the battle, some never to return. British airmen based in France agonizingly realized their limitations. Flight Lieutenant Sir Archibald Hope was sent aloft alone to guard his airfield when all the other planes in the squadron turned out to be unserviceable. He patrolled the base for two hours. "One aircraft!" he later recalled. "What could one aircraft have possibly done if there had been a raid."

From the very start, "kill" claims by pilots were highly inflated, making it difficult to appreciate fully what was happening in the air war. In the heat of battle, it was impossible for a pilot to know whether a plane he had attacked was shot down, only damaged, or merely deliberately emitting a trail of smoke for evasive purposes, a ploy German pilots had mastered. On May 11, the BBC announced that the Germans had lost more than two hundred aircraft in two days of fighting, "ten times more than Britain." RAF fighter pilots in France were reported to be satisfied with nothing less than "ten [kills] before breakfast." If those reports had been accurate, the Luftwaffe would by then have been on its way to being knocked out of the war, which it patently was not.

Knowing how the war in the air over France was actually developing, Air Chief Marshal Sir Cyril Newall, chief of the Air Staff, realized, ". . . we cannot continue indefinitely at this rate of intensity. . . . If we expend all our efforts in the early stages of the battle we shall not be able to operate effectively when the really critical phase comes." But when the French pleaded for RAF assaults on German pontoon bridges across the Meuse to keep the Germans from breaking through into the French heartland, planes of the Advanced Air Striking Force had to be dispatched to do the job. Of seventy-one Blenheims and Battles sent aloft to knock out those bridges, forty were shot down, and still those bridges stood.

French troops reeling under German bombing attacks cursed the failure of their leaders to provide them with aerial cover. The French government repeatedly pleaded for British aerial reinforcements. BEF commander Gort also asked that additional fighter squadrons be urgently sent, as did Air Marshal Arthur Barratt, who commanded British air forces in France. In London, Chief of Staff Ironside moaned, ". . . these calls . . . will continue until we have little left, but this battle may be decisive of the whole war. . . ."

By May 15, the seriousness of the RAF's losses in France was seen in London to be taking on an additional alarming aspect. Advising against the dispatch of additional fighter planes to France, Newall expressed concern that Britain's home defenses could be jeopardized by their loss and that airfields the Germans had captured in Holland and might still capture in Belgium were likely to be used by the Luftwaffe for short-hop raids against British cities and military installations. Air Chief Marshal Sir Hugh Dowding, commander in chief of Fighter Command, pressed the point with great insistence. Dowding warned that Fighter Command could be "bled white and in no condition to withstand the bombing attack which will inevitably be made on this country as soon as our powers of resistance fall below a level to which we are already perilously close."

Earlier calculations lent credence to such forebodings. It had previously been estimated that the RAF needed sixty fighter squadrons to defend the country adequately, and that had assumed that the Luftwaffe would be operating from airfields in Germany. But now the Germans had access to fields in Holland, which were much closer to targets in Britain, and Fighter Command was down to a mere thirty-nine squadrons and was losing planes every day. Even before the extent and significance of the French setback on the Meuse was understood in London, a sense of foreboding was beginning to incubate there.

The people of France meantime were being kept in the dark about what exactly was happening at the front, except of course those in the immediate vicinity of the fighting. That the situation was serious was apparent from the way accelerated efforts were made to prepare the Paris subways for use as air raid shelters and the way armed police took to scouring cafés in search of suspected fifth columnists. The grief-stricken, tear-smeared, bewildered Dutch and Belgian refugees who arrived at the French capital's Gare du Nord testified to the misery caused by the fighting in progress beyond France's borders. But official communiqués gave no indication that France was genuinely in trouble.

The same was true in Britain, though further emergency measures were being implemented there as well. Men between the ages of nineteen and thirty-seven were required to register for military service and the registration procedure was accelerated. There was no great rush to the colors by enthusiastic volunteers anxious to don uniforms and get a crack at the enemy as there had been at the start of the First World War a generation earlier. This war was, after all, already nine long, dreary months old. Conscripts turned up when summoned, but in a number of cases, Scotland Yard was called in to investigate able-bodied men suspected of having hired unfit stand-ins to take their places at preinduction medical examinations.

A citizens' militia was called into being on May 14 to supplement the regular army. Though consisting of men too old or unfit for active military service, this Home Guard, initially called Local Defense Volunteers (and later, with derisive affection, Dad's Army), was supposed to be subject to military discipline. But in a society so comparatively free of legal restraint, it depended largely on the dedication and morale of the recruits, few of whom at that stage were equipped with so much as a pistol to fend off an invading enemy if one appeared.

The threat believed posed by enemy aliens resident in Britain was dealt with soon after the battle began. German and Austrian nationals living along the east and southeast coast of England were taken into custody for shipment to internment camps. By nightfall of May 12, three thousand of them, most living near airports, military installations, docks, munitions factories, power plants, and bridges, had been rounded up. Ironically, many were refugees from Hitler's Third Reich domain, driven away by fear of Nazi persecution.

The Home Office urged people to remain alert for enemy agents landing by parachute and, if they spotted any, to "report at once to the nearest police station giving the most accurate information possible as to place and numbers of persons landing." Across the country, people took to scanning the skies, and road directional signs were taken down almost everywhere to deny enemy agents who managed to evade detection any assistance such signs might provide. Innocent travelers who didn't know their way were of course also confounded and confronted by suspicious locals when asking directions. CBS correspondent Edward R. Murrow reported back to the United States, "The only thing to tell the traveller that Canterbury is Canterbury is the big cathedral rising out of the plain."

Foreign correspondents based in Berlin were assured by government spokesmen there that the German onslaught was purely defensive, that it had been launched to head off aggression by Britain and France. But not even isolationists in the United States, to which the Allies continued to look for help, were prepared to believe that. Instead, the German offensive swelled the ranks of Americans who insisted that German expansionism could imperil the security of the United States. Roosevelt declared on May 10 that his government would act "to defend by every means . . . our culture, our American freedom and our civilization." Secretary of State Cordell Hull declared that the world was threatened with "an orgy of destruction not only of life and property, but of religion, of morality, of the basis of civilized society." *The New Republic* magazine warned that the United States must be prepared for an Allied disaster in Europe.

Expressions of support for the Allies and sympathy for victims of the Germans reverberated across America. The government froze the American assets of Belgium, Holland, and Luxembourg so that the Nazis would not be able to take possession of them through puppet governments. Growing numbers of Americans came to believe that the security of the United States itself was now under threat and agreed that the country's defenses should be strengthened. But they thought in terms of a stronger navy and enhanced air power to warn off any potential threat from abroad. The idea of mobilizing a large army that might be sent to fight in Europe and once more plunge the nation into a foreign quagmire remained anathema to most Americans.

Whenever pressed, Roosevelt felt obliged by prevailing public opinion to repeat that he saw no reason to revise his belief that the United States could stay out of the war. Nevertheless, the president paid close attention to what was happening at the front. He called for continual updates from the War and State departments on how the battle was proceeding and how the British and French governments were dealing with their troubles.

Reynaud pleaded for rush shipments of American arms. Churchill did the same.

The voice and force of the United States may count for nothing if they are withheld too long. You may have a completely subjugated, Nazified Europe established with astonishing swiftness. . . . All I ask now is that you should proclaim non-belligerency, which would mean that you would help us with everything short of actually engaging armed forces. Immediate needs are, first of all, the loan of forty or fifty of your older destroyers. . . . Secondly, we want several hundred of the latest types of aircraft. . . . Thirdly, anti-aircraft equipment and ammunition. . . .

Roosevelt replied sympathetically but explained that Congress would have to agree. The president did what he could to persuade Congress to bend America's neutrality status so that arms and munitions could be supplied to Britain and France to save them from defeat. But congressional resistance was formidable. California Republican Senator Hiram Johnson warned that any attempt to repeal or modify the neutrality act would be "vigorously contested." Most Americans appeared to agree that no matter which side deserved sympathy in the European war, it was really none of America's business.

Despite the intimate tone of Roosevelt's direct communications with Churchill, and though the president was relieved that a dynamic prime minister was now in charge in Britain, he wasn't absolutely certain that Churchill had the leadership qualities the pressures of the moment required. Having once served as assistant secretary of the navy, he knew well the value of naval power and considered the British fleet to be America's first line of defense against ambitions Hitler might harbor in the Western Hemisphere. But the president was not impressed with the way, under Churchill stewardship, the Royal Navy had mishandled the Norway episode. He felt that "if things kept up the way they were going, the English were going to get licked."
Presidential advisers also entertained doubts about Churchill's abilities. Ambassador Bullitt, who kept pressing for stronger American support for the Allies and whose views were much respected in the White House, thought as little of Churchill as he had of Chamberlain. He believed, "There are no real leaders . . . in all of England in this time of grave crisis," a sentiment which he said was shared by Reynaud and other leading Frenchmen.
It was to be expected that Ambassador Kennedy, whose coterie of well-placed London contacts tended to be Cham-

berlain cronies and partisans, would be critical of Churchill too. It was no surprise in Washington when Kennedy urged on May 15 that despite Churchill's calls for help, the United States should take care not to find itself "holding the bag for a war in which the Allies expected to be beaten." But Kennedy's influence in the White House continued to dwindle. Roosevelt was annoyed when he took it upon himself to advise Americans living in Britain—about eight thousand at the time—to make for home as soon as possible. But the advice having been offered with all the authority of the American government's official representative in the country, the State Department felt obliged to help make the necessary arrangements. The British liner *Athenia,* bound for Canada with three hundred Americans among her fourteen hundred passengers, had been torpedoed by a German submarine the day after the war broke out. Twelve Americans had been among the dead or missing. In view of the continuing danger of German submarine attack, it was decided to send a clearly marked vessel across the Atlantic for those who wished to return to the United States from Britain and, as a further precaution, to inform both the British and German governments.

During the early months of 1940, the most important political question in Washington was whether Roosevelt would seek a third term in the White House. If he did so, he would break the tradition of a two-term limit for the presidency. Roosevelt was under strong pressure from the liberal wing of the Democratic Party to run again and frustrate the hopes of conservatives, including those among his own Democrats, to capture the presidency and repudiate or dilute his New Deal social policies. But tiring of office, Roosevelt had been thinking of a tranquil post-presidential career. He thought of retiring to his home at Hyde Park in New York's rural Hudson Valley, where he would take on the role of an elder statesman. He could gather his presidential papers for posterity and write about his time in office and about current events. After eight years in the White House, the prospect of a change of circumstances and scenery was attractive. As an invalid who had contracted polio many years before and who was confined to a wheelchair during most of his waking hours, he also found relief from the immense physical pressures of the presidency a tempting prospect.

Developments across the Atlantic now became a factor in Roosevelt's ponderings about whether to run again. The desire to educate the American people to the dangers they faced because of the war in Europe inspired Roosevelt to a new dedication and a renewed sense of his own importance. But it still did not provide a conclusive answer to whether he would agree to be a candidate for reelection. He told intimates that he did not intend to run "unless . . . things got very, very much worse in Europe." However, as he must have known, if things did get much worse, it was likely that Congress and the American public would be even more reluctant to get involved overseas. It would lumber Roosevelt—more than ever convinced that Hitler had to be stopped—with an even more difficult task than he had already undertaken. A presidential intimate believed, "The question of whether Roosevelt would run is being settled somewhere on the banks of the Meuse River."

The decision was a matter of crucial importance to the Allies. Any candidate hoping to be elected would have to promise never to tie America's future to the fate of any of the European combatants in any way. And he would have far greater difficulty than Roosevelt, who was a masterful political tactician and who was already working on ways to circumvent the congressional ban on sending arms to the Allies, in wiggling out of that promise. If he decided to step down, America was more likely to keep its distance from Europe's turmoil, with incalculable consequences.

Rampage

Muddle and disarray was the French response to the German onslaught which had taken Hitler's panzers through the Ardennes Forest and across the River Meuse in the four turbulent days between May 10 and May 14. But the moment had not yet passed when counterattacks could demolish the enemy bridgeheads across the river. General Corap established a containment line from which such efforts could be mounted. However, the failure of communications and the collapse of morale, both shattered by air attack, unhinged the French response where it was not paralyzed altogether.

While most of the German panzers were still lined up front to rear on the far side of the Meuse, waiting their turn to cross, a French tank unit moved into position behind French lines to participate in a planned counterattack. Word of its identity and mission not having gotten through, it was mistaken for German. Local commanders thought enemy armor had zoomed forward in an encircling maneuver, and whole units fled, believing they were about to be surrounded.

After rushing forward, the elite French 1st Armored Division was a mere twenty-five miles from where General Rommel was consolidating his bridgehead but didn't know it. It just sat there waiting for instructions which didn't come.

Out of touch with who was where, some French units fired on each other. Other units disintegrated, the men making pell-mell for what they hoped would be safety. Reinforcements rushed in to bolster defense lines found that bridges over waterways they had to cross had been destroyed and no one was available to explain why or who had given the order.

Unfounded rumors of German advances reached command headquarters, where, for want of more accurate intelligence, they were believed, further confounding commanders who from the moment the battle had started had had only limited information on what was happening and where. With few coherent orders being issued, the fallback gathered momentum. Men many miles back from the Meuse found themselves descended upon by swarms of troops who had bolted from the front, allegedly under orders of their commanders.

French units which did put up fierce resistance were undermined by the panic of those which did not. Their flanks endangered, they were forced to join in the retreat. Many men threw away their rifles and tore off their stripes or insignias of rank, thereby signifying they were personally finished with the army and the war. Platoons, companies, whole battalions ceased to exist. Fearing attack from the air, some men abandoned their military vehicles in their retreat and took to the road. Many French tanks rolling unhesitatingly into battle ran out of fuel and had to be put out of action by their anguished crews, who then had no alternative but to join the humiliating ragtag race to the rear. Many troops went into hiding in villages, farms, or woods, waiting for the moment when they might safely surrender to Germans.

At his Vincennes headquarters, General Gamelin was trying to function as overall Allied commander without a radio—without even a carrier pigeon, one of his staff officers moaned—and with unreliable civilian telephone links. He only belatedly grasped the extent of the setback on the Meuse. To receive information and issue instructions, the commander in chief relied on motorcycle riders who careened back and forth with reports and dispatches over roads jammed with vehicles and hordes of refugees. Some dispatch riders were killed or seriously injured in accidents, with no one at either end aware that, regardless of urgency, whatever messages they carried would never be delivered.

Commanders lower down the line of command were similarly cut off from contact with the forces they believed were at their disposal. Some had no idea where their units were, or indeed where the shifting front line was. Nevertheless, late on May 14, with the French defenses around Sedan on the verge of disintegration, General Georges, overall commander of Allied forces in the northeast, reported, "The German advance appears to be blocked." He had no idea of the actual state of affairs.

Attempts were made to reestablish control. "When the destiny of France is in balance," General Corap warned his troops, "no weakness will be tolerated. At all levels, leaders have the duty to set the example, and if necessary force obedience. Pitiless sanctions will fall upon any leaders who fail." It was futile. Battered and dispersed, Corap's Ninth Army was on its way to extinction. The entry in its official diary on the morning of May 15—Corap would be relieved of his command before the day was out—was a whimper of hopelessness: "No information—communications cut—liaison unworkable—back areas blocked with convoys and wrecked columns—petrol trains in flames—wholesale chaos." The rout was well underway.

Even if the French High Command had grasped what was happening, it would have required greater military skills than it possessed to do something about it. Many of the best Allied fighting troops were deeply committed in Belgium, and well before the Germans had been expected to get past forward Belgian defenses, they had begun battering hard against points along the newly established Allied Dyle-Meuse defense line farther back. General Blanchard's First Army, guarding the right flank of that line and best positioned to rush back south to reinforce General Corap's disintegrating Ninth Army, was locked in battle. Its disengagement was beyond the capabilities or imagination of Blanchard under pressure.

Too much was happening too fast to be assimilated, understood, and responded to with sound judgment. A French officer recalled seeing General Blanchard trying to absorb the information which had reached him.

> I spent more than an hour in the same room as the general. . . . He sat in tragic immobility, saying nothing, doing nothing, but just gazing at the map spread on the table between us, as though hoping to find in it the decision which he was incapable of taking.

Blanchard's superior, General Billotte, commander of the First Army Group, charged with coordinating the actions of the Allied forces which had swiveled so confidently into Belgium a few days before, also seemed too shattered by developments to make a decision of any kind. When one was extracted from him, it was soon withdrawn or revised.

This lethargy was infectious. It was communicated right down the line to forces which were not yet seriously engaged. According to Colonel A. Goutard, who later recounted the course of events:

> No one really wanted to counter-attack. It was passed from one headquarters to the next like some unpopular fatigue. The armies, the corps, the divisions, the regiments were never ready. Sometimes, however, some good units—regiments or improvised groups—did attack in real earnest, and met with such astonishing success that the High Command became nervous and called them back hastily.

The inadequacy of their senior commanders infuriated many of the French staff officers. The British liaison officer attached to Billotte's headquarters recorded in his diary that younger members of the staff there "were quite frankly in despair and poured out to me the measure of their disgust and contempt at the supine futility of their commander and higher staff." Many broke down in tears as reports came in of the disarray and impotence of their army. Officers of the British Expeditionary Force tended not to show their feelings so dramatically. Gallic emotional display was not their style, and it was, after all, not their country which was being invaded and bombed. It was not their magnificent Maginot Line that was being proved a catastrophic folly. It was not their once-proud army that was proving feeble and ineffectual. And at first, it was not their troops who were being blasted by German armor and aircraft.

But to the exasperation of much of his staff, Lord Gort, like Gamelin, isolated himself from his major conduit of information on how the battle was developing. While most of his intelligence and operations personnel, receiving and collating whatever reports were available on German movements, remained at BEF headquarters at Arras, Gort had set up a command post at the village of Wahagnies near Lille on the first day of the German offensive, and then moved on May 13 to Renaix, closer to the front, and then on May 15 to Linnick St. Quentin, which was still closer. For communications with his headquarters, he was compelled to rely on dispatch riders and the civilian telephone system, which was abandoned by its operators during air raid alerts. Anxious not to sit back and let things take their own course (which they did nevertheless), the BEF commander was also away from his forward command post for long hours at a time, seeing for himself what was happening. Communications with key sections of his staff were thus impossible to maintain.

Not until the day the Germans had crossed the Meuse on May 14 did Gort learn that an enemy thrust in that direction—three days in the making—had materialized! And not until May 16, the day after they had broken through in strength at Sedan, did he learn that it had happened, though by doing so the enemy was positioned for a drive that could slice through his supply lines. The BEF was in serious danger and he had received no warning.

Much of the fault lay with the command structure. Gort was in charge of the British Expeditionary Force, but he remained subordinate to the French army command. His immediate superior, Army Group Commander General Billotte, was supposed to be coordinating the activities of the Allied forces in Belgium. But Gort had little idea what this coordinator was up to. Battles were raging at various points along the western front, but the BEF commander, whose troops were supposed to play a key role in the struggle, was told nothing by his French superior.

The French had much more pressing matters to deal with than the fate of the British Expeditionary Force, which for the most part continued at this stage to be spared serious combat. French armies were being pummeled and trounced. German troops were once more thundering over the soil of France. The enemy was dominant in the skies above the country. Paris itself could soon be under threat. These were serious distractions, though not serious enough for the British to appreciate being ignored and neglected. Bitterness and recrimination began to creep into relations between the Allies.

In Paris, less than two hundred miles from the front, a different mood prevailed. Parisians had been led by radio and newspaper reports to believe that though there was a battle raging in Belgium, French territory remained inviolate. To American journalist Clare Booth, newly arrived in the French capital, things appeared normal.

Taxis hooted on the boulevard, glasses clinked on the marble
tops of the bistro tables, the flower market at the Madeleine
was madly colorful, and the clocks in the towers calmly
struck the hours.

Reynaud himself hadn't been informed until the afternoon
of May 14, after German armor had begun pouring across the
Meuse, that things were turning very disagreeable for his nation
and his people. In addition to the military debacle, an estimated
two hundred thousand civilians in the north were fleeing before
the enemy.

The French premier had a message telephoned to London
that evening to inform Churchill that the situation had deteriorated: "The German army has pierced our fortified lines south
of Sedan. . . . Between Sedan and Paris there are no fortifications comparable to those. . . ." France urgently needed more
help. Reynaud asked Churchill, who had previously promised
the dispatch of four fighter squadrons to beef up RAF forces
already in France, to send ten additional squadrons immediately. Without them, Reynaud said, his forces might not be
able to stop the Germans from crashing through to Paris.

Though detailed reports had been sparse in London, the
War Cabinet already had reason to believe that problems which
had arisen at the front were more than the initial battle setbacks
for which allowances could be and had been made. Those informed of the heavy losses the RAF was sustaining in France,
and of the implications those losses had for Britain's home defenses, were particularly alarmed. Though Churchill was a firm
advocate of always meeting an enemy at a forward position
rather than with a back-to-the-wall posture, he fully appreciated
the dangers of further depleting the country's aerial strength and
had reluctantly agreed with his chiefs of staff that no further
fighters should be sent abroad.

But that was before London had learned of the German
breakthrough at Sedan. Churchill and his advisers had still believed that the main battle would be in Belgium and that the
Allied line there would block the enemy's advance, finally bringing Hitler's aggressive adventures to a halt. The prime minister
was therefore astonished to hear Reynaud's anguished message
about Sedan and his plea for help. It was thought possible that
the French premier was suffering from a bout of Gallic hysterics,

triggered by excessively gloomy communiqués reaching him from the front. But at 7:30 the next morning, May 15, Reynaud telephoned Churchill personally. This time his message to the prime minister, who, having gone to bed in the early-morning hours as usual, had to be awakened to take the call, was even more desperate. "We are beaten," Reynaud sobbed down the line. "We have lost the battle. . . . They are pouring through in great numbers with tanks and armored cars."

Churchill could not believe it. He had been dealing with defeatists too long to be convinced that things were as bad as Reynaud insisted. He had "seen a good deal of this sort of thing in the previous war, and the idea of the line being broken, even on a broad front, did not convey to my mind the appalling consequences that now flowed from it." He told Reynaud there was no chance that the war would be lost and tried to convince him that the onrushing Germans would soon have to stop and wait for their supplies to catch up. That was when the Allies would be able to administer a savage counterblow. Unable to reassure Reynaud on the telephone, Churchill decided there was no alternative but to fly personally to Paris to discover the true military position and to persuade the panicky French that the outlook was not as bleak as they thought.

But Reynaud was right and Churchill was wrong, as War Minister Daladier discovered to his horror that night when General Gamelin, who had just presented the War Council in Paris an encouraging report, telephoned to change his tune. German panzers, he now reported, had broken out of their bridgehead at Sedan. Not only did he not have the resources to mount any sort of counterattack, but there was nothing to stop the Germans from roaring on to the French capital itself.

"What you tell me is not possible!" Daladier shouted back over the phone at the French commander. "You are mistaken!"

Gamelin assured him that he was not mistaken. American Ambassador Bullitt, who was visiting Daladier at the War Ministry when he took the call, cabled Washington, ". . . unless God grants a miracle . . . the French army will be crushed utterly." Even if a miracle had been in the offing, it would have come too late for the French Ninth Army, which was "in an indescribable disorder, troops are falling back on all sides, Army HQ have lost their heads, they do not even know where their divisions are."

At times the situation was reduced to the level of farce. Senior members of General Gamelin's staff were gathering protectively around the ineffectual supreme Allied commander. When Colonel Marie-Joseph-Victor de Villelume, Reynaud's military adviser, went to Gamelin's headquarters to try to unravel confusing reports on developments at the front, Colonel Petitbon, Gamelin's chief of staff, strongly protested what he considered his excessive curiosity and threatened to impose a news blackout on the head of the French government. "If this goes on," he warned de Villelume, "I will not give any information at all."

In view of the fact that nothing that was happening at the front reflected credit of any sort on Gamelin, that sort of petulance, though absurd, was understandable. Unperturbable until now, Gamelin was panicking. Having relied exclusively on a strategy of preventing the enemy from penetrating the nation's borders, he had no idea what to do now that those borders had been breached. That night, he urged the French government to prepare to abandon Paris because the capital was in danger of falling to the enemy—and only six days had passed since the first shots had been fired! Plans were set in train to transfer the government to another part of the country. Where it was to go was not decided. In the developing frenzy, a total evacuation of the city—an impossible task—was suggested.

Resistance to the German breakthrough was fast crumbling in France, but people in London had no idea how the battle was progressing. The London *Times* story on the morning of May 16 was almost euphoric.

> Under a seemingly endless torrent of bombs, backed up by an artillery barrage from the French forces, the Germans wavered and then began to fall back. They found the roads to their rear choked and blocked in many places by wrecked and overturned lorries, tanks, armoured cars and supply transport.

It was exactly what might have been happening but was not. Though his sources were not confined to wishful press reports, Churchill remained unaware of the magnitude of the French setback. But his assumption that the excitable Reynaud had been wildly exaggerating the rout of his army evaporated when he landed in France later that day. To General Ismay, who was in the party accompanying the prime minister, the gloom of the French officers who greeted them at Le Bourget airport made it "obvious that the situation was far more critical than we had suspected." He was told that the Germans were expected to reach Paris in a few days' time at most. Paris police that day were being issued rifles as well as revolvers, stepping up their raids on cafés frequented by foreign nationals, and stopping cars on main raids into the capital to search for fifth columnists.

At a remarkable emergency meeting at the Quai d'Orsay that afternoon, attended by the leaders of Britain and France and their senior aides, Gamelin summed up the situation at the front. He had brought his panic under control, and his presentation seemed like a lecture to students at a military academy on how to go about losing a war. Everyone there, all standing throughout, listened in either despair (the French) or astonishment (the British).

Gamelin left no doubt that the plight of the Allies was indeed extremely serious. The Germans had rammed a hole at least fifty miles wide through the defenses around Sedan, and their armor was racing forward at remarkable speed, heading either for the English Channel or Paris; he did not know which. The French forces in their path had been either scattered or destroyed. "Where is the strategic reserve?" Churchill demanded. "There are none," Gamelin replied. His exact words may have been misheard or misreported. But the meaning was the same. The battle had barely begun but the commander in chief of the French army, and officially commander as well of the British Expeditionary Force, the man who at that moment was responsible for the fate of his country, appeared reconciled to defeat.

Believing that the British leader might not yet have fully grasped the gravity of the situation as outlined in Gamelin's stilted presentation, Reynaud recapitulated, explaining, "The hard point of the German lance has gone through our troops as through a sand hill." But Churchill needed no elucidation. In case Gamelin's lecture hadn't been enough, he had been treated to a graphic display of the French government's desperation— through a window of the conference room he could see bonfires being made of Foreign Ministry archives in the courtyard to keep them out of the hands of the momentarily expected Ger-

mans. To ward off panic, Reynaud earlier that day had assured
his Chamber of Deputies that there was no question of the government's abandoning Paris, but that was exactly what it was
preparing to do.

Churchill had no choice but to accept that his confidence in
the might of the French army had proved illusory. He was bitter
with the French for having neglected the elementary precaution
of backing up their front-line defenses with reserve forces to
meet the kind of emergency with which they were now threatened, and he was angry with the British War Office for not
knowing about that extraordinary omission. "We had a right to
know," he fumed. "Both armies were fighting in the line together."

Nevertheless, the prime minister believed that the French
leaders were overly despairing and that France should and could
fight on. He would not accept that a large and powerful country
could win or lose a war in a matter of days. He was not alone in
failing to appreciate that France was managing to do exactly
that. General Ismay also optimistically believed that getting the
French "into a warlike mood" was only a matter of time.

Churchill had reacted angrily (and foolishly) when one of
his senior military advisers had briefed him on a contingency
plan for the British Expeditionary Force to give ground in
Belgium because of the panzer onslaught farther south. Averse
on principle to the idea of retreat except when no viable alternative was possible, he was not convinced that a speedy strategic
withdrawal by the Allied forces had become essential. Seeking
to inject the same sort of fight into the French leadership, the
prime minister reluctantly, and contrary to a War Cabinet decision in London the day before, agreed—with the grudging approval of the War Cabinet that night—to Reynaud's request for
six more RAF fighter squadrons to be sent to France in addition
to the four squadrons already promised. Despite his concern
about frittering away the RAF's stock of fighter aircraft, the
prime minister was persuaded that "the first necessity was to
support French morale and give them a chance to recover themselves" to deal with the German invaders.

In agreeing to the dispatch of the extra squadrons, the War
Cabinet had not suddenly grown less concerned about the danger of jeopardizing Britain's home air defenses. Its agreement
was an almost reflexive response to the terrifying implications of

the German breakthrough, the extent of which it had just learned. Holland had surrendered to the Germans the day before. Brussels was about to fall. The French army and possibly the BEF as well were in serious danger. And all of that had happened in less than a week! The main thing was to bring Hitler's steamrolling forces to a halt, and obviously the place to do that was where they were steamrolling forward. The additional squadrons would help considerably. That British air operations in France and Belgium had so far failed to make any dent in the German advance was not so much overlooked as not yet comprehended.

Fighter Command chief Dowding, deeply distressed by the RAF's losses in France, was appalled by the decision. "Stuffy" Dowding was less inclined than most to be swayed by the pressures of the moment. For him the primary emphasis had not been stopping Hitler on the far side of the English Channel but defending the British homeland from air attack. He understood that the French might soon capitulate if convinced that the British declined to commit more of their forces to the battle. But he thought that a French surrender was imminent in any case, and he believed that the RAF was so outnumbered and outmaneuvered in the skies over France and Belgium that sending a few more squadrons would just be adding to the futile sacrifice already being made there.

Dowding was already jealously guarding his Spitfires, Britain's most advanced fighter aircraft. He had nineteen squadrons of them but refused to permit even a single Spitfire to be sent to the continent to run the same risk as the Hurricanes he had been obliged to send over. The number of Hurricanes being lost was mounting worryingly. Even more worrying, scores of experienced pilots were being killed. It was understandable that some British leaders had been persuaded by the extreme pressures of the moment to believe that France, as Britain's forward line of defense, had to be saved from defeat at all costs. But Dowding saw his fighters as the only means of Britain's salvation from foreign domination. It was essential, he insisted with nagging persistence, for the country to conserve its air power in order to prevent the Germans, with their larger fleets of bombers and fighters, from achieving the same mastery of the air over Britain as they had seized over Europe.

Others were mesmerized by Hitler's blitzkrieg across the

Low Countries and the Wehrmacht's breakthrough into the French heartland. But Dowding was obsessed exclusively by the danger to the British mainland. On May 15, he told the Air Ministry in London that it was necessary to face the fact that the Allied armies in France and Belgium might be defeated. He complained that Britain's home air defenses were already well below their previously calculated minimum strength. And he warned that if his fighters continued to be "drained away in desperate attempts to remedy the situation in France, defeat in France will involve the final, complete and irremediable defeat" of Britain.

It was a statement by an officer who for social and personality reasons was, despite his rank, not really a member of the military establishment. He was overdue for retirement and thought by many of his fellow senior officers to be a tiresome fussbudget. But his warning focused attention on what had become a consideration only within the previous forty-eight hours and on what was still too fantastic for some senior figures to grasp—that Britain's survival as an independent nation could be at stake. The question at issue was reviewed yet again, and Churchill this time regretfully ruled that no more squadrons of fighters would leave the country "whatever the need of France" except, if necessary, to cover an evacuation of troops.

In Belgium, General Billotte, coordinator of the northern Allied armies, remained bewildered by the pace of events. He continued to agonize over the fate of France and the failure of its once glorious armies. Belatedly, on May 16, instructions were drawn up at his headquarters for the French First Army, on the right of the British Expeditionary Force, to prepare to pull back from the Dyle-Meuse line to save itself. Lord Gort, whose flank would be left totally exposed if his divisions did not withdraw at the same time, was not informed.

It was not deliberate. It was an oversight that no doubt would soon have been rectified. Billotte and his senior aides had other things on their mind. But not until later that day, when Gort offered the French on his right a brigade of British reserves to help close a gap the Germans were hammering in their lines, did the BEF commander learn that they were preparing to pull out. Outraged by Billotte's inexcusable failure yet to instruct the BEF to do the same, Gort dispatched a senior officer of his staff to demand that the distraught coordinator finally issue coherent instructions. Orders for a coordinated Allied pullback were then forthcoming. It was to be a staged withdrawal westward, the opportunity to swivel back south to block the German breakthrough at Sedan having by then been lost. The Allied line in Belgium was to withdraw immediately to the River Senne, then on May 17 to the River Dendre, then on May 18 to the River Escaut, where it was to stand fast and where the German advance, if it had not ground to a halt by then, would be met and halted.

Only after that exercise began did the French command in the north finally provide Gort with a thorough reading of developments as far as they were known. Hard pressed, the French had come to recognize something that hadn't featured much in their thoughts in the two harrowing days since the Sedan debacle—that the BEF, though a fraction of the size of the French army, might play a key role in their increasingly desperate struggle to save their country from being overrun.

But by then Gort had grown irreversibly exasperated with the indecisiveness of his French superiors, and the unreliability of French commanders generally. He later complained, "It was no uncommon occurrence to agree with the French to retire at say, 9 P.M., and to find that the troops on the line had, in fact, begun to go back at 4." When his forces had withdrawn to the River Escaut, he found the water level so low that the German tanks could easily have followed his men across because the French had opened sluices to flood regions downriver for defensive purposes but hadn't informed the British.

A whole series of major and minor acts or omissions by the French riled Gort, compounding his sense of frustration at how the battle was turning out. He was still under their command but had begun thinking that under the circumstances, his primary immediate responsibility was not defeating the common enemy, which did not seem a likely prospect in the immediate future. His main concern had become the fate of the BEF.

The orders to withdraw from the positions they had just taken up were not well received by British troops on the line. Their morale had been good. They had been certain they were a match for their German adversaries. But now the confidence with which they had sped into Belgium and had dug in sagged badly. Belgian civilians who had welcomed their arrival with cheers and flowers a few days earlier turned cold and resentful as they watched those same troops abandoning them to the invader with barely a shot having been fired. When a company of Grenadier Guards took a wrong turning and had to double back to find the right road, they were cheered once more by people who thought the British were advancing again to meet the enemy. When they turned again to resume their retreat on the right road, those cheers faded into scornful disappointment.

Unlike the French to their right and the Belgians on their left, few of the British had yet been subjected to serious attack. Having unwaveringly held the sector to which they were assigned, they were baffled when told to pack up and move back. Having been nurtured on a diet of regimental pride from the moment they had first donned their uniforms, men of the front-line units felt humiliated at having to cut and run even before being put to the test. And it became one retreat after another. Troops barely dug in at new rear positions when the "withdrawal party prepare" order was again issued.

> We weren't given much information. We were kept in almost total ignorance. But it didn't need a very bright man to know there was a hell of a fight going on somewhere and we weren't doing very well in it.

In a letter home from Flanders, a soldier wrote, "We have slept in the most queer places [during the withdrawal]—wine cellars, cow-byres, haylofts, stables." Rumors of disaster circulated freely. Belgian positions were said to have been blasted by two hundred German dive-bombers at a time. The Germans were said to be using a secret weapon which prevented guns from firing. "Germans have broken through the Maginot Line and are now south of us only ten miles away," one British officer scribbled in his diary. Another feared that once they had begun retreating, the troops would be "in no mood to halt."

Aside from the reproaches and glum faces of the civilians through whose towns and villages they withdrew, the contrast for the troops between their initial arrival and their retreat was depressing. Most had arrived the previous autumn, passing through the pretty French countryside dotted with charming villages, fruit orchards, and beech forests in which owls hooted at

night. They had been cheerily welcomed in local cafés, where
the drink was good and cheap. The retreat, along a route farther
north, was through a dreary industrial landscape, along the cob-
bled streets of "endless mining towns . . . blocked with military
traffic, guns, lorries and staff cars going one way and refugees
going both ways—the position is so fluid that nobody knows
where any one German division is." On their way back, there
was neither time nor mood for dropping into bistros for a beer
and a laugh. And when they, like their French comrades in
arms, were subjected to the attentions of Stuka dive-bombers,
many of them came to know absolute terror for the first time in
their lives.

> It seemed all hell had been let loose. A plane is screaming
> earthwards; airbrakes wide open, tearing through the sky;
> then its engines seem to cut out as it pulls out of the dive,
> and out of the ensuing silence comes the shrilling whistle of
> the falling bombs. It is the most hellish experience I have
> known. For those few seconds the embryo of life hangs sus-
> pended on the edge of eternity. The world stands still. The
> past, present and future is now. Brace your body. Tension
> every nerve and muscle against the impending shock. For
> those few seconds, it seems, the soul flits away to a safer
> place. One bomb falls closer than the rest, shattering the
> barn roof [beneath which he had taken shelter] and bringing
> heavy tiles crashing down, narrowly missing my head. I'm
> lucky. I'm still wearing my tin-hat. Then the planes climb to
> dive again, and the whole beastly process is gone through
> over and over again until one wonders how long one can
> retain one's sanity.

The wretched refugees fleeing the German invader, some
for the second time in their lives, were both pathetic and trou-
blesome. Vast numbers of them had taken to the road to get out
of harm's way—individuals, couples, whole families with children, young people, old people, many loaded down with as
many of their belongings as they could carry. The lucky ones
traveled in cars, mattresses tied to their tops in a vain attempt to
shield them from aerial strafing attacks. Others were in horse-
drawn wagons or farm carts loaded with furniture, cooking uten-
sils, and everything else that could fit on board. Some were on
bicycles. Hearses, ice cream vans, and other incongruous vehi-

cles joined this desperate exodus. Some refugees pushed baby carriages or wheelbarrows stuffed with their things. But most were on foot, and some had walked so far, or had been so ill equipped for such an excursion, that their shoes had given out and they hobbled along with their feet covered in rags tied with string. Among the refugees were countless Belgian soldiers, fleeing from the German tide either individually or in groups.

The seemingly endless processions of panicking people in flight served German purposes. Luftwaffe fighter planes strafed towns and villages to drive inhabitants into fleeing, to clog roads and disrupt the passage of the Allied forces. Once on the roads, they were strafed and bombed and sent plunging for safety into roadside ditches from which, if they were not hit, they emerged covered in mud. The roadsides were dotted with the bodies of those who were not so lucky.

Unable to move quickly along choked lines of retreat, troops withdrawing in vehicles seized the moment when strafing planes zoomed over, and refugees dove to the side for safety, to speed down suddenly cleared roads and make up for lost time. That was, however, a risky stunt for which a price sometimes had to be paid. Later, in France, as the roads grew increasingly clogged, the French High Command ordered that refugees be driven off the roads into the fields, except for limited, specified hours, if they obstructed military movement.

It wasn't only the Allies who were apprehensive about developments. Recalling the disaster which ultimately overtook Germany's invading armies in France in the First World War, Hitler did not trust the triumph of his armored forces. "The Fuehrer is terribly nervous," General Halder noted in his diary on May 17. "Frightened by his own success; he is afraid to take any chances and so would rather pull the reins on us."

General Guderian complained that Hitler, who had strongly backed the blitzkrieg strategy, was now "frightened by his own temerity." Superstitious, emotional, a gambler who agonized over his rash gambles, he was now convinced that his tanks were moving too far too fast, that their lines were too extended, and that French forces sheltering behind the Maginot Line would rush up from the south to pinch off and obliterate his offensive. As always in moments of stress, Hitler's paranoia shone through. He raged and bellowed and alleged that his generals were well on their way to ruining the whole campaign, almost as if they were deliberately trying to foil him.

The fact was, however, that the blitzkrieg was turning into an unstoppable spurt. The Germans were following hard on the heels of the retreating Allied armies in Belgium, and the panzers which had crashed through around Sedan and had successfully broken out of their bridgeheads across the Meuse were poised either to rush toward Paris or make for the sea.

In the French capital, Reynaud was trying desperately to retrieve French honor and bolster French morale. On May 18, after Daladier had informed him that Gamelin had no plan for stopping the Germans, the premier personally took over the War Ministry, shifting Daladier, whom he considered most responsible for French military unpreparedness, from there to the Foreign Ministry. He brought in tough-minded Georges Mandel as minister of interior both to put a firm hand in control of domestic matters, which also threatened to plummet out of control, and to gain another ally against the defeatists in his government. He also recalled the aged Marshal Pétain from his post as ambassador to Spain to become vice premier. The presence in the government of this First World War "Victor of Verdun" was supposed to demonstrate France's will to win. That, however, was not how Pétain saw his summons to Paris. "My country has been beaten," he confided before leaving Spain. He said he was being brought home to sign an armistice with the Germans.

Knowing nothing of this and studying less than candid Allied battlefield communiqués for the slightest glimmer of hope, some western observers suggested that the German advance was about to become unstuck. It was said that by sending their armor plunging recklessly across northern France, the Germans rather than the Allies were heading for a trap; they would be caught between the Allied armies in Belgium and the French forces shunted up from positions in the south. Besides, too much was being asked of the panzers by their German commanders. They were only machines, bits of metal, which would soon suffer mechanical breakdown or outdistance their fuel supply lines. Cavalry horses could feed off the land and rest up from their exertions without the need for parts replacements. Tanks could not.

For Gort, such musings had no significance. For him the

facts were bleakly simple. Having been spared serious German
challenge during the first days of the offensive, some of his
forces were now being pressed hard by the enemy. Once again
he was being told very little by his befuddled French superiors.
But he finally became aware that if, as reports indicated, the
German breakthrough to the south had not been halted, there
was a distinct danger that his supply lines would be cut. Rations
and ammunitions were already running short. If, as now seemed
likely, the Germans were steamrolling toward the sea rather
than veering off toward Paris, the BEF could soon be caught in
a trap. It was an uncomfortable position to be in, made no
easier by Billotte, who, instead of producing an emergency battle plan for the northern group of armies under his command,
confessed on May 18, "I am shattered with fatigue. I have nothing that can deal with the panzers."

That was tantamount to a confession by the coordinator of
the northern armies of his belief that defeat was inevitable,
which meant that the BEF was in even greater danger than Gort
had previously imagined. Though subject to French command,
he was not without options. His instructions from the War Office
in London, and agreed to by France, had been that if any order
he received appeared to endanger his forces, he would "be at
liberty to appeal to the British government before executing that
order." That could certainly be interpreted as applying to a situation in which orders were simply not forthcoming to deal with
threatening circumstances.

On May 19, Gort's chief of staff, General Pownall, telephoned the War Office in London detailing the BEF's predicament. He reported that it didn't look as if the French would be
able to close the gap the Germans had opened in their lines. The
BEF, he said, had three options. It could stand and fight with
the danger of being cut off; it could counterattack southward in
the unlikely hope of joining with French forces attacking north
to snip off the German advance; or it could withdraw to the
Channel coast for possible evacuation. Pownall made it plain to
the War Office's director of military operations, with whom he
spoke, and whom he described as "singularly stupid and unhelpful . . . knowing nothing of the reports which were being
made," that this last option, though extreme, had to be considered very seriously.

The War Cabinet met later that day to consider a response

to what was, in effect, a totally unexpected cry for help from BEF headquarters. Gort had not been given authority to make his own strategic decisions. Despairing of his French superiors, he had now turned to London for instructions, advice, encouragement, and support. The response was not what he expected. His warning that the BEF might be driven into the sea shocked Churchill. It was obvious to the prime minister that the Germans had pulled off a daring maneuver in crossing the Meuse at Sedan and breaking out of their bridgehead there. But no indication had yet reached the British capital that a million Allied troops, including the BEF, might be caught between German pincers. Surely Gort was being irresponsibly premature in suggesting that such a possibility existed.

Those at the War Office and elsewhere in senior positions in London who had never been overly impressed by Gort's command talents were tempted to conclude that their judgment of the man was now being proved accurate. As far as Churchill and the War Office were concerned, evacuations had to be last resorts. The BEF was on the continent not to withdraw but to engage the enemy. It might be momentarily compelled to retreat some distance. It might withdraw to new positions for strategic reasons. But to fall back on the Channel ports was insane. Churchill believed that once it did that, it would be in a "bomb trap" and its total annihilation or capture would then be inevitable, only a matter of time. Ironside was dispatched to Gort's headquarters to put the BEF commander straight.

However, as a matter of standard policy, all options were to be considered. A meeting was called at the War Office later that same day to examine the points Pownall's telephone call had raised. Two main items were on the meeting's agenda: first, how to supply the BEF through the French English Channel ports—Boulogne, Calais, and Dunkirk—now that the Germans had rendered its supply lines from the coast farther south inoperable; and second, the "unlikely" possibility of having to evacuate "very large forces" from France through those same Channel ports.

Contingency planning was set in motion under the supervision of Vice Admiral Bertram Ramsay, naval commander at the port of Dover, twenty miles across the Channel from Calais. Further meetings on May 20 and May 21 looked more closely at evacuation possibilities. Such a momentous operation was still considered improbable and, if ultimately necessary, unlikely to be overly successful. The hazards involved, both for those being evacuated and those doing the evacuating, would be nightmarish. Nevertheless, emergency options had to be examined, however unlikely they might be.

Admiral Ramsay's staff was to be beefed up to include shipping and transportation specialists, among others. A roster was to be drawn up of all available ships to be put at Ramsay's disposal. These were to include as many passenger vessels as possible, capable of carrying large numbers of troops and of loading them quickly. It was decided also to compile a list of small vessels, including pleasure craft, which could be called upon to participate in an emergency evacuation from French beaches if that became necessary, though it was obvious that lifting great numbers of men from beaches would be an extremely hazardous undertaking, totally dependent on the actions of the enemy, the tides, and the winds. Ramsay's communications facilities were to be improved and he was to liaise directly with Fighter Command for aerial cover if circumstances required. All of this was still considered hypothetical.

Hypothetical or not, the operation needed a code name for convenience and security. Though charged with drama and purpose, the name it was given had mundane origins. Naval headquarters at Dover were situated in rooms built in tunnels which had been carved into the cliffs above Dover city by French prisoners of war more than a century before during the Napoleonic Wars. One of those chambers had housed an auxiliary electrical power generator during the First World War and had been known as the Dynamo Room ever since. Hence the name given to what would soon become one of the most critical operations in the Second World War—Operation Dynamo.

Like other paranoiacs whose fears are only partly imaginary, Hitler did have genuine reason to worry about the rapid advance of his tanks. They had covered a lot of ground. There could be trouble if their supply lines proved overextended, if their infantry backup did not move up quickly enough to guard their flanks, and if the Allied command seized the opportunity to do something about it. In fact, on May 19, in his first decisive move since the day more than a week earlier when the offensive began, General Gamelin ordered a maneuver of the kind Hitler dreaded.

Allied forces in the north were to wheel southward while French forces south of the Somme were to rush north to link up and chop off the German advance. The armored units which were the vanguard of the German offensive would be isolated and picked off and the offensive itself would be crushed. The concept was sound, though it may have been too late for Gamelin's proposed maneuver to have a chance of success. His forces in the north were too deeply engaged to be easily or quickly redeployed, and the breakdown in communications would have conspired against it.

Whatever the possibilities, the Gamelin plan was never to be tested. Horrified by developments at the front and regretting that he hadn't put Gamelin out to pasture before, Premier Reynaud relieved him of his command that same day. General Weygand, a seventy-three-year-old First World War hero, was to replace him as Allied supreme commander. Weygand immediately canceled the north-south linkup operation. He was very much his own man. He wanted to examine the situation before deciding on a course of action. While that was happening, German generals were left to marvel at the failure of the Allies even to try to block their advance.

As instructed by the War Cabinet in London, General Ironside arrived at Gort's headquarters on the morning of May 20 to disabuse the BEF commander of the foolish idea his chief of staff had floated about withdrawing toward the coast. Neglecting to consult Gort's French superiors, the British chief of staff instructed him to prepare to drive southward instead. He was to take action very much like that proposed in Gamelin's canceled join-up plan. The order baffled and infuriated Gort and his staff. Ironside was told the maneuver was impossible. Of Gort's nine divisions, seven were in combat on the line and could not easily disengage to move in a different direction. Even if they could, the Germans would quickly rush through the gap that would be left, nullifying the purpose of the proposed maneuver. Pownall said it would be "a scandalous—i.e. Winstonian—thing to do and in fact quite impossible to carry out—it would have involved a flank march across a gap which we know had some enemy mechanized parties in it." On the spot to see for himself, Ironside was persuaded that the maneuver, which had seemed logical and feasible when examined in the remote, calm setting of the War Office in London, was indeed ill-advised.

From Gort's headquarters, Ironside proceeded to Lens, north of Arras, to consult with Billotte at the headquarters of Billotte's Northern Army Group on what should be done. Also there when he arrived was French First Army commander Blanchard. For the first time, Ironside understood Gort's frustration with the chain of command. Neither of the French generals, in whose hands the fate of the BEF lay, inspired confidence. Ironside found them "in a state of complete depression. No plan, no thought of a plan. Ready to be slaughtered. . . . Très fatigués and nothing doing." Awestruck by what seemed to him to be unmitigated defeatism, Ironside, like Gort, concluded that the survival of the BEF rather than beating the Germans had to be the main immediate priority. He saw no grounds for optimism. "Situation desperate," he noted in his diary. "Personally, I think we cannot extricate the BEF. Only hope a march southwest. Have they time?"

Time was, in fact, running out. At 7:00 P.M. on May 20, a mere eleven days after the Germans had launched their offensive, Guderian's 2nd Panzer Division had reached Abbeville near the mouth of the Somme River, where it empties into the English Channel. One of its battalions had rolled on to reach the Channel at Noyelles in time to admire the sunset. The Allied armies in the north were now closed in on three sides, having only the sea by which their escape might yet be achieved, unless, as seemed unlikely, they could gather the strength to break out southward. Despite Hitler's anxiety, each stage of the swoop of his forces across northern France had been easier than the one before. Resistance had grown weaker rather than stronger. Now the Germans were ready to pivot along the coast to take the Channel ports and close the trap they had so speedily forged.

Word filtered back to the United States of how desperate the Allied position on the battlefield had become. Washington had been shocked by the rapidity of the German conquest of Holland. That shock intensified as reports told of the retreat of the Allied forces in Belgium when the battle had barely begun. "Worst of all," said Under Secretary of State Sumner Welles, "was the increasing apprehension that the German war machine was so overwhelmingly superior in might, quality, strategy, matériel, and morale to the available forces of the western European powers that Germany might well become the supreme master of all Europe before the summer had passed."

Churchill and Reynaud continued to press Roosevelt to find ways to circumvent congressional restrictions and release arms and supplies for urgent shipment to their forces. The president was also being urged by Ambassador Kennedy in London and Ambassador Bullitt in Paris to take action, though their advice about what should be done differed fundamentally.

Kennedy had sent word on May 16 that an "absolutely reliable" informant in London had told him "nothing can save [the Allies] from absolute defeat unless the President with some touch of genius and God's blessing can do it." This hint that the United States should intercede to plead for an armistice was not well received in Washington. If achieved, it would have left Hitler with virtually all of Western Europe under either his command or his shadow. A stiff return message to Kennedy from the State Department warned him that the United States was not in the business of trying to solve Europe's problems. With Roosevelt in charge in Washington, it certainly did not intend to do so by undermining Allied resistance to Nazi Germany.

Ambassador Bullitt's forebodings were more troubling. He had been frantically pleading for arms and supplies to be sent to France to enable the French to beat back the Germans. Now, in a message "personal and secret" to Roosevelt, he said, "I think it may possibly be of the utmost importance for the future of the United States that you should have in mind the hypothesis that, in order to escape from the ultimate consequences of absolute defeat, the British may install a government of Oswald Mosley and the Union of British Fascists [which Mosley led] which would cooperate fully with Hitler. That would mean that the British navy would be against us."

The British ambassador in Washington, Lord Lothian, didn't hesitate to draw advantage from American fears that circumstances existed under which the Royal Navy could fall under German control. Lothian stressed that the British fleet was crucial to American national security. He spelled out a predicament which already worried Roosevelt: if the American fleet patrolled the Pacific, American security would be endangered if Britain went under. If the American fleet was in the Atlantic, the expansionist Japanese might grab Hawaii. If the fleet was split to patrol both oceans, it would not be sufficiently strong in either to take on an aggressor. America, Lothian explained, had no logical alternative but to make certain Britain was not defeated.

Roosevelt suggested that if Britain was forced to succumb

to Hitler, the Royal Navy could be sent for safety to the United States. Lothian shrewdly replied that it would be difficult to convince the British public to agree to such a plan if America remained proudly aloof in a struggle in which Britain had suffered grievously in the name of freedom and justice. No, the fleet, if it could get away, would more likely head for far corners of the Empire—to Australia, perhaps, or New Zealand. In such circumstances, the United States would have to do without it. It was a form of blackmail that Roosevelt, not averse to such tactics himself when dealing with congressmen, well understood.

Churchill, whose friendship with the president permitted him certain liberties, was blunter still. He echoed Bullitt's blunt warning about the possibility of the emergence of a regime in London prepared to do a deal with Hitler if the situation seriously deteriorated further. On May 20, he cabled the president a warning of what might happen if his government was forced out.

> If members of this administration were finished and others came in to parley amid the ruins, you must not be blind to the fact that the sole remaining bargaining counter with Germany would be the fleet, and if this country was left by the United States to its fate, no one would have the right to blame those then responsible if they made the best terms they could for the surviving inhabitants. Evidently I could not answer for my successors who in utter despair and helplessness might well have to accommodate themselves to the German will.

Churchill's suggestion that a government sympathetic to Hitler might actually come to power in London had the intended effect of deeply troubling Roosevelt and others in Washington responsible for American security. But the president knew he was still unable to bring the American public with him in his wish to provide the Allies with substantial material aid. Sympathy for the plight of the Allies soared as word spread of the German blitzkrieg, dramatically reported in the American press. However, the news from Europe also reinforced the hope of most Americans that the United States would not be drawn into the struggle.

Still publicly vowing that it would not happen, Roosevelt risked a great deal by maintaining his secret personal correspondence with Churchill. If that correspondence was publicly disclosed, isolationists could claim it was proof that the president was covertly violating the neutrality he professed to be defending. After all, he engaged in no such personal correspondence with Hitler. It could be turned into a serious political embarrassment for Roosevelt and a serious setback for American supporters of the Allied cause. As the position of the retreating Allied armies turned critical, that almost happened.

On the morning of May 20, Scotland Yard Special Branch detectives, armed with a warrant, went to the home at 47 Gloucester Place, London, of Tyler Gatewood Kent, a code clerk at the American embassy. As a member of the embassy staff, Kent had diplomatic immunity, but that had been waived by Ambassador Kennedy at the request of the Foreign Office. When the twenty-nine-year-old bachelor, inside in his pajamas, refused to open his door to police, they broke it down and began a thorough search of his bed-sitting room flat. In a closet, they found folders containing copies of fifteen hundred secret documents which had passed through the embassy code room during the previous seven months. Kent had been handing the documents to Nazi sympathizers in London, who had in turn passed them on to the Italian embassy in London, from which they had presumably made their way to the German embassy in Rome and from there to Berlin. Included had been the Churchill-Roosevelt correspondence.

Kent had been under surveillance for some time. It may have been that Kennedy hadn't been informed of it earlier because, in view of the ambassador's well-known defeatist attitude, he himself was under discreet surveillance by British counterintelligence. After being arrested, Kent was incarcerated in London's Brixton Prison. The United States did not ask for him to be extradited to stand trial in America. The American government wanted no publicity for the case or for the reasons Kent gave for his actions.

At his London trial *in camera* later that year, Kent maintained that he had acted as a responsible American citizen, that the American people had the right to know about Roosevelt's efforts to provide support for Britain while pretending to be keeping America out of the European conflict. It was hardly a plea that would gain sympathy from a jury in Britain, which, at the time of the trial, was being blasted nightly by German bombers. Kent was sentenced to seven years in prison for violating the British Official Secrets Act.

Assistant Secretary of State Breckenridge Long believed that Kent's activities meant "not only that our codes are cracked a dozen ways but that our every diplomatic maneuver was exposed to Germany and Russia." Of even greater danger to the Allied cause was the possibility that the Germans would make the Churchill-Roosevelt correspondence public and that their propagandists would seek to persuade Americans that their president had been brazenly dragging America into the war against their will. Such a charge could have damaged Roosevelt's chances of winning a third term in the White House. Coming at a time when the president was making up his mind, it might even have discouraged him from running, leaving the candidacy open to someone much less concerned about the fate of Europe. As it was, details of the Kent case were to be kept secret for many years.

Few armies under pressure can retreat gracefully. The better prepared they are for combat, the more cumbersome they become when routed. For the BEF, that meant that thousands of its soldiers—men in the labor battalions, Pay Corps, Dental Corps, support troops of all kinds—though they had to be fed, quartered, and transported, no longer performed a pressingly useful purpose. Reconciled to the likelihood that their services would not be needed in the immediate future, Gort ordered some twenty-eight thousand "useless mouths" evacuated back to England. From then on, the BEF would travel light—but not always in retreat.

On May 21, under pressure from London and Paris for the BEF to put up more fight, Gort patched together an emergency strike force consisting of elements of his two reserve divisions and a tank brigade to counterattack vigorously. The aim was to block roads south of Arras and sever German lines of communications and supply. Two French divisions from General René Altmayer's V Corps were to launch a simultaneous attack but failed to do so. Having been heavily engaged and badly battered for more than a week, the French troops were exhausted, though some units did join the counterattack a day late and fought with much spirit until forced to withdraw twelve hours later.

The British strike force was outgunned and outnumbered, but in this first major clash between the BEF and Hitler's armored forces, the Germans took a heavy beating. Many of their tanks were destroyed and four hundred of their troops were taken prisoner, more than the Allies had captured since the beginning of the German offensive. The elite SS Totenkopf Division was forced to withdraw in little less than panic before overwhelming German armored superiority was able to reassert itself. But the British operation was overly ambitious and doomed to be short-lived. Within forty-eight hours, Gort's counterattack was snuffed out and his troops were forced to scamper unceremoniously back to avoid being encircled.

Nevertheless, their momentary achievement had an important bearing on the course of events. Guderian's newly committed crack 10th Panzer Division was quickly pulled back into reserve to meet any further surprises the British might come up with. Had it been permitted to race directly for Dunkirk as planned, any hope of the Allied escape by sea from the German trap would have been dashed even before the need for it was seriously considered.

From the moment General Weygand had assumed command of the French-British forces on the continent on May 19, he had been carefully studying the situation. He had even exposed himself to great danger by traveling to forward positions to consult personally with his immediate subordinates. Given the circumstances, it was no casual jaunt for a man of his advanced years. Having examined the possibilities, on May 21, the day the British Arras counterattack was launched, Weygand produced a plan to seize the battlefield initiative from the Germans. French forces south of the path the German tanks had blasted open across northern France and French-British forces north of that path were to launch simultaneous drives to link up, slicing off and isolating the enemy spearhead. It was essentially the same operation General Gamelin had proposed and Weygand had canceled three days before, on the day Gamelin had been dismissed, except that its chances of success had then been somewhat less remote.

Gort was to be required to commit three of his divisions to play a key role in the Weygand plan. When he learned of it, the BEF commander was appalled. A farcical series of timing and travel errors had caused him to miss the meeting with Weygand at which the north-south linkup was planned, so, though suspicious by now of French generalities and assurances, he had been unable to question details of the operation or the operation itself. He was, in any case, unable to comply immediately with Weygand's orders because all the BEF's available reserves were committed at the time to the Arras counterattack. It was therefore accepted that the linkup drive would not be launched until the battlefield situation had stabilized, not until May 26 at the earliest.

But now Churchill, exasperated by the setbacks the Allied forces had suffered, interceded. Back in Paris the following day, May 22, he was characteristically still not persuaded that the situation for the encircled forces was desperate. Reynaud took him to meet Weygand at Vincennes, where the new supreme commander vividly and buoyantly outlined to the prime minister the campaign he had devised for beating the enemy. Though it clearly resembled Gamelin's canceled plan, in contrast to his predecessor's despair, Weygand displayed the confidence of a forceful, resolute soldier who knew exactly what he was doing and how to achieve his objectives. This caused difficulties.

Churchill was both relieved and deluded by the sudden, overdue signs of decisiveness, lucidity, and fight in the French military leadership. He told the septuagenarian Weygand, "The only complaint that I have got to make about you is that you are a little too young." The prime minister did not understand that the new commander was offering far more than he could deliver. He did not know that British divisions expected to participate in the Weygand campaign were in the process of being forced by superior German forces to abort their operation near Arras and, their supply lines cut, were too low on ammunition to undertake any new major campaigns. Churchill did not know that the French First Army, far from being ready to go on the offensive alongside the British in the north, had been severely battered and was still under relentless German pressure from which it could not disengage to take part in fanciful schemes. And he did not know that the French forces south of the Somme were far weaker than Weygand suggested and that they were nowhere near ready to lunge northward across the German line of advance. Churchill also knew nothing of the agreed timetable for the planned synchronized north-south offensives. But excited by new signs of French resolve, he cabled Gort, ordering him to adhere to what the prime minister mistakenly understood to be the Weygand plan.

The BEF commander was instructed to begin his attack southward in concert with the French "at the earliest moment—certainly tomorrow with about eight divisions." It couldn't be done. Even if it could, it didn't make sense. The prime minister's intercession provoked undiluted outrage at BEF headquarters. Pownall was particularly incensed.

> Can nobody prevent him trying to conduct operations himself as a super Commander-in-Chief? How does he think we are to collect eight divisions and attack as he suggests. Have we no front to hold which if cracked would let in the flood? He can have no conception of our situation and condition. . . . The man's mad.

Pownall had not held Churchill in high regard even before, but his fury was doubly understandable. Not only were the prime minister's instructions impossible to carry out but one object of the proposed offensive was to prevent the Germans from getting to the English Channel despite the fact that they had reached the Channel two days before and had already begun their drive up the Channel coast. To raise the level of vexation at BEF headquarters to new heights, though disaster was looming for the British forces, London was persuaded by complaints from Paris that the BEF wasn't really pulling its weight. Pownall was bitter about "criticism . . . that the BEF was not doing enough."

> Clearly at home they do not understand how much we have done and are still doing. That everyone is in the line, that everyone has been marching or fighting or digging in for sixteen days without rest or relief, that we have held our ground and inflicted heavy casualties on the enemy.

Whatever appreciation or lack of same London had for the achievements of the BEF, word was passed along to Gort that he ought to stop moaning and get on with his job.

The BEF commander was, in fact, not without partial responsibility for the damage done to understanding and confidence between himself and London. Obedient soldier and gentleman that he was, at no time up to this point had he done more than intimate that he had grave doubts about the competence of his French commanders and their grasp of the situation. Neither Churchill nor Ironside knew what he was thinking. He neglected to take the advice of his friend Admiral Sir Roger Keyes, who was representing the British government at the Belgian royal court and who urged Gort to "tell the government to go to the devil, and insist on being given a free hand to extricate your army from the appalling situation into which it has been placed, through no fault of yours."

Confusion reigned supreme in the Allied High Command. Whatever his intentions and expectations, Weygand had little to offer on the battlefield. Proposals, plans, direct orders had little affect on the situation. Commanders couldn't locate one another to convey orders, exchange information, and resolve misunderstandings. Many officers and troops were left without orders. Even priority messages arriving at signals sections could not be delivered because nobody knew where to find the units or officers for which those messages were intended. Intelligence on German movements was virtually nonexistent. When, on May 22, Weygand instructed the exhausted, ill-equipped Allied forces, struggling for survival, to box in the triumphant German panzer divisions and starve them out, it was apparent that the French command had completely lost contact with reality.

The Allied armies in the north were enduring agonies of deprivation. Fighting and running, the men of the BEF had been put on half rations and were often not even fed those. Many of the troops, both French and British, were living off the land. It was, one officer said, "a sort of licensed pillage." The hungry troops did not always respect proprieties as they pulled back, but many farmers had joined the streams of refugees and eggs and poultry were up for grabs, as was milk from cows. In towns and villages, foraging soldiers found stores abandoned as well and took what they could use—cheese, canned food, coffee, tea, beer, and wine. However, such scavenging could not satisfy military requirements. Ammunition was increasingly in short supply. For the BEF, it had to be parachuted in from England.

The indecisive Billotte, from whom Gort had received nothing resembling an order in the four previous days, had been fa-

tally injured in a car accident on May 21. False rumors
circulated that he had committed suicide. Blanchard, named his
successor as coordinator of action in the Northern Army Group,
wanted to be formally appointed before getting on with the job.
There being no direct communications link between the French
army command and army group headquarters, that was not
easily accomplished.

Nor was it likely that speedy confirmation of Blanchard's
appointment would remedy the situation. Aside from the fundamental inability of the Allies to seize the initiative in the battle,
the British considered him a dangerous incompetent. At one
point, General Brooke saw him standing studying a map of the
battlefield and "gathered the impression that he might as well
have been staring at a blank wall. . . . He gave me the impression of a man whose brain had ceased to function." Nor did his
senior French subordinates have much faith in his abilities.
Shortly after finally assuming command of the army group,
Blanchard was overheard by a French officer suggesting that
perhaps capitulation was the wisest course of action. General de
la Laurencie, commander of the French III Corps, one of the
few senior French officers to emerge with credit from the debacle—twenty-five French generals were relieved of their commands by May 25—urged that Lord Gort take charge of the
army group in place of Blanchard. He said he believed
Blanchard incapable of command. Marshal Pétain also suggested to Spears, shortly after he arrived in Paris to be Churchill's personal representative there, that Gort take overall
command of the armies in the north, though his object may have
been to shift the blame to Britain for France's impending defeat.

The retreat of the BEF strike force which had mounted the
short-lived counterattack near Arras outraged Weygand. He was
convinced Gort had abandoned Arras without being compelled
by the Germans to do so. With communications disrupted and
the French command in the north completely muddled, the supreme commander had no way of knowing, or any reason to
believe, that the retreat had been ordered to save the strike
force from annihilation when it was imperiled by enemy flanking
movements. What he did know was that it would undermine his
plan for snipping off and destroying the German armored advance. Aside from that, it appeared that the British were aban-

doning their French comrades in arms, thus further demoralizing his troops. To the secretary of the French War Council in Paris, Weygand appeared "overcome by the defection of the English." He was wrongly but firmly convinced that Gort would never have acted on his own but must have retreated on orders from London. How could France fight a war when its ally behaved so despicably?

By now, meetings of the War Council were being regularly punctuated by futile moanings about how France had been militarily unprepared for the war, how it had been "criminal" to send its troops into battle without sufficient tanks, antitank guns, and aircraft. Though Reynaud had to accept some responsibility for that, he did not spare the feelings of the French military command. He told the Senate in Paris that "incredible mistakes" had permitted the Germans to cross the Meuse and that those responsible "will be punished." Reynaud was also beginning to share with his generals growing resentment of the apparent British desire to get their troops out of Europe as fast as possible. He complained that the British "always made for harbors." But he made it clear that as far as he was concerned, France was determined to fight on.

The premier's perseverance was not easy to sustain in the climate of despair in Paris, repeatedly heightened by disheartening news from the front. When, on May 25, one of Blanchard's staff officers, Major Joseph Fauvelle, was sent to Paris from Northern Army Group headquarters to report on the situation, he was brought along by Weygand to a meeting with Reynaud and told the premier, "In the voice of a seasick passenger asking a passing steward for a basin . . . 'I believe in a very early capitulation.'" General Spears, who was at the meeting, was appalled.

> I felt cold fingers, turning my heart to stone. I have in my time seen broken men, but never before one deliquescent, that is in a state when he was fit only to be scraped up with a spoon or mopped up. . . . Nothing short of throwing Fauvelle out of the window would have been adequate.

Spears was also more than a little surprised at that meeting, where the fate of France was being discussed, when Reynaud tolerated seemingly trivial telephoned interruptions by his mistress and from someone who appeared to be a politician asking that his son-in-law be transferred to a sector of the front where he was less likely to encounter Germans. Such distractions were perhaps emotionally and politically necessary for Reynaud, who was under enormous stress and who realized far better than Spears the extent of despondency with which he had to contend.

Few defeatists in Paris were any longer troubling to conceal their doleful sentiments. At a meeting of the War Council that day, when Weygand presented a report on the wretched state of what remained of French defenses, President of the Republic Albert Lebrun suggested that an understanding with the German invaders might be possible. Lebrun recognized that the French and British governments had agreed that neither would engage in separate negotiations with the enemy without the consent of the other. But, he said, if Germany made "any relatively advantageous offer we ought . . . to examine it closely and objectively."

Minister of Marine César Campinchi, who was not numbered among those prepared to give up the fight, was worried that worsening circumstances might lead to the formation of a government in Paris prepared to seek a separate armistice with the Germans. In the spirit of Allied solidarity, Campinchi urged Reynaud to warn Churchill of that possibility. But Marshal Pétain was not overly concerned about British sensibilities. It was his contention that the Allies had a duty toward each other only in proportion to the effort they made in the common struggle, and Britain had contributed far less than France. Air Force Commander General Vuillemin concurred, claiming that while the French air force was sustaining heavy losses, little was to be seen of the RAF in the skies over France—exactly the complaint in reverse that RAF pilots made about the French.

Whatever arguments were presented at the War Council meeting, it was evident that what was happening on the battlefield was developing important political dimensions. It was decided that Reynaud would fly to London the following day, May 26, to confer with Churchill on the possibility of considering German peace proposals if such proposals were forthcoming.

In London, the War Cabinet, still trying to discover what was happening at the battle front, or indeed where the front was, could not fathom what Gort was up to. Churchill was grow-

ing increasingly impatient with the BEF commander. Reynaud
had protested angrily to the prime minister about the BEF's allegedly unnecessary and certainly unauthorized withdrawal from
Arras after its successful counterattack there. Unaware of Gort's
reasons, Churchill agreed that the French had grounds for complaint. He said Gort should have informed both London and his
French superiors of the action he was taking. He cabled Reynaud, "We know nothing of the evacuation of Arras, and this
would be absolutely contrary to our wishes." To Ironside, Churchill said, "I must know at earliest why Gort gave up Arras, and
what actually he is doing with the rest of his army." But while
not yet persuaded, Churchill reluctantly allowed that circumstances might make it necessary for the BEF to fight its way to
the coast.

Cadogan noted in his diary, "Gort seems—inexplicably,
rather—to have withdrawn 40 kms! But everything is complete
confusion: no communications and no one knows what's going
on, except that everything's as black as black. . . . If *only* that
Great French Army could give them a smack on the flank, we
should have defeated Hitler. They *may* be preparing something,
but there is no sign of it, and I haven't heard of a Frenchman
fighting anywhere."

Frustrated by the dearth of reliable, up-to-date information
on what was happening at the front and not convinced that Gort
knew what he was doing, the War Cabinet grew increasingly
worried, and not only about day-to-day developments. A dazzling, unnerving realization was beginning to fester in the upper
reaches of the government and the War Office. It was suddenly
conceivable that the BEF, constituting virtually the entire British professional army and all its equipment, might be lost to the
Germans! And the fighting war had just begun. Frighteningly
awesome in itself, it could also have calamitous consequences
for the fate of Britain. The Germans were already in a position
to cross the English Channel to mount an invasion.

Examination of the enemy's military threat to the country
was intensified. The review was not confined to dangers posed
by conventional attack. A report to the Chiefs of Staff Committee said that the Germans had large reserves of mustard gas and
other poisonous chemical substances and that they had experi-
mented with spraying them from aircraft. Intelligence had reported that on two occasions the year before, German planes

had released mysterious large white balloonlike objects over France. These had disintegrated and covered an area of several square kilometers with a substance resembling cobwebs. It had been impossible for people in the immediate area to avoid getting these cobwebs on their hands and faces, though with no noticeable ill effect. There had been no further details or explanation, but evidently the Germans were experimenting with new dimensions of chemical warfare. They were believed also to be experimenting with thorium and uranium bombs which could have formidable powers of devastation, but it was considered doubtful that the necessary techniques for their development and use were sufficiently advanced to present an immediate danger. Another report said that the Germans might have produced crewless tanks which could be remotely controlled from aircraft overhead.

Meantime, rumors were spreading in Britain about the kind of measures to which defense forces might have to resort if the Germans invaded. The War Cabinet was informed that "there appeared to be a general feeling abroad that, in the event of the enemy gaining a foothold on the East coast, the only means of ejecting them would be to bombard the area with artillery and from the air." Regional officials felt obliged to put through formal requests for total evacuation of civilians from the targeted region before such drastic action was taken. They were assured that such matters were under consideration.

There could be no doubt that if the BEF was doomed to be captured or destroyed and if the Germans then proceeded with an attempt to invade armyless Britain, the challenge to home defenses would be formidable. Arrangements were made for the government to take total authority over all persons and property in the country. The minister of labor was given the power to assign anyone in Britain to whatever job he thought would help the war effort.

Belated awareness of the dangers helped concentrate minds in London on the chances of extricating the British forces from France. On May 25, the War Office sent Gort a telegram telling him what he had known for a week—that he "might be faced with a situation in which the safety of the British Expeditionary Force would be the predominant consideration." He was informed that every endeavor would be made to provide ships for an evacuation of his men, as well as aircraft to provide aerial cover, if such an operation became necessary.

Boulogne had already fallen to the Germans, which left only Calais and Dunkirk among the Channel ports where an evacuation might be attempted. But Calais was under German bombardment and siege; retreating troops would have to fight their way into the city to be evacuated from its harbor—an unlikely prospect. If an evacuation was to be attempted, it could reasonably be made only from Dunkirk. A message was dispatched to Brigadier Claude Nicholson, commanding British troops holding out in Calais, informing him that his men would have to fight to the end. By holding out, they would delay the German advance up the coast to Dunkirk. Indicating the extent of the sacrifice that was expected, Churchill himself informed Nicholson, "His Majesty's Governments are confident you and your gallant Regiment will perform an exploit worthy of the British name." A great deal was being asked of Nicholson, who was later to die in a German prisoner of war camp. Not only were his forces greatly outnumbered but he had been short-changed on essential equipment. He had only eight antitank guns to fend off German armor; the others with which his troops were supposed to be equipped were still at Dover, waiting for cargo space to be found on ships crossing the Channel.

At this stage—May 25—the attempt to evacuate the BEF, though increasingly likely, was still no more than that. No one—not Churchill, not Gort, not Admiral Ramsay, who would superintend the operation—believed it would be able to produce more than a very limited success of the kind that, while saving some of the men, would underline the enormity of the Allied rout. General Brooke wrote in his diary, "Nothing but a miracle can save the BEF now and the end cannot be very far off." It was possible that the evacuation operation would collapse into catastrophic panic. Such was the intimation at Dunkirk, where Gort's assistant adjutant general, Colonel G.H.F. Whitfield, had already begun evacuating the "useless mouths" among the troops. Whitfield was appalled by the conduct of many of them and worried about the effect of German bombing.

> On many occasions both officers and men hurried into the report centre [at Dunkirk] at a speed which made one sup-

pose that the enemy were at least only a few yards behind
them. It was clearly impossible for me to check up on the
credentials of so many arrivals coming, as so many did, without an authority of any kind to support their application for
embarkation. . . . Men who belonged to untrained or poorly
officered regiments and corps broke to pieces when the
heavy bombing raids occurred. . . . [But] I am doubtful if
even the best disciplined troops could have stood such attacks for long so that I am not surprised that small bands of
men, utterly helpless and lost, were reported to me as wan-
dering about Dunkirk trying to find shelter from the next
raid. . . . In many cases . . . the officers departed for the
boats leaving their men behind. . . . Officers whom I detailed for jobs which might delay their departure for a day or
so disappeared and I have no doubt embarked for England
without permission.

Counterattack rather than sending the fighting troops
streaming back for evacuation was still officially the plan of operations. Despite Weygand's conviction that Gort had turned
tail, and though the BEF commander had grave doubts about its
prospects, on the evening of May 25 he was still prepared to
fulfill his allotted role in the Weygand plan. His two reserve divisions were braced to drive southward to attempt the elusive
linkup with French forces supposedly preparing to lunge northward. But enemy action once again dictated the course of
events.

That evening, the BEF commander received word that German pressure on the sector of the front line held by Belgian
forces to his left was becoming irresistible. The Belgians were
sustaining tremendously heavy casualties. Some Belgian units
had dissolved under German battering. Troop morale was disintegrating. Many Belgian soldiers had personally bowed out of
the war—a British liaison officer who had been dispatched to
assess the situation had seen some of them knocking back liquid
refreshment in cafés without a care about what might be happening at the front barely a mile away.

What was more, those Belgians who did fight on were determined to resist as best they could, but only within the borders
of their own country, regardless of the demands of concerted
Allied tactics. Instead of preparing to fall back into northern
France, they were closing ranks toward Bruges, where their gen-

eral headquarters were situated. As a result, a gap was opening
between British and Belgian defense positions. If the Germans
rushed through that gap—and captured enemy documents indicated that was their intention—they would be able to cut the
Allied line of withdrawal to the coast, trapping the BEF and
what was left of the French First Army as well as the Belgian
army. Indeed, the German High Command declared that evening that "the ring around the British, French and Belgian armies has been definitely closed."

Gort was faced with a dilemma. The only forces available to
him to prevent that German breakthrough were earmarked for
the drive south the following morning, May 26. If he sent them
north instead to block a German breakthrough in Belgium, he
would be disobeying orders, undermining the Weygand plan for
seizing the initiative in the battle, and confirming French suspicions of British betrayal. The decision had to be made immediately. Delay could be calamitous. An officer found Gort sitting
at his table alone at his new command post in a house in Pre-
mesque, "looking rather bewildered and bitter. . . ." Uncharac-
teristically, he voiced his frustration at his treatment at the
hands of the French.

> He said . . . not only had their Army continually pleaded
> that it was too tired to fight, and their staff work broken
> down, but from start to finish there had been no direction or
> information from the High Command.

A few minutes later that same evening, Gort's bitterness at
being let down found new grounds. He was informed that instead of the three divisions and two hundred tanks that the
French were to contribute to the planned joint British-French
drive south the next morning, only one division would be available. And that was a do-or-die operation scheduled to be
launched in a few hours' time! His conviction that the proposed
southward drive was doomed to failure was now unshakable. He
no longer had doubts about which course to follow. The two
BEF divisions earmarked for the operation Weygand had ordered were instructed to shift north instead to cover the gap
opening up between the British and Belgian positions. A line of
march to the coast was to be kept open for his troops, and,

regardless of whatever hopes for counterattack Churchill and Weygand might entertain, that march was about to begin.

The urgency of the situation and communications inadequacies led the BEF commander to make this critical decision without informing either London or his French superiors. General Blanchard, newly confirmed as Northern Army Group commander in place of the deceased Billotte, could not be found by British liaison officers and didn't learn of it until much later that night. The French military command was to see this delay, as well as Gort's unilateral decision, as further proof of the bad faith of their British allies.

Had Gort's decision proved to be a mistake, it might have gone down in history as one of the great military blunders of modern times. Weygand's plan for chopping off the German armored advance may have been based on a questionable assessment of Allied capabilities, but it was the only existing strategy for challenging the German onslaught, and it hadn't yet been proved faulty. Now that strategy was in ruins because of the insubordinate BEF commander, who hadn't bothered to consult either his French or British superiors before going off on his own. The Allies—and certainly the Allied armies in the north—could not now even attempt to snatch victory from the Germans.

Weygand bitterly declared, "The defection of the English compels me to abandon finally any offensive movement." Despite his earlier declarations about saving the honor of France by fighting to the last cartridge, he concluded that it was now necessary to consider how to "prevent a useless massacre" of French troops. As for the British, a hard-pressed retreat to the coast and the evacuation from France of a comparatively small number of their men seemed the most they could hope for.

Even before Gort had wrestled with the decision to withdraw to the sea, he had initiated efforts to guard the threatened right flank of the shrinking Allied pocket in northern France and southern Belgium. To block a thrust by German panzers across the rear of the Allied armies, a defense line had been established along the continuous chain of canals that ran from Gravelines on the coast through St. Omer and Bethune to La Bassée. A remnant of the French army which had rushed confidently into Holland at the start of the German offensive and which had then hastily withdrawn held the section of this Canal Line closest to the coast. Marshy and streaked with waterways, much of this area was extremely difficult terrain for tanks. Such was not the situation along the rest of the Canal Line. There the German panzers, now poised to bolt forward to close the trap around the Allied northern armies, would encounter no natural obstacles aside from the line itself.

This sector was held by a hastily improvised BEF force in which infantry units, artillery and antiaircraft troops (mostly without their big guns), and engineer and signal troops were supplemented by an assortment of normally noncombatant soldiers who had not yet been withdrawn to be evacuated as "useless mouths." They included medical orderlies, transport troops, technical instructors, and even men from mobile bath units. For many of these men—some ten thousand in all—experience in handling weapons amounted to no more than hurried instruction as they took up their positions. All infantrymen now, they fought with desperation but were outgunned, short of supplies, and under repeated air attack. By the morning of May 24, German armored units had secured four small but dangerous bridgeheads across the Canal Line and were only fifteen miles from Dunkirk! Troops in one of their forward positions could already see the towering belfry of St. Eloi Church in the center of the city. Dunkirk appeared to be theirs for the taking.

But the Germans were not without problems. In virtually continuous motion for two weeks, under the strain of battle, their troops were nearing exhaustion. They had suffered heavy losses in equipment, some through combat, most through mechanical breakdown. But victory carries its own momentum. Aside from the momentary thrashing suffered at Arras, the German advance had been relentless. Troop morale was high. Though recognizing the weariness of the men and the equipment problems of the panzer divisions, Chief of Staff General Halder had no doubt that they were capable of one last spurt along the coast to seal the fate of the Allied armies of the north. Cornered, badly mauled, and groggy, the bulk of the Allied forces could be closed off from the sea in relatively short order, after which it would be a simple mopping-up operation. But on the morning of May 24, before the final blow could be struck, the advance of the panzers trying to force the Canal Line was suddenly called off.

This strange, totally unexpected development originated with a decision by General von Rundstedt, commander of Army Group A. Rundstedt was worried that his tanks had pushed too far too fast and that his lines were overextended. He thought it would be best to close ranks before bringing the campaign in the north, which was practically won anyway, to a close. What he had in mind was a brief pause for rest and recovery before his panzers resumed their advance. But not only did Hitler endorse Rundstedt's judgment when the destruction of the Allied armies of the north was within his grasp, but he turned it into a firm order to halt right across the Canal Line and angrily canceled an effort by Army Commander in Chief, von Brauchitsch, to circumvent it. He made it clear that the panzers must stay put on the far side of the line.

For the Allies, the order to halt, when it came, was an astoundingly well-timed mercy. It happened just before Gort decided to abandon the Weygand Plan and shift the only two divisions he had in reserve to block the threatening German breakthrough on the Belgian sector on his left. Had the advance of the German tanks on his right not been halted, he would have had to cope simultaneously with closing the gap in Belgium and bolstering his fragile defenses on the Canal Line. It is not easy to see how, under those circumstances, the BEF commander could have prevented the Germans from breaking through, either on the Canal Line or in Belgium or in both places, to slam closed their trap on the Allied armies in the north.

Various explanations have been offered for Hitler's halt order. Though the campaign across northern France and Belgium had received his backing from the start, he had been deeply worried about its prospects for success, as demonstrated by his earlier attempt to slow down the panzer advance. As a soldier in the First World War, he had experienced the chaos of combat at first hand and particularly the German battlefield disappointments in the mud of Flanders. He knew that best-laid battle plans could go sour. He realized how great a gamble the entire operation through the Ardennes and northern France had been—with his tanks racing ahead of both their supply lines and the infantry—and had difficulty convincing himself that it was already virtually a total success.

His panzers had not been an unrelieved joy in the past. Some had broken down embarrassingly en route to Vienna during the annexation of Austria in 1938. During the Polish campaign, there had been extensive mechanical breakdowns. Now his tanks had been pushed harder than before and were not bearing up well. Panzer group commander von Kleist said that 50 percent of his tanks had been put out of action. Hitler may have feared that his armored units would grind to a halt or suffer greater losses than they had already if pushed on without rest and repair.

He also feared that the Allied forces had not yet been enfeebled and were still capable of reversing the course of events, that they might recover, regroup, and counterattack as they had at Arras, only in a more sustained fashion. The Belgian, French, and British armies in the north still amounted to a million men. It was not beyond the realm of possibility that they would break out of the pocket in which they were enclosed to participate in a modified Weygand Plan. If they succeeded, not only would the German offensive be wrecked but the very survival of his Nazi regime in Germany might be put at risk. Great care had to be taken in this endgame.

It was also true that now that the Allied armies in the north were being pressed against the sea, Paris had become the priority objective. Hitler had already declared, "The principal thing now is to husband the armored formations for later and more important tasks." When Paris did fall to his troops three weeks later, wiping out the shame he felt for the Versailles Treaty two decades earlier, it was to be one of the most ecstatic moments of his life.

In halting his panzers, Hitler was also bowing to pleas from Goering. The Luftwaffe commander had been pressing him to permit the German air force to finish off the trapped forces as a token of gratitude for the tremendous contribution it had made in the campaign. Goering reminded Hitler that while few of his army generals were devout National Socialists, the Luftwaffe was a Nazi creation. Its pilots were blindly loyal to the Fuehrer and deserved the honor of achieving this triumph over the decadent democracies. Goering told Hitler that if he gave the order that this operation was to be left to the Luftwaffe alone, he "would give an unconditional assurance that he would annihilate the remnants of the enemy; all he wanted . . . was a free run; in other words, the tanks must be withdrawn sufficiently far . . . to ensure that they [would not be] in danger from our own bombing." Goering said that after his planes had done their work, all that would be required of the army would be to "occupy the territory."

There was also the question of Hitler's determination to demonstrate to his generals that he was as much the supreme ruler on the battlefield as he was in politics at home. He insisted on being implicitly obeyed regardless of any contrary thoughts they might entertain. He was increasingly exasperated by senior officers who presumed to engage him in wrangling over strategy and tactics, questioning his grasp of military matters and his judgment. Halder noted in his diary that the "divergence of views [beween Hitler and some of his generals] results in a tug-of-war which costs more nerves than does the actual conduct of the operations." During his rise as leader of the Nazi movement in Germany and then as German dictator, Hitler had often felt obliged to demonstrate his authority forcefully to prove to recalcitrant subordinates that he was in charge, and he may have felt the same as the battle of Flanders neared conclusion.

There is, finally, the possibility that Hitler had been informed that the stars weren't right at that moment for a land operation by his tanks that would have cut the Allies off from the sea. He was reputed to place such great faith in astrologers that later in the war, the British consulted some as well to learn what sort of advice he might be receiving.

Whatever the reason or combination of reasons, the German dictator ignored the complaints of officers who saw no justification for the panzers to be reined in when they had been doing so well. Guderian was furious. It had been his tanks, in the vanguard of the panzer charge across northern France, which had established bridgeheads across the Canal Line when the order to halt reached him. He noted bitterly in his diary, "It was forbidden to cross that stream. We were not informed of the reasons for this. . . . We were utterly speechless."

That last wasn't particularly true. They were far from speechless, though careful not to let word of the tone of their reaction to reach the Fuehrer. Noting in his diary that the panzer force "which has no enemy before it" was being "stopped dead in its tracks," Halder was convinced Hitler's interference was jeopardizing the successful conclusion of the campaign. Word that Dunkirk was to be left to the Luftwaffe did not mollify those men who knew the possible consequences. The chief army operations officer called the halt order "insane." "Are we going to build golden bridges for the British?" he demanded. "Are we going to allow them to embark? This is ridiculous." Panzer group leader General von Kleist tried to ignore the order and sent his tanks forward but was emphatically ordered to withdraw them.

Spared the fierce attentions of German armor, the hastily patched-together forces which constituted the thin shield guarding the Canal Line could be reinforced. They dug in and consolidated their positions. Hitler's order to halt, tacitly recognized as a mistake, was lifted two days later. But the Germans had to contend with far stronger resistance on the line than they would have met initially as they renewed their attempt to sever what was about to become the Allied corridor to Dunkirk and the sea.

PART TWO

PART TWO

Sunday, May 26:
Day One of Dunkirk

Dunkirk is comparatively new upon the face of the earth. Not much more than a thousand years ago much of where it now stands was barely more than a sandbank, slipping in and out of the tide. Soon after the sea receded, a chapel was built and the village of Dunkirk—Church of the Dunes—grew around it. It was a sleepy fishing community on the shore of the English Channel, just north of the narrowest point of that marine trench which separates France from England. Four hundred years ago, when Dunkirk was part of the Spanish Netherlands, the Spaniards turned it into a garrison town for the armada that gathered for an abortive attempt to invade and conquer Britain. In the seventeenth century, it was twice besieged by the English and for a while came under English rule and had to be bought back by France.

Dunkirk subsequently became a thriving port city. By the nineteenth century, freight vessels from around the world berthed at its docks. In due course, two long breakwaters were built, converging toward each other in the outer harbor to protect it from the swirl of the tide. The stretch of coast east of the port constituted one of the longest unbroken sand beaches in northern Europe. Backed by wide expanses of desolate, rolling dunes studded with clumps of coarse grass, it extended well beyond the Belgian border eight miles away.

The beach here shelves gently into the sea. At low tide, a person can wade hundreds of yards into the sea with the water reaching no higher than his knees. At high tide, the farther reaches of that same stretch of coast is under several feet of water, though still not deep enough for large ships to approach closer than a half mile from the shore.

Though the sea passage to Dunkirk harbor provides little danger to navigators familiar with the sea lanes, it can be treacherous to those who do not know their way or do not have the appropriate charts. Waters even well away from the coast are laced with shallows. Channels between ribbons of sandbank can be as little as twelve feet deep. During most of the year, even on mild, sunny days, the waters off Dunkirk are more often than not buffeted by winds which make crossings bumpy and which can threaten small craft manned by inexperienced sailors with beachings and swampings.

The landscape immediately enclosing Dunkirk city is flat and largely treeless. It would make ideal tank terrain were it not for the impact of the sea on the region. It is a marshy countryside with four major canal systems and many lesser canals and streams. In the spring of 1940 while the evacuation from Dunkirk was in progress, these waterways provided screens behind which defense lines could be established to delay the advance of the German forces which had thundered across northern France.

A National Day of Prayer had been declared in Britain. The BBC broadcast a morning service from Westminster Abbey during which the Archbishop of Canterbury, senior primate of the Anglican Church, led prayers "for our soldiers in dire peril in France." Similar prayers were offered in churches and synagogues throughout Britain that day. In London, the famous Petticoat Lane market was empty for the first time in living memory on a Sunday so that the market traders who tended the pushcarts there could take part.

For many people in Britain, it seemed the first firm proof that things were turning out desperately wrong across the English Channel. It was a very worrying omen. When the broadcast of a prayer service at London's Catholic cathedral was abruptly cut off for no apparent reason, an official explanation was hastily concocted to reassure the public at a time when people were being warned to beware of saboteurs. It was announced that the interruption had been caused by a woman worshiper standing near the microphone who had been overwhelmed by religious emotion and that the incident had no po-

litical significance. In fact, she had shouted "Peace" during the
sermon by Cardinal Hinsley and the transmission had been suspended until she had been ejected.

Early that morning, Gort was able to contact London and
passed word on that he was shifting the reserve troops which
had been earmarked for the drive south northward to close the
gap opening on the Belgian sector of the front. Whatever reservations may have persisted at the War Office, it was pointless for
anyone there still to insist that southward was the way out for
the BEF. Gort had made the decision, and everyone concerned
had to live with it. Later that morning, a cable from Eden to
Gort revealed that London was indeed finally coming to accept
that the sea was the only possible escape route for the BEF. The
secretary for war told Gort that he might find himself faced with
a situation which, as far as the BEF commander was concerned,
already prevailed.

> I have had information all of which goes to show that French
> offensive from Somme cannot be made in sufficient strength
> to hold any prospect of functioning with your Allies in the
> North. Should this prove to be the case you will be faced
> with a situation in which the safety of the BEF will predomi-
> nate. In such conditions only course open to you may be to
> fight your way back to West where all beaches and ports East
> of Gravelines will be used for embarkation. Navy will pro-
> vide fleet of ships and small boats and RAF would give full
> support.

Exasperatingly, this still was not firm confirmation or approval for Gort's unauthorized, unilateral action. Churchill was
to review developments with Reynaud when the French premier
arrived in London later that day. ". . . in the meantime," Eden
told Gort, "it is obvious you should not discuss the possibility of
the move with the French and Belgians," neither of whom were
likely to take kindly to the idea of being abandoned by the British forces.

Gort was relieved that at least London finally appeared to
understand his dilemma in remaining under French command
while trying to ensure the BEF's survival. He was, however, not
convinced that the War Office had yet grasped the full extent of
the crisis. The withdrawal to the coast for evacuation, about

which London was still dithering, would be an extremely difficult, hazardous operation. A quarter of a million men had to be
shifted back fifty miles through a corridor fifteen miles wide with
the enemy snapping at their heels and hounding their flanks.
Gort cabled Eden, "I must not conceal from you that a great
part of the BEF and its equipment," constituting virtually all of
Britain's heavy guns and all its tanks, "will inevitably be lost
even in best circumstances." To an aide, he confided, "I never
thought I'd lead the British army to its biggest defeat in history."

Mutual distrust and recrimination had by now become ha-
bitual between the Allied military leaders. The British saw
breathtaking incompetence of the French senior commanders as
the only possible explanation for the precipitous collapse of the
illustrious French army, to which the BEF had been expected to
lend only marginal assistance. The French meantime were bitter
that Britain, with a population as large as France's, had fielded
such limited forces in the struggle against the common enemy—
and that those forces made for the sea at the earliest opportunity. And where was the RAF, of which so much had been
expected? Their essential communications having become virtually nonexistent, almost all RAF squadrons based in France
had already packed up and scrambled home.

To complicate matters still further, another divergence on
strategy developed between the British and French. As far as
Gort was concerned, the BEF would be withdrawing for one
purpose only—to be evacuated back to England. But
Blanchard, even if he had known Gort's objective, which he did
not, wasn't about to authorize the abandonment of his homeland by the troops under his command, which officially included
the BEF. Blanchard believed the pullback was only to shorten
defense lines in order to maintain a bridgehead based on Dunkirk for continued spoiling operations against the Germans.
"This bridgehead," he declared in accordance with instructions
from Weygand, "will be held with no thought of retreat."

A factor influencing the attitude of the French was their
difficulty in fathoming the concept of escape by sea, which the
British, a seafaring people, grasped instinctively. French navy
commander Admiral François Darlan was asked to examine possibilities for "reembarkation" of French troops caught in the

Dunkirk pocket, presumably so that they might be shifted to safety farther down the French coast. But that request aroused little urgency—Darlan's reflexive response was that an evacuation was impossible—and none of the commanders in the north were informed that anything of the sort was being contemplated. Attending a meeting of the French government's War Council in Paris, General Spears "suddenly realized . . . that to [its members] the sea was much the same thing as an abyss of boiling pitch and brimstone, an insurmountable obstacle no army could venture over unless they were specially organized colonial expeditions endowed with incomprehensible powers such as had once been enjoyed by Shadrach, Meshach and Abednego."

Morale among the British troops drooped markedly, as might have been expected from men on half rations if they were lucky, most of whom had done nothing but retreat, dig in, and retreat again for the better part of ten days. It seemed a strange way to run a war after messing around for nine months doing nothing. Frontline regular infantry units were highly disciplined and pulled back in good order to new positions when the command came, but the same could not be said for reserve and support units. They had neither intensive training nor regimental pride to fall back on. Some units disintegrated under attack when they lost experienced officers and senior NCOs. The men then made their way back as best they could. Many were told, "It's every man for himself." Word reaching the men that a National Day of Prayer had been proclaimed for them at home—"as though we were an army of the doomed!"—did little to lift their spirits.

Gort's decision to withdraw to the sea did nothing to improve spirits in London among members of the War Cabinet and the chiefs of staff. Their forebodings about the fate of the BEF were compounded by fear that a German invasion of Britain could be imminent. General Ironside noted in his diary, ". . . the Germans may try to reduce this country by air-attack alone [before invading]. . . . The position is serious." Many on the fringes of power in Whitehall got wind of what their seniors were pondering in the endless series of top-level emergency conferences taking place and also began to fear the worst. Harold Nicolson, parliamentary secretary at the Ministry of Information, advised his wife to have a suicide pill handy "so that you can take your quietus when necessary. I shall have one also. I am not in the least afraid of such sudden and honourable death. What I dread is being tortured and humiliated." Lord Weymouth feared what had happened to Czechoslovakia and Poland "will seem trifling compared to what Hitler will do to the hated English once he gets the chance."

Senior figures in Berlin were confident that the British as well as the French were on the verge of total defeat. They forecast a British capitulation and the occupation of London "within a few weeks." There were hints about a "great secret weapon" that would bring Britain to its knees. The Germans were not alone in forecasting Hitler's imminent total victory over the Allies. Ambassador Bullitt in Paris cabled President Roosevelt, "I believe that the British, French and Belgian armies in Flanders will be obliged to surrender within two or three days." British leaders assumed that Reynaud was coming to London that day to announce his government was considering a separate peace with Germany that would leave Britain fighting on alone against Hitler. Churchill prepared to plead with the French premier not to take that course of action.

Reynaud would be reminded that France and Britain had joined in a solemn undertaking not to conclude a separate peace and that it would be dishonorable to violate that undertaking. Churchill would warn him that France would become a vassal, if not a slave, to Germany if it succumbed, no matter how generous were the peace terms Hitler would pretend to offer. He would tell him that if his government did sign a separate peace with Hitler, Britain would have to include France in its maritime blockade of Germany and this might regrettably lead to widespread hunger and starvation among the French people. France would be cut off from its overseas empire—a hint at a possible British seizure of France's territories in Africa, the Caribbean, and elsewhere. And it would not be spared death and devastation from military action the British armed forces would be obliged to take against German forces on French soil. French cities would be bombed by the RAF.

At the same time, Churchill intended to try to convince Reynaud that the situation was not as serious as it seemed, that the invading German forces were fully stretched and on the verge of exhaustion, that Hitler was in trouble at home because of domestic economic pressures, and that continued joint resistance to the Nazis by the Allies would soon bring the United

States to their side. Finally, if unable to persuade Reynaud, Churchill intended to press the French to make a supreme effort to help the BEF get back to England before the French capitulation and to transfer the French navy and air force to British command so that the Germans would not gain control of them.

As expected, Reynaud did little to lift hopes in London when he arrived. Weighed down with despair, he confirmed the reports the prime minister had earlier received from Paris that instead of performing the tasks for which Marshal Pétain had been brought into his government—to imbue the French with determination to prosecute and win the war—his new deputy premier had revealed himself to be leader of the defeatist faction in France. Reynaud said that he feared the Germans would soon be marching on Paris and said he had no means of stopping them. He said they outnumbered the French defenders 150 divisions to 50—impossible odds.

Reynaud said France was prepared to fight to the death for its independence. But he pressed the possibility of persuading Italy to undertake diplomatic efforts that might lead to an honorable armistice and save his country from total disaster. He said Mussolini had to be convinced that it would not be in Italy's best interests for Germany to dominate Europe. The Italian dictator had to be persuaded not to join the Germans in their attack on France and instead to use his influence to get peace talks going. France was willing to offer him some of its African colonial empire as an inducement.

Reynaud suggested that Britain might be willing to make similar friendly gestures. It was no secret that Mussolini felt humiliated by British control of the Suez Canal and Gibraltar. They guarded the two portals of the Mediterranean Sea which Il Duce liked to think of as an Italian lake, controlled by Rome as it had been during the days of the Caesars. Perhaps Britain would be prepared to internationalize the Canal and Gibraltar, and maybe the mid-Mediterranean island colony of Malta as well.

Churchill responded cautiously. A staunch believer in the British Empire, he was appalled by the suggestion. Besides, he was convinced that a resort to diplomacy at that stage would serve only Hitler's purposes. But he knew the pressures to which Reynaud was subjected back in Paris. He told him he would have to take the matter up with his War Cabinet, which he did.

But he cautioned those of his ministers who were tempted by the idea of an approach to Italy, "We must take care not to be forced into a weak position" by inviting Mussolini "to go to Herr Hitler and ask him to treat us nicely."

With regard to the fate of France, he wasn't sure what would be in Britain's best interests. He knew Reynaud was no defeatist. But the premier's unrelieved despair indicated that France could indeed be on the verge of collapse. German propaganda was already directed at convincing the French that Germany's quarrel was not with them but with Britain and that the perfidious British were determined to fight to the last Frenchman.

It was likely that the French would be offered by Hitler comparatively moderate capitulation terms, which, Churchill warned his ministers, "we would not." That Britain might find itself alone at war with a triumphant Germany was a painful prospect. But the prime minister insisted that whatever happened to France, it would be better for Britain to go down fighting than for it to be enslaved.

That noble sentiment was shared by all in the cabinet. But a sharp divergence of opinion developed between Churchill and Halifax over whether an effort should nevertheless be made to discover whether an honorable peace could be negotiated before the coast of Britain became the front line in the war. The foreign secretary was not yet reconciled to Churchill's style of leadership. Nor was he convinced of the prime minister's perspicacity. A clash of personalities figured in their differences, but it was more than that. Halifax was not a vindictive man. He genuinely doubted whether the prime minister was able to comprehend the extent of the devastation that the Luftwaffe, flying from captured airfields in Belgium, Holland, and northern France, would soon be able to inflict on British cities.

It didn't have to happen. Halifax believed that the situation had to be calmly appraised and that conclusions should be drawn without resort to emotional speechifying. He told the War Cabinet that, in contrast to Churchill, he believed that if Britain was prepared to make certain compromises, it might be "possible to get out of our present difficulties." He said that he attached "rather more importance" than the prime minister to the "desirability of allowing France to try out the possibilities of European equilibrium"—which very likely meant a peace conference which, by virtue of the German army's conquests, Hitler would dominate. Halifax said he was not convinced that "the Prime Minister's diagnosis was correct [or] that it was in Herr Hitler's interest to insist on outrageous [peace] terms." He believed that if terms could be found which did not "postulate the destruction of our independence, we should be foolish if we did not accept them."

The foreign secretary, who in the House of Lords had been loyally praising the prime minister's leadership skills, may by then have regretted not taking over leadership of the country instead of Churchill when he'd had the chance two weeks earlier. He was not alone in his growing impatience with Churchill's rousing war oratory. It did not always have the same morale-boosting effect on senior officials as it had on the general public, which was cushioned from the alarming details of how badly the situation had deteriorated on the other side of the Channel and of the perils facing Britain.

Sir Alexander Cadogan, the permanent under secretary at the Foreign Office, observed in his diary that he considered the prime minister "too rambling and romantic and sentimental and temperamental. Old Neville [Chamberlain] still the best of the lot." Apparently dismissing Churchill's obstinacy, "Old Neville," still active in the cabinet, wrote in his diary, "If we could get out of this jam by giving up Malta and Gibraltar and some African territories, we would jump at it."

His country on the brink of disaster, Reynaud also had reservations about Churchill and his talk of the need to struggle on to the last if necessary against tyranny. "The only one who understands," the French premier said upon his return from London to Paris that evening, "is Halifax who . . . realizes that some European solution must be reached. Churchill," he complained, "is always hectoring."

In Paris, General Weygand, though bitterly accepting that his plan for a north-south linkup of Allied forces had to be canceled, was still certain that it would have had a chance of success. But he realized there was now no alternative but for the armies in the north to withdraw toward the coast, and he issued the appropriate orders. However, Eden did not intend for Gort to wait for formal pullback instructions to filter through France's

shattered communications. He cabled the BEF commander the
official go-ahead.

> Prime Minister has had conversation with M. Reynaud this
> afternoon. Latter fully explained to him the situation and
> resources French Army. It is clear from this that it will not
> be possible for French to deliver attack in the south in suffi-
> cient strength to enable them to effect junction with north-
> ern armies. In these circumstances no course open to you
> but to fall back upon the coast. . . . You are now authorized
> to operate towards coast forthwith, in conjunction with
> French and Belgian armies.

Gort finally had approval for the action he had taken. The
BEF had already begun trickling back, as had elements of the
French First Army. But the Allied command remained plagued
by misunderstanding and cross purposes. General Blanchard still
did not know, and was not informed, that the British troops
were pulling back in order to be evacuated to England. Equally
in the dark about British intentions was Admiral Jean Abrial,
the French officer in command of the Dunkirk area, whose permission was by rights required before the mass evacuation could
proceed. He could only be informed through the chain of command which went through Paris, from which he heard not so
much as a whisper on the subject.

Calais was still holding out. For Brigadier Nicholson and
the men under his command besieged in the city, it was another
day of German air raids, artillery bombardment, and ground assaults. The attacks grew heavier as the day wore on and German
impatience with the stubbornness of the defenders intensified.
Sustaining heavy casualties, the defenders were forced back,
fighting as they went, district by district, street by street, separated into smaller and smaller groups in the rubble to which
their positions were methodically reduced. Brigadier Nicholson
was captured in the afternoon. Though low in ammunition,
many of his men fought on until they were overwhelmed. By
nightfall, their resistance was crushed and the survivors were
taken prisoner and led away in captivity as well.

It is difficult to determine whether the defenders of Calais
were needlessly sacrificed. Two days before the city fell, plans
had been afoot to evacuate them. But then Nicholson was in-

formed that the French commander of the Channel ports, in accordance with orders from Paris, "forbids evacuation." By holding out, the men would disrupt the German advance up the coast. But by the time Calais fell to the enemy, some German units had already bypassed the city on their way toward Dunkirk. The question remains whether the men stayed put only "for the sake of allied solidarity," as the War Office put it, at a time when the French were openly indignant about British abandonment or whether the Calais defenders served a useful purpose right to the end by tying down at least one German armored division, giving Allied forces farther along the coast more of a chance to strengthen the defense lines between the enemy and the last remaining bolt hole at Dunkirk.

The value of that bolt hole was still in doubt. It depended on whether the BEF could withdraw through the narrow corridor to the sea and then be successfully lifted off. General Pownall noted in his diary, "Whether we ever get to the sea, how we get off the beach, how many of us survive is on the knees of the Gods. But it's the only thing to be done. We cannot stay here without being surrounded and there is no other direction in which to go." General Brooke, one of Gort's three corps commanders and later chief of the Imperial General Staff, believed that ". . . we shall be lucky if we save 25 per cent of the BEF."

The Canal Line, guarding Gort's right flank, was now as organized as it would ever be. It was composed of four BEF divisions, none at full strength. Facing them were six German armored and four motorized divisions of von Rundstedt's Army Group A, still waiting for permission from Hitler to resume their advance. Three of the British divisions on the Canal Line were Territorial reserves; one had originally been sent to France only for training and support duties. Now its task was to stand fast and shield part of the BEF's line of retreat.

On Gort's left sector, four of his other divisions confronted von Bock's Army Group B, which, not equipped with any significant amount of armor, was not subject to Hitler's halt order. Guarding the line covering the last twenty miles to the sea on that flank were the Belgians—pummeled, bloodied, and near to collapse. Their condition had been fast deteriorating during the day. A succession of Stuka onslaughts followed by sustained infantry assaults had them reeling. If they caved in completely, the

Germans would plunge through and race down to take Dunkirk from up the coast.

Weygand was informed in the afternoon that the Belgian army would fight on to block the enemy advance so long as its supplies held out but that it had "nearly reached the limit of its endurance." There was nothing he could do about it. He didn't bother to reply. He was more concerned about the fate of the remains of the badly mauled French First Army, which was under fire around Lille, at the far end of the corridor to the sea, farthest from Dunkirk, to which it still had not been ordered to retreat.

By late in the day, Hitler, ever fearful of an unexpected reversal of his fortunes, was once again agonizing over the progress of the campaign. Though Boulogne had been taken, Calais was about to fall, and aerial bombardment had shattered Dunkirk harbor, the complete destruction of the Allied armies in the northern pocket was taking too long. Despite Goering's promises, the Luftwaffe had failed to do the job, and Army Group B, which should have been moving in for the kill through Belgium, had not yet crashed through Belgian lines and was meeting very stubborn resistance from British troops protecting most of Gort's left flank.

The crescendo of complaints among Hitler's generals about the immobilized panzers on the Canal Line mounted during the day. "Our armored and mechanized forces are standing motionless," Chief of Staff Halder moaned, ". . . as though they were rooted to the ground. . . . At this rate it can take weeks to clear up the cauldron. . . ." Hitler found that prospect intolerable. His earlier fears that the Allies were preparing to break out toward the south to snip off his advance had proved groundless; no move was being made in that direction. It was time, he decided, to wind up the operation.

Late that day, he canceled the order which had kept his armor from closing the trap around the Allied troops beginning to scamper back toward the sea. At about the same time, the machinery that would give the name Dunkirk a unique place in military history was being set in motion across the English Channel.

At 6:57 at night, Admiral Ramsay at Dover received a signal from the Admiralty in London—"Operation Dynamo is to commence." A subsequent message told him, "It is imperative

for Dynamo to be implemented with the greatest vigor." The
object would be to lift "up to 45,000 men" from Dunkirk within
two days, "at the end of which it is probable that evacuation will
be terminated by enemy action."

No word was given on what was expected to happen to the
rest of the BEF—almost a quarter of a million troops. Were
they to be written off? Things were happening too quickly to
give that question the attention it deserved. Thoughts focused
on getting home as many men as possible. Ironside believed that
even the low estimate in Operation Dynamo's launch orders of
the number of men who could be rescued was optimistic. He
thought the BEF would be lucky to evacuate thirty thousand.
The desperation with which Dynamo was launched was thickly
clouded by premonitions of debacle.

It was also complicated by limited appreciation of what exactly was involved. Available to Ramsay for evacuation purposes as the operation began were thirty-five passenger ships
(mostly cross-Channel ferries), sixty-two coasters, barges, and
flat-bottomed Dutch "skoots," and a variety of supply craft.
Ramsay had jumped the gun and had sent rescue vessels over to
Dunkirk that afternoon. But aside from small ships, he was
planning a flow of only "two vessels every four hours." At that
stage, comparatively few troops had yet reached Dunkirk to be
evacuated. The order for them to make for the coast was only
just beginning to circulate among units which were not deployed
keeping the Germans from cutting the escape corridor. It was
pointless and dangerous to dispatch vessels for whom no evacuees would yet be available, and destroyers were too badly
needed for protection purposes in the Channel and elsewhere to
be earmarked for evacuation duty. It was as if bringing home
only a small fraction of the BEF in the forty-eight hours before
the Germans were expected to close in was to be a self-fulfilling
prophecy.

Hopes of lifting men from the Dunkirk beaches, as well as
from what was left of the harbor, were dimmed by the fact that
at that stage Admiral Ramsay had few craft at his disposal capable of getting in close to the shore without grounding—only
some motorboats from the Anti-Smuggling Control Base at
Ramsgate, a few fishing drifters, and four passenger launches.
Ramsay pleaded with the Admiralty to find him additional small
craft to work the beaches. But it seemed certain that the bulk of

the British army was about to be left in France at the mercy of
the Germans, a prospect which Gort, increasingly impatient
with his superiors as the situation grew more critical, was convinced London was unable to comprehend.

The experience of ships returning to English ports that day
after having run the gauntlet to and from Dunkirk harbor did
nothing to convince anyone that Operation Dynamo could succeed. They had been attacked from the air and shelled by enemy
guns on the coast, and the harbor itself was a heap of rubble.
Arriving off Dunkirk during a heavy air raid, the passenger ferry
Maid of Orleans was forced to turn back to Dover and had to
make a second crossing later to get on belatedly with its assigned
task.

Just as Chamberlain had to make way for a more dynamic
British leader sixteen days earlier, so General Ironside was required to shift on May 26 from his position as Chief of the Imperial General Staff. Top-level military misunderstandings and
confusions by the British High Command as well as by the
French were recognized as having been partly responsible for
the blunderings in France and Belgium. Besides, the Germans
were demonstrating that this was a totally different sort of war
than had ever been fought before. Under the circumstances,
General Sir John Dill, an expert in mechanized warfare, was
thought better suited to be Britain's top soldier and was named
to replace Ironside, to the relief of many senior officers who
believed the move was long overdue.

His extensive command experience still valued, the former
chief of staff was put in charge of the British Home Forces instead. It was a much less prestigious post than the one he was
leaving, but with an invasion threatening, it was taking on ever
greater significance. A substantial catalogue of measures for
home defense had already been implemented. Now they needed
tightening and extension. Coastal defenses had to be improved,
and the expansion of the army—there were only three trained
divisions on home ground at the time—had to be rapidly accelerated.

Civil defense measures also had to be more vigorously implemented across the country. Instructions were, for example,
issued that day for car owners all over Britain to make certain
their vehicles were immobilized at night so that enemy agents

landed under cover of darkness would not be able to use them, and for garages to put their gas pumps out of commission at the end of each working day. Britain was to be ready for the enemy on home ground. Even Buckingham Palace had sandbagged machine-gun emplacements at its gates.

With almost all of the army's heavy equipment expected to be lost in France, the production of war supplies, already receiving priority attention, became an even greater concern. The minister of supply, Herbert Morrison, a former chairman of the Labour Party, warned workers against anything that might impede war production. "In war," Morrison told people working in war factories, "you are all public servants." He cautioned them against "irresponsible mischief-makers who . . . may be 'Fifth Column' elements—even direct or indirect agents of the enemy."

> If any man should come whispering in your ear that you should go slow on your job, that for the nation to demand of you sacrifices for victory is to attack your security and your future—know that man for what he is: a traitor, an enemy more insidious, more dangerous than any parachute trooper.

In Washington, the American government was short on details, but President Roosevelt had a good idea of how desperate the Allied position had become. Personal messages from Churchill conveyed a sense of deepest anxiety, and cables from Ambassador Bullitt in Paris reported the mood of imminent doom which permeated the French capital. American military attachés in Berlin, Paris, and London passed word along of the general state of play on the battlefield. A U.S. military attaché in Berlin reported that "whether the Allied forces can counter-attack effectively enough to hold the German advance and stabilize the front is a question which will decide the outcome of the entire war."

The remarkable speed with which Hitler's forces had smashed through Allied defenses and the prospect of an Allied collapse aroused profound consternation in Washington. In New York's Times Square, hushed crowds watched news bulletins about the German onslaught flash around Times Tower. Whatever people thought about rights and wrongs in the war, few had previously considered American interests to be seriously and perhaps immediately imperiled. But now it was realized that Nazi Germany might very soon be in a position to directly threaten the national

security of the United States. Until then, the War Department's
basic contingency defense plans—code-named Rainbow—had
concentrated on the western Pacific and the threat posed by Japanese expansionism there. Now the department's Joint Planning
Committee hurriedly began revising Rainbow.

It proceeded on the worst-case assumption that Britain as
well as France was about to be defeated and that after that
defeat, the United States would be faced by a hostile German-
Italian-Japanese coalition. The naval power of this axis of adversaries, bolstered by portions of the British and French fleets
seized by the Germans, would considerably exceed that of the
United States. Reports circulated that Hitler had threatened to
exact a toll of a million British lives if the British fleet was not
turned over to him at the time of his victory. While Britain and
France pleaded for American war supplies, the White House
was urged by its military strategists to consider drastic measures
closer to home. Roosevelt was advised to order the "protective
occupation" of the British West Indies and other British,
French, Dutch, and Danish possessions in the Western Hemisphere if Nazi conquest of the Allies appeared about to be
achieved. Roosevelt was bombarded with advice from experts
and others on the subject.

> . . . if the bad boys win, or even gain a definite temporary
> advantage over the more decent boys abroad . . . it is an
> absolute certainty that we will be baited and badgered and
> insulted and annoyed with all sorts of incidents of a political,
> commercial or colonizing nature, which eventually will force
> some sort of violent unpleasant showdown. . . . Nothing the
> present administration could do would more intrigue both
> public and press than a sound, vigorous program for com-
> plete West Indian control for all time and the center of that
> control being moved to Washington D.C.—not dictated by
> squabbling capitals in Europe.

Roosevelt took such warnings and advice seriously. In a
message to Congress, he spelled out his worries about the dangers of German incursions in the Western Hemisphere.

> . . . if [the British colony of] Bermuda fell into hostile hands
> it is a matter of less than three hours for modern bombers to

reach our shores. From a base in the outer West Indies, the coast of Florida could be reached in 200 minutes. The islands off the west coast of Africa are only 1,500 miles from Brazil. Modern planes starting from the Cape Verde Islands can be over Brazil in seven hours. And Para, Brazil, is but four flying hours to Caracas, Venezuela, and Venezuela but two-and-a-half hours to Cuba and the Canal Zone, and Cuba and the Canal Zone are two-and-a-quarter hours to Tampico, Mexico; and Tampico is two-and-a-quarter hours to St. Louis, Kansas City and Omaha.

Though most eyes were focused on Europe, Latin America was the area of priority concern for the United States government and military command. There were large and politically active German minorities in several South American countries. Unconfirmed reports said that armed Germans were already in training in southern Brazil, where there had been an attempted fascist coup the previous year. Large German embassies were maintained in all Latin American capitals, and Germany had developed extensive commercial interests throughout the region, including control of several commercial airlines which flew mostly seventeen-seater, three-engine Junker aircraft, easily converted into bombers.

A War Plans Division memorandum to the State Department suggested that the United States "initiate conversations at the earliest practicable date with all American republics" for the purpose of defending them "against all foreign interventions and activity that may threaten them." It was pointed out that this might "require the employment of means beyond the present ability of individual American states to provide," in which case the United States would be ready and willing to lend a hand. The implication was that American dominance in the hemisphere would be invoked if necessary to persuade Latin American countries disinclined to cooperate. "Assurances should be sought . . . that their existing airdromes, ports and port facilities, as well as anchorages in their territorial waters, will be available to the United States as required." A War Department general staff memo was even more explicit.

The only sure way of preventing the surprise overthrow of existing South American governments by German inspired activities is to have adequate force or what appears to be adequate force present on the spot prior to the need for its employment. . . . A naval vessel or vessels ostensibly on courtesy visits can be put into critical South American harbors without delay. Detachments of sailors or marines from such vessels might provide the necessary deterrent or the necessary force to accomplish our object.

Countries of particular concern included Argentina, Chile, Colombia, Uruguay, and Venezuela. But the primary focus was on Brazil, where the U.S. embassy staff reported that many government and army officials were pro-German. Even the Gestapo had established a presence in Rio de Janeiro, and German influence was spreading. The *New York Times* ominously reported that a German visitor to Rio de Janeiro had told an elevator boy there to learn to speak the German language because "You're going to need it."

The Admiralty in London did nothing to discourage American alarm at German incursions in the Western Hemisphere. On May 24, it had passed along word—which the United States was in no position to confirm or contradict—that six thousand Nazis had been boarded onto German merchant ships and might be heading for Brazil, where they could join Nazi sympathizers already there to seize the government. The following day, President Roosevelt directed his chief of naval operations to prepare secret plans for transporting an advance guard of ten thousand American troops to Brazil by air if and when a German threat materialized there. They were to be followed by one hundred thousand troops sent by sea. A plan—code-named Pot-of-Gold—was drawn up earmarking four battleships, two aircraft carriers, nine cruisers, and three squadrons of destroyers for the operation.

On the night of May 26, Roosevelt went on radio to broadcast one of his fireside chats. His aim was to prepare the American people for the disagreeable steps that he believed the United States would ultimately be compelled to take.

Tonight over the once peaceful roads of Belgium and France, millions are now moving, running from their homes to escape bombs and shells and fire and machine gunning, without shelter and almost wholly without food. They stum-

ble on, knowing not where the end of the road will be. . . .
There are many among us who in the past closed their eyes
to events abroad—because they believed . . . that what was
taking place in Europe was none of our business; that no
matter what happened over there, the United States could
always pursue its peaceful and unique course in the
world. . . . To [them], to those who would not admit the
possibility of the approaching storm . . . the past two weeks
have meant the shattering of many illusions. They have lost
the illusion that we are remote and isolated and therefore
secure against the dangers from which no other land is free.

The president assured Americans that whatever steps were
needed would be taken to guarantee the defenses of their country. "We shall build them," he promised, "to whatever heights
the future may require." He did not confine his thoughts to domestic defense. "We defend," he said, "and we build a way of
life, not for America alone, but for all mankind. Ours is a high
duty, a noble task."

Roosevelt's comments were derided by isolationists as another of his moves to nudge the United States into the European
quagmire. Frank Gannett, a candidate for the still-to-be-decided
Republican Party's presidential nomination, dismissed Roosevelt's speech as a charade meant to scare the American people,
much like the famous Orson Welles radio fantasy about an invasion of Earth by Martians.

Though Roosevelt was more concerned about security in
the Western Hemisphere, he was indeed giving close consideration to the incessant pleas from Britain and France for planes
and other war matériel. But even if Congress would give its approval for the shipment of war supplies, almost everything was
in short supply and could not be spared. The army had only 160
P-40 fighter planes for its 260 fighter pilots, and only fifty-two
bombers. The army's Ordnance Division allowed that it could
release five hundred First World War field guns, a half million
Enfield rifles, thirty-five thousand machine guns, and five hundred mortars. But Roosevelt was barred by law from sending
abroad any war matériel that was not surplus to the defense
needs of the United States, and questions were raised about
whether those weapons could really be considered surplus in
view of America's military unpreparedness. So as Britain

launched a desperate, apparently hopeless operation to rescue its trapped army, the American government could offer nothing but sympathy and good wishes.

By midnight on this first day of Operation Dynamo, 27,936 men had been brought back to England from Dunkirk. But these were still "useless mouths" whose evacuation had earlier been ordered. The fighting troops, the men upon whom Britain depended to guard its shores against invasion and form the core of a resurgent army, were still a long way from home and in deep trouble.

Day Two—Outlook Grim

With Dynamo made operational the previous night, the exodus from Dunkirk began in earnest on May 27. *Mona's Isle,* a Royal Navy armed boarding vessel, was the first back that morning. Its journey was not the kind to raise hopes. It had reached Dunkirk the previous night during a German bombing raid but had managed to take 1,420 troops on board. However, on its return voyage, it was hit by shells from enemy guns on the shore and strafed by German aircraft. By the time it had completed its run back to Dover, twenty-three men on board had been killed and another sixty wounded. Five other vessels sent to join in the evacuation that day came under such heavy fire from shore-based enemy artillery before they reached Dunkirk that they turned back without a single evacuee. And two strings of small boats towed by a tug for use in picking men up off the beaches for transfer to ships offshore were scattered and lost en route after their lines were severed.

German control of the coast below Dunkirk dangerously complicated the rescue operation. Because of the sandbars and shallows that made the waters off Dunkirk a graveyard for ships, the shortest run from Dover, covering a distance of thirty-nine miles, skirted part of the French coast and brought vessels within range of German shore batteries on the coast above Calais. Alternate routes had to be followed. An indirect fifty-five-mile route traversed waters that had been mined by the Germans. It had not yet been fully swept and only warships had been degaussed against magnetic mines, but time was pressing and vessels were sent through them anyway to begin loading men. An eighty-seven-mile route took vessels into the North Sea before turning southwestward off Ostend to reach Dunkirk. The longer two routes were out of range of the enemy artillery but exposed ships to more protracted danger from German air and torpedo attack. The time factor was also important. Vessels navigating those sea lanes took far longer than the two-hours-each-way more direct run. It meant even fewer men than expected were likely to be evacuated before the Germans moved in to capture Dunkirk and close down Operation Dynamo.

It meant also that it was even more essential than before that the operation be efficiently superintended on the Dunkirk end. A senior officer was needed on the shore to organize the lift-off and maintain direct liaison between the BEF and the Royal Navy. That assignment fell to Royal Navy Captain William G. Tennant, chief staff officer of Britain's first sea lord. Named senior naval officer Dunkirk, Tennant hurried from London to Dover that morning to be briefed and to gather together a staff of twelve officers and 160 seamen, before setting off across the Channel to get on with the job. Given no idea what their assignment was to be but instructed to travel light, one of those officers brought along tennis shorts. Summoned at a church service in Portsmouth, another officer went directly to Dover still attired in full service dress.

Across the Channel, senior Allied army officers met that morning to plan the defense of Dunkirk and its surrounding area. Lieutenant General Sir Ronald Adam, commanding the BEF's III Corps, was assigned by Gort to organize a defense of the Dunkirk perimeter. At 7:00 A.M., at the Hotel Sauvage in the hill town of Cassel, twenty miles inland from Dunkirk, Adam met with Lieutenant General Marie Fagalde, the French officer officially in command of all Allied troops on the coast. The two men examined possibilities for establishing the perimeter defense and decided how to go about it. The British would guard a line stretching from Nieuport on the coast across the border just inside Belgium, and leading to and along the Berques-Furnes Canal running roughly parallel to the coast about six miles inland, as far as the town of Berques. The sector of the perimeter defense held by the French would extend from Berques westward along the canal to Gravelines on the coast. A supply system for the perimeter was to be organized. Ammunition dumps and food stores were to be set up, with ships making the perilous run from Dover ferrying in the needed supplies.

After these arrangements had been made, Adam and Fagalde were joined at the hotel in Cassel by General Louis Koeltz, representing General Weygand, Admiral Abrial, General Blanchard, and General Prioux, to review the overall situation. None of the French gathered there had yet been informed that the British were falling back on Dunkirk to be evacuated. Adam, who knew, had no authority to confer with them on that question; his assignment had been only to deal with setting up the perimeter defense. Koeltz, Abrial, Blanchard, and Prioux still understood that the fallback was only to establish a bridgehead from which the Germans would be unable to dislodge the Allied troops. They had no orders or intention to plan the abandonment of what was about to become the last enclave of northern France which had not fallen to the enemy.

This element of unreality had other dimensions as well. Koeltz transmitted to the assembled officers a proposal from Weygand for a counterattack to relieve the troops defending Calais, unaware not only that the city had fallen to the Germans the night before but that French forces had even been driven out of Gravelines closer up the coast to Dunkirk. It was from there that German guns on the shore were shelling rescue vessels attempting to negotiate the shortest Dunkirk-Dover route. Even a German bombardment of Cassel itself while their meeting was in session there did not deter Koeltz from harboring such far-fetched aspirations.

But he was not alone in conjuring up fantasies. Though the French at the Hotel Sauvage conclave knew nothing of evacuation plans and would have been appalled if they had, the story was different in Dover. At a meeting there that morning, during which French naval officers actually conferred with the British on procedures for evacuating both French and British troops from Dunkirk (they hadn't known about the British evacuation plans until that meeting), it was agreed that the Allies should attempt to recapture part of the French coast as far south as Cap Griz Nez, past Calais—a very unlikely prospect given the prevailing situation. It would facilitate the evacuation, which otherwise was considered likely to be "extremely difficult if not impossible."

At that Dover meeting, the representatives of the British

and French navies agreed that Admiral Ramsay would be responsible for regulating sailings of French and British vessels to Dunkirk and that Admiral Abrial, who still knew nothing about Operation Dynamo, would be "the only authority in charge of all arrangements for berthing and loading ships at Dunkirk and on the coast." Captain Tennant, on shore at Dunkirk organizing the evacuation of British troops, was to be under Abrial's command. The ground (and sea) rules having been established, accelerating the operation took top priority.

With the realization that great numbers of small craft would be needed to lift men from the beaches came the task of finding those craft and getting them quickly in shape for the operation. That assignment went to the Ministry of Shipping. Early that morning, H. C. Riggs of the small craft section of the ministry contacted Douglas Tough of Tough Brothers Boatyard of Teddington, whose family had worked on the Thames for almost a century and who had a comprehensive knowledge of the coast and waterways of southeast England. Empowered to act as agent for the government and escorted by naval personnel, Tough went out to find the small craft, and not only those which had previously been registered with the Small Vessels Pool. Many were less than shipshape.

> There they lay in muddy estuaries and creeks, in deserted moorings, along the coast of Kent and Sussex and in the quiet reaches of the Thames . . . tarpaulined and forlorn, paintwork dirty, brasswork tarnished, water gurgling morosely in their bilges, or high and dry in a builders' yard.

The search went as far north as The Wash on the east coast of England and as far west as Cornwall. If the owners couldn't be contacted, their craft were taken away anyway. Few who could be contacted objected when informed that their vessels were needed by the navy for an urgent, secret operation. Even if details of the BEF's predicament weren't common knowledge, Britain's growing peril was widely understood. Some owners were asked to deliver their vessels to coastal rendezvous points and hand them over there to the navy. Others insisted on helping out by doing so.

*   *   *

It was one thing for the generals who had gathered at Cassel early that morning to plot out a perimeter defense for Dunkirk and for Admiral Ramsay to calculate how many ships might be needed at what intervals to get the men home. It was another thing to get the troops to the coast for those plans to have any relevance. The harsh reality for the officers charged with that task was that the initiative and overwhelming might remained with the enemy and that their own immediate problem was to find troops to plug gaps in defense lines while trying to manage an orderly, staged withdrawal down the corridor while under fire.

Men under such pressure did not react well to instructions from afar that made no sense. When Gort received a "personal appeal" from Weygand for strong British participation in unspecified joint counterattacks—"Situation demands hard hitting," he was told—it confirmed his suspicion that the Allied supreme commander had taken leave of reality. The only rational objective of counterattacks now was to keep the escape corridor open. Nor was Gort's confidence in the judgment of other senior French officers restored by General Prioux's announcement that despite the detailed arrangements made that morning for establishing a perimeter defense around Dunkirk, his First Army would not withdraw to the coastal area. Prioux declared that there would be no further retreat by his troops. They would stand and fight. In view of superior German strength, it seemed a brave but pointless gesture even if it delayed the German advance and helped screen the BEF withdrawal to Dunkirk.

Gort was now making only the most necessary gestures toward acknowledging French command over himself and his troops. He no longer worried overly much about behaving in an insubordinate fashion. After days of misunderstanding and cross purposes, he and London were finally in full accord. A message from the War Office in London that afternoon made it "quite clear that sole task now is to evacuate to England maximum of your forces possible."

Though Gort agreed fully, it did raise a delicate question. Was he not to concern himself at all with the evacuation of French troops? Some had already pulled back to Dunkirk. What was he to do about them if the question arose? There were dif-

ferences about that in London. Mindful of Britain's obligations
to its ally and still hoping that France would not capitulate, or
that it would hand over its air force and navy to Britain if it was
forced to, Churchill wanted nothing done to make the French
believe they were being deserted by the British. That meant special consideration for potential French evacuees at Dunkirk. The
War Office, however, was now concerned exclusively with bringing home as many British troops as possible to fight off the Germans when their inevitable assault on the homeland materialized.
In regular contact with the BEF, the War Office was for the
moment able to prevail without troubling Churchill and arousing
his unwanted advice.

Gort was told that while it was eminently desirable that
nothing should be done to suggest a lack of cooperation with the
French, the safety of the BEF was to be his primary consideration. The French Admiralty, he was told, was taking steps to
provide vessels for its end of the operation. When they appeared, evacuation facilities could be shared equally beween
British and French personnel. "Until French ships materialize
however you are authorized to use British ships for British personnel."

That was the way the BEF commander preferred it. But
from what he had been informed of Operation Dynamo, he was
convinced its evacuation plans were totally inadequate. In anguish, he had the previous night dispatched Group Captain Victor Goddard, his air aide, to London to crash a meeting of the
chiefs of staff in Whitehall in the morning to demand from the
navy a much greater effort. "I have been sent by Lord Gort,"
Goddard declared, "to say that the provision made is not nearly
enough. . . ." In addition to Channel ferries, he said it was essential to send "pleasure steamers, coasters, fishing boats, lifeboats, yachts, motorboats, everything that can cross the
Channel."

The audacity of this uninvited junior officer presuming to
lecture his superiors was not appreciated, especially when neither Gort nor Goddard had full command of the facts. The assembly of small craft from the Thames estuary and southeast
coast ports was at that moment underway, and preparations
were being made to dispatch them to Dunkirk to assist the
larger vessels in the evacuation.

*   *   *

Meantime, the two German army groups which had blud-geoned their way across Belgium and northern France were pro-ceeding with their bid to close the trap around the Allied forces before they could reach the coast. Hitler's order to halt having been lifted late the previous day, the panzers which had been frozen in place on the other side of the Canal Line for the better part of three days now launched withering attacks, resumed their forward momentum, and were firmly across the line well before nightfall.

Once more, the disparity in force strengths was glaringly displayed in set battles. Guarding its sector of the line, the Brit-ish 2nd Division, most of whose antitank guns had been re-moved to Dunkirk, faced three panzer divisions, an SS division, and parts of two other German divisions. Fighting determinedly nevertheless, it was mauled practically to extinction during the course of the day, though its sacrificial perseverance made it possible for elements of four other British divisions and more than two divisions of the French First Army which might other-wise have been surrounded to slip back toward the coast after darkness had fallen. Then, still under fire, its battered remnants fell back as well.

It was a hard day for British troops clear across the Canal Line, but hardest of all for the men of the 2nd Battalion, Royal Norfolk Regiment. They took very heavy casualties, and what remained of the unit was forced to fall back. Enraged by their stubborn resistance and recalling their humiliating setback at the hands of the British at Arras the previous week, men of the SS Totenkopf Division took cruel vengeance on the survivors, most of whom were wounded. They had been driven back to a farm near the town of Paradis. Surrounded, outgunned, and far out-numbered, they had surrendered, only to be marched across the farmyard and cut down by machine-gun fire. Those who were not killed were bayoneted and finished off with pistols. Two of the men succeeded in feigning death, were captured by other German troops, and survived to tell the story. After the war, the SS company commander primarily responsible was convicted by a war crimes tribunal with the help of testimony of a woman at the farm and was executed.

At virtually all points of the front, the Germans surged for-ward, but not without paying a price. A German officer reported, "At every position heavy fighting has developed—especially at every village and indeed in every house. . . . Casualties in personnel and equipment are grievous. The enemy are fighting tenaciously and, to the last man, remain at their posts: if they are shelled out of one position, they shortly reappear in another to carry on the fight."

German aircraft dropped leaflets on which rough maps had been printed showing how desperate the Allied position in the north had become and calling on the troops to surrender.

BRITISH SOLDIERS!
YOU ARE ENTIRELY SURROUNDED!
PUT DOWN YOUR ARMS!

Except for men who were in no position to do anything but surrender or die, those leaflets had little effect.

Meantime, line troops were receiving orders for their staged withdrawal to the coast. These men had been fighting, retreating, digging in, fighting again, and retreating once more for days without any idea of what their objective was except to stay alive. The instructions they now were given aroused both alarm and relief among junior officers of the 2nd Battalion, Coldstream Guards, who were gathered at their makeshift headquarters in a house they had commandeered just behind the line to be told what they were to do.

We sat down on chairs making a circle round the room, and waited. The Commanding Officer looked up and, after a pause, said, "We are to march 55 miles back to the coast"— he paused and looked round at us. Our hearts sank. Fifty-five miles seemed a bit too much. Then he went on—"and embark for England!" Immediate sensation. No one had expected this. We had had vague ideas of falling back as the armies of 1914 had fallen back until, somehow, sometime, we too should stand and fight our victorious battle of the Marne. But this! There was a sudden loosening of the tenseness we had been living in for so long. We felt a surge of contentment beneath our anxiety about the war news in general and our own immediate prospects in particular. Then we thought again of the 55 miles, and wondered.

Reports began reaching German commanders that a systematic evacuation, such as it was at that stage, was in progress at Dunkirk, that men were being loaded onto British ships in some sort of organized fashion and carried back to England. They did not yet suspect how massive an operation had been launched. But Major General Kurt Brennecke, chief of staff of the German Fourth Army, was informed, "Large ships are being made fast to the quayside [at Dunkirk harbor], planks are laid across and men swarm aboard." Brennecke was bitter at the prospect of German troops having to meet those men in combat at a subsequent date, fully rested and once more fully equipped. The Luftwaffe was called upon to step up its attacks, and German forces pressing up along the coast forced French defenders back to positions a mere four miles from Dunkirk, within easy artillery range of the city.

Farther inland, along the escape corridor, road congestion was gravely complicating the withdrawal to the coast. Operation Dynamo had barely begun, but already the main roads leading back from the front to the comparative safety of the Dunkirk perimeter were clogged with human and vehicular traffic. In addition to the problem of the refugees, attempts to assign separate withdrawal routes to the British and French commands proved futile. French troops did not appreciate being told that certain roads in their own country were reserved for use by the British. As his report later indicated, Gort was enraged by the resulting muddle.

> The [withdrawal] plan, as agreed [with General Blanchard], envisaged the reservation of certain roads for the exclusive use of the BEF. In fact, however, French troops and transport continued to use them, and this added very considerably to the difficulties of the withdrawal of British troops. The roads were few and for the most part narrow, and . . . they were badly congested with marching troops and horsed transport of French formations, and with refugees.

General Pownall, for whom the tragedy of France at that moment was dwarfed by the BEF's predicament, complained, "It is no good having boundaries and roads allotted as between ourselves and the French. They pay no attention and do exactly what they damn well like."

The danger of congestion within the Dunkirk perimeter also posed a problem. If all vehicles heading that way were permitted to enter the perimeter, nothing would be able to move within it. BEF headquarters accordingly ordered that vehicles be abandoned off the road outside the coastal defense zone. Troops heading for evacuation were to be required to make their way on foot the last few miles to the harbor and the beaches. That was easier to decree than enforce.

The withdrawal to the coast came under relentless air attack. Messerschmitt fighters strafed the retreating troops and the positions screening their fallback. Dorniers and Heinkels bombed them. Stukas screamed out of the sky at them to release their deadly payloads. Gort pleaded with London to supply his men with the strongest possible fighter cover, but RAF Fighter Command was finding the role it was assigned in the operation impossible to fulfill.

It was instructed to "ensure the protection of Dunkirk beaches (three miles on either side) from first light until darkness by continuous fighter patrols in strength" and in addition to "have due regard to the protection of bomber sorties and the provision of support in the BEF area." Fighter Command couldn't possibly do all of that, not if the skies over Britain itself and British cities were to be guarded against the expected massive Luftwaffe onslaught from the continent.

For purposes of air defense, Fighter Command chief Dowding had divided Britain into four geographic areas, each the responsibility of a Fighter Command "group." The task of providing aerial cover for Operation Dynamo fell to 11 Group, whose bailiwick was southeast England, closest to the coast of northern France. 11 Group commander Air Vice Marshal Keith Park had at his disposal sixteen squadrons—about two hundred planes, depending on serviceability. The Germans were throwing three hundred bombers, with 550 fighter escorts, into this stage of the battle.

To cover the operation, RAF fighters had to fly at least fifty miles from their bases in southeast England—at Biggin Hill, Hawkinge, Kenley, and Manston—and then fifty miles back, their planes devouring so much fuel in the process that if they engaged in dogfights they might be limited to as little as twenty minutes over the Dunkirk area before having to head home. They were beyond the range of British radar stations and had to rely entirely on visual contact, which meant they had to patrol the area in search of the enemy. Under those conditions, there was no way they could possibly provide uninterrupted cover seventeen hours a day for the BEF falling back on Dunkirk, as well as for the troops already there, and for the ships which were to carry them home.

But cover had to be provided, and a system had to be devised to provide it as adequately as possible. None of the three possible solutions was satisfactory. Committing Fighter Command's entire fleet of aircraft, with the possibility that it would be decimated and that mastery of the air over England would thus be delivered to the enemy, had to be ruled out. Dispatching regular large patrols of fighters would mean there would be long intervals between patrols in which there would be no RAF presence at all in the skies over the Dunkirk pocket. Sending smaller patrols would make it possible to shorten those intervals, but they would be at a greater disadvantage against the large formations of attacking aircraft the Germans were sending aloft.

The last of these options was chosen. Small patrols of between eight and twenty fighters were dispatched to keep the intervals between flights as brief as possible. That first full day of the evacuation, British fighters, taking off in small groups from first light until nightfall, flew 287 sorties, reverting automatically to on-call status for home defense after and between their missions. Coming up against waves of up to fifty enemy aircraft, they shot down ten enemy aircraft and lost fourteen of their own—an ominous ratio.

Many of the British pilots had never been in combat before. Dunkirk provided a jolting baptism of fire for them. No matter what sort of training they had had, not till their first dogfights did they really learn what their Spitfires and Hurricanes, or the enemy aircraft, were capable of.

> We were jumped by [Messerschmitt] 109s. It was the first time we had met the enemy. All of a sudden the sky was full of aircraft with black crosses on them. It was frightening, because I realized for the first time that there was somebody up there who was really trying to kill me. It was a moment of truth.

German squadron leaders took full advantage of the lack of experience of their British counterparts. They would send over a single decoy aircraft. When British fighters roared in to shoot it down, Messerschmitts hovering in the sun thousands of feet above would come thundering down to deal with them.

But inexperience and being outnumbered were not the only problems with which British fighter pilots had to contend. The flight and combat tactics they had been taught, and still were being drilled into them by their commanders and instructors, added enormously to their difficulties. Unlike the Germans, they flew in V formations so tight that all except the formation leader had to concentrate on staying in place rather than on scanning the skies for the enemy who might be swooping in from above, behind, or the side. In addition, back armor for fighter pilots—soon to be provided—was mistakenly thought to add too much weight to the Spitfire and make it less maneuverable. Pilots who would have survived were lost as a result. One squadron lost five pilots and five Spitfires during the first two days of Operation Dynamo and had to be pulled out of the patrols to be reconstituted.

The Spitfires and Hurricanes at first approached the combat zone too low—ten thousand feet or lower—and were pounced on by 109s plunging down at them out of the sun from much higher vantage points. The pilots quickly learned that was a mistake. It took them longer to learn that the Germans were monitoring their radio chatter and would often wait until they told each other they were heading for home before beginning their attack on the troops on the ground and the ships offshore.

Criticism of the RAF had already become a steady refrain among the troops on the ground. They had been repeatedly strafed and bombed but had rarely seen a British aircraft come to their defense. Nevertheless, even on that first full day of the evacuation, despite its problems, the RAF succeeded in disrupting many of the German aerial attacks. Its efforts weren't much observed or appreciated on the ground because of its limited resources and because of the fairly extensive stretch of land it had to cover, both along the coast and inland. But without the RAF's contribution to Operation Dynamo, German mastery of the sky would have gone unchallenged over the evacuation zone and the Dunkirk episode very likely would have ended in slaughter and surrender for the BEF.

*   *   *

In Paris, the sense of impending doom was taking ever tighter hold. Rumors that a German drive to take the city was imminent circulated widely. Police raided hotels and patrolled streets looking for enemy saboteurs and fifth columnists. Thousands of people were stopped and required to produce identification papers. Parisians who could afford to do so fled to the south and southwest of the country to escape, their cars crammed with whatever valuables they could carry. So many left that within the capital, vehicle traffic was down to a trickle.

The government was convinced that Italy, taking heart from Germany's military successes in the north and France's disarray, was about to invade the country from the southeast and that Mussolini's forces could no more be effectively repelled than Hitler's had been. Pétain no longer made much effort to disguise his belief that the war was already lost. He was more concerned that troops be alerted to deal with the danger of domestic disorder, leading to a Communist coup. Beginning to lose heart as well, Weygand spoke openly of Britain's "refusal to fight" and wondered how France could be expected to struggle on when its allies did nothing but retreat. The countdown to capitulation had begun.

In London, an understanding of the gravity of the situation continued to percolate down through the corridors of government. On learning that the British troops were to be evacuated from France, Minister of Transport Sir John Reith wrote in his diary, "This is awful and awful the slaughter that will be done them in the process." Expressions of concern were everywhere in Whitehall. Those who were not privy to restricted information asked questions about what exactly could be happening across the English Channel about which little was being revealed but which continued to engage grim-visaged senior officials in a seemingly endless sequence of emergency conferences. Nothing could be learned from the newspapers or the BBC about Operation Dynamo and very little about the circumstances which had brought it into being.

At one of those emergency conferences, Churchill instructed his chiefs of staff to examine how Britain would manage fighting on alone against Germany if that became necessary. The reply later that day was depressing. The prime minister was told that Germany held "most of the cards," that the deciding factor

would be air power, and that the German air force outnumbered
the RAF in the skies by a ratio of four to one. As long as the
RAF could fight off the Luftwaffe, a seaborne invasion of Britain was unlikely. But if the Germans did gain superiority in the
skies over England, all might be lost. If the enemy succeeded in
landing forces in strength, the country's ground defenses, as
they then existed, might not be capable of repelling them. It
would be essential to deal promptly with initial landings either
from the air or on the coast.

Defense plans had to be prepared for any eventuality. They
could not be blinkered by conventional thinking. The Germans
had shown themselves to be shrewd adversaries capable of imaginative exploits. While it was natural to plan for dealing with
scattered landing attempts, it was essential to consider how to
prevent enemy tanks which might be landed piecemeal from
converging to form an armored division against which defense
on the flatlands of southern England would be difficult indeed.

According to the chiefs of staff, morale of the troops and
the civil population would be a critical factor in determining the
outcome of the struggle. Churchill was a distinct asset on that
score. Building and sustaining popular morale were among his
greatest achievements as a war leader. Appearing always confident, always indomitable, he was determined never to display
the slightest suspicion that defeat could be on the cards. However, Lord Halifax remained unswayed by expressions of hope
and defiance when the BEF was on the verge of extinction and
when the facts threatened death and destruction. A junior official at 10 Downing Street noted in his diary that "there are
signs that Halifax is being defeatist."

At a meeting of the War Cabinet that day, Halifax pressed
Churchill to be realistic. "Suppose," the foreign secretary said,
"the French army collapsed and Herr Hitler made an offer of
peace terms. Suppose the French government said [to the Ger-
mans], 'We are unable to deal with an offer made to France
alone and you must deal with the Allies together.' Suppose Herr
Hitler, being anxious to end the war through knowledge of his
own internal weaknesses, offered terms to France and England,
would the Prime Minister be prepared to discuss them?" Refus-
ing to be cornered, Churchill replied that in such circumstances,
he would not join France in asking for terms but would be prepared to discuss them if told what they were.

Halifax was not at all reassured by either the prime minister's response or his general attitude. His own attitude had shifted since he had told Oxford students three months earlier that "evil must be met by force." Now deeply anxious about Britain's prospects, he was convinced that Churchill was ignoring the grave danger that confronted the nation and was offering little but emotional responses embellished with fine phrases. After what he called the "long and rather confused discussion" at the War Cabinet meeting, he wrote in his diary, "I thought Winston talked the most frightful rot." He felt that if the prime minister continued to act the way he did, "our views must separate. . . . It does drive me to despair when he works himself up into a passion of emotion when he ought to make his brain think and reason." To Cadogan he declared, "I can't work with Winston any longer." "Nonsense," Cadogan replied. "His rhodomontades probably bore you as much as they do me, but don't do anything silly under the stress of that."

Reports and rumors of a serious rift within the War Cabinet spread beyond Whitehall. Ambassador Kennedy cabled Washington, "If the Germans made Britain along with France an offer of peace there would be a row in the Cabinet between the 'do or die' group and the 'group that want a settlement.'

> Only a miracle can save the British Expeditionary Force from being wiped out or . . . surrender. . . . Churchill, Attlee, and others will want to fight to the death, but there will be other members who realize that physical destruction of men and property in England will not be a proper offset to a loss of pride. . . . The English people, while they suspect a terrible situation, really do not realize how bad it is. When they do, I don't know which group they will follow—the do or die, or the group that wants a settlement.

That Britain might succumb, leaving Hitler triumphant and unchallenged, intensified concern in Washington. Secretary of State Welles recalled later, "Those were the days in Washington when maps of the European front appeared in all government offices. Every morning an officer of the G-2 [Intelligence Section] of the War Department would bring to the Department of State a map of France with the latest progress of the German Armies marked upon it."

On the Haymarket off Piccadilly Circus in central London,
Americans lined up at the offices of the United States Lines to
book sea passage home. The ocean liner *President Roosevelt,*
named after Theodore rather than Franklin Roosevelt, was
being dispatched to pick up United States citizens paying the £75
fare who could make their way to Galway in Ireland, where the
liner was due to dock the following week.

Despite prevailing isolationist sentiment in the United
States, anglophile White House and State Department officials
kept British diplomatic personnel in Washington reasonably well
informed of American government thinking and planning. Word
that the United States was pondering annexation of the British
West Indies and other British territories in the Western Hemisphere for national security reasons did not sit well in London.
Lord Lothian, British ambassador in the American capital,
cabled a suggestion to London that Britain offer to lease bases
in Newfoundland, Bermuda, and Trinidad to America so that
American forces might merely take over responsibility for their
defense, relieving Britain of that obligation. But Churchill, for
whom the possibility of American annexation at that stage must
have seemed both farfetched and outrageous, wasn't interested
unless Britain was offered something more substantial in return.
Despite his intimacy with Roosevelt, he was exasperated at the
failure of America to contribute to his righteous crusade against
the forces of wickedness in Europe. He told the War Cabinet
that Britain had received from the United States "practically no
help in the war"; it appeared to be interested exclusively in its
own defense.

Churchill knew that Roosevelt was genuinely sympathetic to
the Allied cause and that he was hamstrung by public opinion.
He did not take offense at Roosevelt's suggestion that if dire
circumstances required and the Royal Navy remained intact, the
war against Germany could be carried on by the British from
Canada. He and others in London had already pondered the
possibility. However, the War Cabinet was not overly impressed
when the president suggested that if the British government and
royal family were forced into exile, the king should go to Bermuda rather than Canada because Americans wouldn't take
kindly to the idea of a monarchy based on North American soil.
Deeply offended, some ministers wondered whether Roosevelt

might be thinking of how nice it would be "to pick up the bits of the British Empire" if Britain was vanquished. The United States had to be cautioned not to be hasty. Secretary of State for Air Sir Archibald Sinclair said Washington had to be made to understand that Britain intended to fight on despite its setbacks.

Churchill agreed emphatically. But he was more troubled by the possibility that people in Britain itself might be led to believe otherwise and that they might succumb to a desire for a short-cut solution to the country's dilemma—an agreement with Hitler that would leave Germany dominant on the continent and well placed to challenge Britain's independence sometime in the future. Halifax, an honorable, patriotic Englishman who could not be accused of underestimating the malevolence of Hitler and the Nazis, was already providing the argument that could easily grasp the popular imagination. The reasoning was deceptively simple: Yes, fight on at all costs if Britain's independence is at stake. But if guarantees can be extracted from Hitler that British independence would not be jeopardized by an armistice, why not consider an offer from Berlin which would save British cities from the kind of devastation that had flattened Rotterdam? What could be lost by just talking with the Germans about it through intermediaries when things otherwise looked so grim?

With preliminary reports from Dunkirk not at all reassuring, with the bulk of the British army possibly heading for captivity, Churchill was keenly aware of how delicate his own position remained. His speeches were well received, but he had yet to show any significant contribution to the cause of Britain's survival. There had been nothing to change the view of many in the Tory Party that he was nothing more than a pushy political lothario and windbag while Halifax remained a much-respected figure throughout the land. If further serious setbacks lay ahead for Britain on the field of battle, Churchill knew he could be made to take the route Chamberlain had just traveled to political oblivion. He, and his moving call for an outlay of "blood, toil, tears and sweat" to ensure Britain's survival as an independent, proud nation, could be brushed aside to make way for Halifax and his passionate but potentially disastrous concern to save Britain from the horror and devastation of the war brought home.

By midday, Captain Tennant had been briefed in Dover on the formidable task that would be his as Senior Naval Officer

Dunkirk supervising the evacuation. That afternoon, he and much of his staff crossed the Channel aboard the destroyer *Wolfhound* to begin the job. They soon began to appreciate the hazards with which they and the evacuees would have to contend. En route, the *Wolfhound* was repeatedly dive-bombed and forced to take evasive action while its guns tried to blast attacking Stukas out of the sky. They had no great success at that, but it was frightening to realize amid the din and fury that many of the vessels to be dispatched for the troops would not be well armed and would be capable only of making a gesture at best of fighting back.

Difficult as the crossing had been, it had not been enough to prepare Tennant for the sight that awaited him at his destination. He had never before seen a city on fire. Dunkirk appeared to be an inferno. Flames and a thick curtain of black smoke rose clear across the horizon, and the stench of burning oil was everywhere. German bombers had that day unloaded two thousand tons of high explosives and incendiaries on the city. A thousand civilians had been killed, as had many of the British, French, and Belgian troops who had been separated from their units and who had converged on Dunkirk over the previous few days to take shelter in its nooks and crannies.

The nightmare continued as Tennant and his party, having debarked, made their way to Bastion 32, Admiral Abrial's harborside bunkerlike fortress headquarters, where the local British command had been given office space, and then went to examine the damage Dunkirk had sustained. Bombed for days, the city was rubble, its streets covered with the wreckage of buildings and the remains of burned-out vehicles. Dead bodies and the carcasses of horses were strewn about. Tram wires were down all over.

Some British troops had taken refuge in the cellars of buildings, and some of them were trapped and killed when those buildings collapsed. Among those who survived, some were almost unhinged by the experience. An officer told of an NCO, a decorated First World War veteran, crying quietly in the corner of a cellar and how "several men [there] began to make queer little animal noises—rather like homesick dogs."

By evening, the troops who had sought these makeshift, dangerous sanctuaries in the city had been ordered to head instead for the beaches and dunes, where they would receive further orders. Some soldiers who had thrown away their arms wandered about dazedly or drunkenly. An angry group who hadn't discarded their rifles, apparently crazed by the bombing and infuriated by the sight of the clean, neat naval uniforms of Tennant's party, advanced threateningly on them but were jollied into submission.

Even more than the city, the harbor had been blasted into wreckage by the aerial bombardment. With deepening dismay, Tennant inspected what remained of the port facilities—the smashed docks and shattered cranes. The two long breakwaters shielding the outer harbor were all that remained reasonably intact. But bringing ships in to berth alongside them would be a risky, perhaps even reckless undertaking, and there was nowhere else where large vessels could tie up. It was hard at that moment to see how even a small proportion of the BEF could be evacuated.

The only remaining option was for small boats, great numbers of them, to come in close to the beaches east of the harbor to pick men up from the shore. They would transfer them to larger rescue vessels waiting offshore and then go back for more—a long and hazardous process completely dependent on weather conditions, RAF aerial protection, and the ability of the perimeter defense to hold back the enemy. With word reaching Tennant that the Germans had taken Calais, that their forces were moving up the coast, and that their tanks might be no more than thirty-six hours away, he realized that the evacuation plans he had discussed at Dover that morning were already out of date. He urgently signaled Dover, "Please send every available craft to beaches east of Dunkirk immediately. Evacuation tomorrow night is problematical."

Misunderstandings compounded the difficulties. When the transport *Canterbury* left Dunkirk after having with difficulty boarded 457 evacuees, it was instructed to turn back other ships attempting to enter the harbor. It passed word to three passenger vessels heading for Dunkirk, and they all returned to Dover, although the turnback order was meant only to divert them to evacuation duty off the Dunkirk beaches. Before the confusion was cleared up, the message had been further garbled to become "Dunkirk is in enemy hands. Keep clear." Hearing that, five flat-bottomed skoots turned back to England.

By then, large numbers of men had begun converging on

the sands and dunes east of the city. Each of the BEF's three corps was assigned a different beach—III Corps was to make for Malo, closest to Dunkirk harbor, II Corps was to head for La Panne, across the border on the Belgian coast, and I Corps was assigned to Bray Dunes, in between. But those who had already arrived were only a small fraction of the number of troops to be lifted off. If evacuation the following night was, as Tennant told Dover, indeed "problematical," then it was reasonable to conclude that Operation Dynamo, newly launched, was already in its closing phase and that Britain was about to find itself without an army.

Apprised of the situation prevailing at Dunkirk, Admiral Ramsay, like Captain Tennant, realized that it was the wrong time and the wrong place for his plan for a methodically organized, paced flow of rescue vessels. Never before had Britain faced such a crisis. He would have to improvise, with all possible haste. All available craft at his disposal, including the precious destroyers which had been patrolling offshore, were immediately ordered to the waters off the Dunkirk beaches. All told, a cruiser, nine destroyers, two transports, four minesweepers, and an assortment of other vessels were ordered to take up positions off Malo, Bray Dunes, and La Panne "with utmost despatch and embark all possible British troops. . . . This our last chance of saving them." They quickly moved into place and lowered their small boats to lift off the men ashore whom Tennant's beach control officers had begun trying, with limited success, to organize into orderly queues.

The evacuation process remained agonizingly, impossibly slow. There were too few small boats and just so much the boats available could achieve. Thirty men were picked up here, forty there, a dozen somewhere else. At the pace the boats were coming in to shore, boarding men, ferrying them out to the larger vessels at anchorage offshore, and unloading them there, the evacuation would be a fiasco. It was already failing.

In desperation, Tennant took another close look at Dunkirk's outer harbor. Its breakwaters, a mile apart at the land side, angled toward each other into open water. Made of concrete pilings, covered with boardwalk, they were about eight feet wide. There was much wreckage in the harbor, but ships could still enter. It still seemed very risky to try to bring them alongside the breakwaters to tie up there. The breakwaters had not been constructed for that purpose. But if large numbers of men were to be loaded onto ships to be taken home to England, there was no other way. The western breakwater was only about five hundred feet long, and the water at its near end seemed dangerously shallow. But the eastern breakwater was almost a mile long and might serve as a pier.

A Channel ferry, *Queen of the Channel,* was anchored offshore nearby to board men lifted off the beach by small boats. Tennant signaled it to enter the harbor and tie up at the eastern breakwater. The vessel gingerly eased into place against the breakwater and, to Tennant's relief, was quickly and safely secured to stanchions. There might be boarding problems. The normal rise and fall of the tide in the harbor amounted to a difference of fifteen feet. At high tide, the men might be able to clamber straight from the breakwater onto the decks of rescue ships. At low water, they would perhaps be able to descend along gangplanks and ladders. Dover was immediately signaled that vessels could make for the harbor, and Tennant's men immediately went about organizing a flow of men to tramp from the adjoining beach and along the planking of the eastern breakwater to board the ships when they arrived. It was the first hopeful development all day, though the overall situation remained less than promising.

The impromptu nature of the operation showed through in various ways. Nothing, for example, had been done or said to indicate to the captains and masters of the rescue vessels that many of the men they would be taking on board would be in need of medical attention and that practically all would have gone without food and drink for long periods of time.

The galleys [of the destroyer *Gossamer*] were just as thronged with [evacuated] soldiers as the rest of the ship. However . . . stacks of corned beef sandwiches and gallons of cocoa were produced which were very welcome. In Dover . . . an attempt was made to replenish the stores used [for the next trip] but, apart from fuel and ammunition, there was an astonishing reluctance to part with anything. Food? Ridiculous! Medical stores? Even more so! However, after numerous phone calls and signals our requirements were met, at least in part. . . .

For the Belgian army, May 27 had been a day of disaster. As it drew to a close, King Leopold had to make a painful decision. His army had been under almost ceaseless attack all day, and its situation had become unendurable. It was short of ammunition, virtually defenseless against air attack, and split in two by the enemy. It had already been forced to surrender most of its country to the invaders, who bombed Belgium's cities and strafed columns of its pathetic refugees. The resistance of Belgian forces had been overwhelmed by the Germans at each stop line in its retreat. The last of its reserve troops had been thrown into the battle but had failed to have any impact. To the north, Holland had succumbed. The forces of Britain and France, which had so recently swept confidently across Belgian territory to save it from the aggressor, were in disarray. King Leopold had been informed that morning that the evacuation of the BEF back to England was in progress. All that fate seemed to hold in store for his own troops was defeat and slaughter.

Shortly after noon, Gort had received a message from Sir Roger Keyes, the British liaison officer at King Leopold's court, which foretold a Belgian collapse: "[The king] wishes you to know that his army is greatly disheartened. It has been incessantly engaged for four days and subjected to intense air bombardment which the RAF have been unable to prevent. . . . He fears a moment is rapidly approaching when he can no longer rely upon his troops to fight or be of any further use to the BEF."

That evening, a Belgian officer crossed German lines to ask for armistice terms. He was told that there would be no terms other than unconditional surrender. King Leopold realized he had no other option. Shortly before midnight, the Belgian army, which had been guarding the far left flank of the Allied armies, was ordered by the king to cease fire as of 4:00 the following morning. When informed, Weygand exploded in fury, accusing the Belgians of abandoning the Allies without notice, though he had been told of their difficulties and though it had been apparent for at least two days that they would soon be incapable of resisting a determined German assault.

For Gort, the surrender required immediate remedial action. He had from the start been reconciled to the comparative weakness of the Belgian forces. Two days earlier, he had contro-

versially yanked two divisions away from the abortive drive
south to cover for them. But despite General Brooke's belief
that they "seem to have vanished off the map," Gort had been
relieved that they had at least held a small sector of the line.
Now there would be a totally undefended gap in Belgium twenty
miles wide between BEF positions and the sea through which
the Germans could pour to seize Dunkirk and bring Operation
Dynamo to an abrupt halt.

When the news reached London, the War Cabinet met in
emergency session. Minister of Information Duff Cooper had
issued a public statement the previous day explaining the failure
of the government to release detailed information on developments across the Channel.

> No one in this country would wish to buy news at the price
> of a single British, French or Belgian life. We must all wait
> patiently and confidently till news can be given us with
> safety.

Now Duff Cooper urged in cabinet that the British public
be told how precarious was the position of the BEF. War communiqués issued by the French, and reported in Britain, had a
misleading upbeat tone. The minister warned that the British
public wasn't yet prepared for the shock to which it was about to
be exposed. Churchill agreed but wanted no details released yet.
He felt that the disclosure of the Belgian surrender would go a
long way toward preparing the public for the extremely bad
news it would probably soon have to digest.

As the day ended, there was nothing to indicate that the
BEF was anything but doomed. Ill informed about the pace of
the evacuation, Lord Gort believed that a mere two hundred
men had been lifted off the beaches by the small boats since
morning. The true number, still not enough to arouse great
hopes, was actually a little more than ten times that figure. Including the men who had embarked in the harbor, the number
brought home on May 27, the first full day of Dynamo, was only
7,669. Practically all of the BEF was still in danger of being
killed or captured.

In a brief missive to his wife, Admiral Ramsay despaired of
developments.

The situation is past belief, frightful, and one wonders how the British public will take it when the full implications are realised. It's all too horrible to contemplate. . . . I am directing . . . one of the most difficult and hazardous operations ever conceived, and unless the *bon Dieu* is very kind, there will be many tragedies attached to it.

Vice Admiral Bertram Ramsay, naval commander at Dover, was in charge of Operation Dynamo, leading the team that turned an imminent military catastrophe into a historic triumph. *Imperial War Museum*

Below, from left to right: Chief of the Imperial General Staff General Sir John Dill, Secretary for War Anthony Eden, and British Expeditionary Force Commander General Lord Gort, leaving the sandbagged War Office in London. *Imperial War Museum*

Prime Minister Winston Churchill who, within three weeks of taking office, had to face the probability of monumental military defeat for Britain at Dunkirk. *Imperial War Museum*

Prime Minister Winston Churchill and Foreign Secretary Lord Halifax. During the darkest days of Dunkirk, Halifax tried but failed to persuade Churchill to see if an honorable peace settlement could be reached with Hitler. *Imperial War Museum*

Lines of troops waiting their turn to be evacuated snaked out across the Dunkirk beaches. The men scattered when enemy aircraft zoomed over, bombing and strafing, resuming their places when the queues re-formed. Below, survivors from the rescue passenger ship *Mona's Queen,* which sank in less than two minutes after hitting a German mine off Dunkirk on day three of Operation Dynamo. They were rescued by a destroyer. *Imperial War Museum*

Above, troops in a dinghy rowing out from the beach toward a vessel anchored far enough from the shore not to be beached when the tide rushed out. *William Kershaw*

Soldiers sometimes waded out up to their necks in the waters of the English Channel to meet incoming small boats and dinghies and be rescued. *William Kershaw*

Troops wading out to a rescue ship. During quieter moments, when evacuation vessels were waiting offshore, the operation proceeded in an orderly fashion. But ships were usually in short supply and enemy aircraft could appear over the horizon at any moment. *Imperial War Museum*

Below, no professional or experienced photographer having been active on the beaches during the Dunkirk days, this painting by Charles Cundall offers as good a picture as is available of what the evacuation from the beaches entailed. *Imperial War Museum*

Above, the eastern breakwater at Dunkirk harbor, deserted after the completion of Operation Dynamo and the arrival of the Germans. The sunken vessel in the foreground was but one of the many that were destroyed by German bombs during the evacuation. *William Kershaw*

Below, British troops who dug in on the rolling sand dunes behind the beach had at least the illusion of cover when enemy aircraft attacked. Bottom, for many of the troops, the worst of the operation was waiting up to two days—some waited longer—while being exposed to enemy attack on the beach and the dunes. *Dunkirk Veterans Association*

After the evacuation, German soldiers inspect a makeshift pier constructed by the British out of trucks to enable troops to clamber out toward vessels unable to get in close to the shore. *Imperial War Museum*

Low tide shows a pier of trucks built out into the sea to facilitate the evacuation. The trucks were driven and manhandled into position and then planked over where necessary to permit men to move quickly to board small ships. *National Archives*

Abandoned vehicles litter the beach at the conclusion of Operation Dynamo. X in the left background marks the remains of an abandoned ship put out of action by enemy aircraft. *National Archives*

British soldiers lying dead on the beach east of Dunkirk; many were killed by German air raids and artillery shelling during the evacuation operation. *National Archives*

The wrecks of trucks outside Dunkirk destroyed by the British in order to keep equipment from falling into enemy hands during their retreat to the sea. The British army lost virtually all of its heavy equipment when its Expeditionary Force was driven out of France. *National Archives*

The sunken and beached vessels and other litter turned what had once been a seaside pleasure area into a surrealist vision. *Dunkirk Veterans Association*

Silence in Dunkirk harbor, a place of sunken or abandoned vessels, after the last of the rearguard was withdrawn from the perimeter defense and the enemy arrived to seize control. *National Archives*

Silhouette of some of the first German troops to enter Dunkirk as they rest in the ruins of the city's main square. *National Archives*

A party of German troops on the Dunkirk beach is next to the remains of a British tent, still flying a battered Union Jack. Bombed-out and beached vessels are in the background. *National Archives*

Conquering German troops marching along the beachfront, now abandoned by British and French troops who had been rescued or led off into captivity. *National Archives*

31 May: As a personal experience D.A & Q.M.G.
embarked with 7 other soldiers at dawn on 31 May.
Every man was most unhandy - not one appearing to
know the purpose of an oar. The tide was falling and
it was not possible to get the men to understand that
the boat must be kept afloat. After falling about in
the baot (folding boat R.E manned by one heroic sapper)
saome progress was made in a crab like manner outwards
when after several attempts a tow line was secured to a
naval motor boat. On arrival at destroyer side the
boat was allowed to charge the ship - no man had an
idea how to fend off. The boat did not break and the
very dopey and awkward soldiers climbed on board
somehow. During the town 2 men in a boat in front
threw away their rifles - it was not possible to
identify them. The sappers remained and took back
the boat still in tow. The 'Shikari' Destroyer arrived
at Dunkirk at 0530 & Dover at 0930.

        ✗   ✗   ✗   ✗

                    (Signed)   J.G. HALSTED
                                Brig

Above, personal note by Brigadier J. G
Halsted, the deputy adjutant and quarter
master general of the 1st Corps of the British
Expeditionary Force, on his evacuation from
the beaches of Dunkirk.

14 OLD SQUARE.
LINCOLN'S INN, W.C.2.
HOLBORN 4038

3rd June 1940

NAVAL OFFICER IN C...
★ -4JUN1940 ★
RAMSGATE

Sir,

              Sub-Lieut. Lucey, R.M.

    The above officer was out in command of the Fire
Float "Massey Shaw" for the purpose of embarking troops
from Dunkirk on the afternoon and night of the 31st May-
1st June.

    As a member of the crew, which consisted entirely
of officers and men of the London Fire Brigade and Auxiliary Fire Service, I venture to send you a brief account of the work done by Mr. Lucey on this occasion,
which might not otherwise be brought to the notice of
his superior officers, in the hope that he will be
given proper credit for it.

    The Massey Shaw brought a light skiff in tow from
Ramsgate, but this was swamped in the breakers early in
the proceedings. It was then decided to attempt to get
a grass line on to an R.A.F. motor boat which was aground
on the beach, and so bring out a load of troops to the
Float. After an unsuccessful attempt with a rocket line,
Mr. Lucey and I swam ashore with a light line and made
fast a grass line to the stern of the boat, the grass
line then being hauled in from the Float. As it seemed
unlikely that the motor boat was going to come successfully through the breakers stern-first, we attempted to
transfer the line to the bow, but unfortunately at the
same moment the Float was got under way in order to drag
the motor boat out, and the line took charge and was lost
I swam after the line but was unable to get it back to
the beach and was hauled aboard the Float. From that
point Mr. Lucey was alone on the beach in the gathering
darkness with about 50 or 60 soldiers, who were rather
demoralised, for two, three hours, most of which time I
believe he spent in the water.

    The Float then had to be shifted into deeper water
owing to the falling tide, and various attempts to get
into contact with the motor boat and Mr. Lucey were
unsuccessful. Eventually at, I think, about 11 o'clock
Mr. Lucey got out to the Float in a boat from another
ship. He then immediately insisted upon further attempts
being made to ferry out more men with this boat, and went
ashore in it again himself and remained ashore while
some thirty or forty men were brought out in the boat.

Extract from a report of the senior Na
officer, Ramsgate Harbor, Ramsgate, Kent.

Destroyers, minesweepers and all manner of craft were arriving, loading and leaving the beaches and Dunkerque continuously, but there were often periods when no ships were at one place or another and embarkation had to wait. Bombing of ships and beaches had so far been spasmodic - the day had been overcast and visibility was not good; sound of fighters overhead seemed to account for our freedom from air attack.

31st May.
0400· Report received at 0400 of aircraft dropping mines 1 mile north of La Panne: planes frequently passed close overhead during dark hours.

Dawn Light N.W. wind sprang up right on the beaches: many boats seen capsized, broached to or high and dry, including at least one of the local boats which carried a lot of men and could get close inshore. Not a cheering sight.
Sky cleared and visibility improved; absence of haze all day.

0730 Made contact with KEITH. EXPRESS now fully loaded and left for Dover as soon as I had transferred to KEITH, in which ship I now hoisted my flag - prior to this I had used a Red Ensign (no flag being available before) to indicate which ship I was in.
While I was in KEITH she did not embark any troops - same as for HEBE.

1035 To VA, Dover:- "Majority of boats broached to and have no crews. Conditions on beach very bad due to freshening onshore wind. Only small numbers being embarked even in daylight. Under present conditions any large scale embarkation from beach is quite impracticable; motor boats cannot get close in. Only hope of embarking any number is at Dunkerque. Will attempt to beach ship to form a lee to try to improve conditions."
Reply:- Urging importance of using beaches as long as possible.

(15) 1105 To VA, Dover:- "Dunkerque our only real hope. Can guns shelling pier from westward be bombed and silenced?"
Successful use of Dunkerque depended on being able to put ships alongside Eastern breakwater: my constant fear that this might be so accurately shelled as to render it untenable. Signalled to shore urging movement towards Dunkerque: troops seen moving slowly westward.
Beach events clearly visible from seaward. Bodies of men marched along - some in good order, others in groups and knots. One battalion in perfect order seen marching down through a winding road from dunes to shore - told later it was the Welsh Guards, but not certain if this was correct.
Embarkation going on all the time, with ships leaving as soon as filled; largest numbers came from Dunkerque.
Commencing of day before and continuing on this day, the Army had been driving lorries down to beach to form a barricade and breakwater. At Braye the R.E. had planked a gangway and made a handrail on these lorries so that motor boats could go alongside. As line ran straight out to sea and wind was directly on shore, breakwater gave very little shelter - still it helped.
During forenoon sent Stevenson over to some paddle minesweepers off Braye to get one beached to act as a breakwater. Done; next day she was high and dry at daylight. Don't know to what extent she was used: no ship was long enough to cover distance tide ran out, so could only be of value for part of the tide.

1000 HEBE returned with Bush, bringing plan for embarkation that night. Was as follows:-
Large numbers of boats were now being sent over in tow of tugs, etc. Due to start arriving at 1500; were to be

(16) kept for use of rear-guard for whom embarkation scheme was planned. To take the troops, 11 sloops were being collected and were to rendezvous and proceed in company, arrival being timed for 0130 on 1st June. Given berths in which to anchor in 3 batches, 1 batch off each of the embarkation beaches.

Extract from the report of Rear Admiral Frederic Wake-Walker, who superintended the Dunkirk evacuation from Royal Navy vessels offshore, transferring from one to another as circumstances demanded.

1st June, Sat. Ship in Granville dock. Repaired and ready for service.

0800. Left Dock and proceeded to Dunkirk, by " X " route.

1308. Observed wreck of " Scotia " and another vessel, apparently on Dyck Bank, with H.M.S. M.15 alongside wreck taking off survivors. Closed as requested by M.15, in company with a great number of small craft proceeding to Dunkirk.

Lowered 3 boats, manned by various ratings of all departments, and picked up a few survivors. All other craft doing likewise. Took some survivors from other craft.

1422. When no more could be done, proceeded towards Dunkirk. M.15 had left for Dover, crowded. Scotia was on fire aft and it was apparent that no more men were on the wreck itself, and very few alive in the water.

1445. Passed No 5 buoy. Heavily shelled and straddled by small calibre guns. No hits after about 4 salvoes.

1508. Between Nos 11 and 13 buoys, was straddled by two salvoes from Dive bombers. Bombs were very close, deluging the entire ship with water, but apparently no damage, though ship was badly shaken.

1540. Berthed at inside berth, Eastern arm, Dunkirk. S.N.O wished me to go to Western arm, but tide being low there was insufficient water.

1550. Comenced to embark British troops, and numerous stretcher cases.

1730. Ship full and very congested with about 1800 men. Advised S.N.O I could not safely take more, being considerably worried about stability. S.N.O strongly advised me to wait, under cover of the shore guns, until 2100, when it was high water and getting dark for the passage across. This I agreed with; During this wait of nearly 4 hours, several dive bombing attacks were made by flights of aircraft on two wrecks outside the harbour, which seemed to indicate that they were anxious to get rid of their bombs on anything which did not fire back. as an intense fire was maintained on them from our 8 Lewis guns and several Bren guns which the soldiers had rigged up in various places and worked for me. Several flights of aircraft passed overhead, apparently bombers, but whilst the R.A.F. were about there was peace.

This long wait was trying to all concerned.

Extract from the report of the commander of the armed boarding vessel *Mona's Isle*.

33. About 1900 a telephone message was received from La Panne Military Headquarters through the War Office and the Admiralty to the effect that Dunkirk harbour was blocked by damaged ships, and that all evacuation must therefore be effected from the beaches.

About the same time a corrupt message from S.N.O.,Dunkirk, was received stating continuous bombing, one destroyer sinking, one transport with troops on board damaged and impossible at present to embark more troops, though pier undamaged.

34. In this confused situation the Vice Admiral, Dover, at 2128, ordered all ships approaching Dunkirk not to close the harbour, but instead to remain off the Eastern beach to collect troops from the shore, and the drifters and minesweepers which were about to be despatched to Dunkirk harbour were also diverted to the beaches.

It appeared, therefore, at this time that the use of Dunkirk harbour would be denied to us except possibly to the small ships.

Signals addressed to S.N.O., Dunkirk, MESE, VERITY, who were known to be in the vicinity of Dunkirk, were sent requiring information as to the accessibility of the Eastern pier for personnel vessels. Admiral Nord was also informed that Dover was out of touch with Captain Tennant, and asked whether it was still possible for transports to enter harbour and berth alongside.

No reply to these enquiries could be expected until after midnight.

35. In the event only 4 trawlers and a yacht entered Dunkirk during the hours of darkness, and as enemy activity was much reduced only two bombing attacks being made, it subsequently transpired that a good opportunity had been missed. It is probable that ships to lift some 8000 to 10,000 troops could have been made available for Dunkirk during the night at little loss to embarkation from the beaches.

Extract from the report on Operation Dynamo submitted to the Admiralty by Vice Admiral Bertram Ramsay, concerning happenings on May 29, when it was mistakenly reported that Dunkirk harbor had been closed by enemy action.

"The once fashionable place of Malo les Bains
was packed with what must have amounted to
thousands of deserted vehicles which somehow gave
one a melancholy feeling of disaster. Div. H.Q.
and ourselves marched across the beach to the mole
at intervals. The Mole is about 1¾ miles long and
stands about 20 feet above the water. As we
marched along, accurate salvos of 5/9's continued
every 10 minutes. The noise was somewhat
frightening, but again our luck held as they were
shelling the forward end of the mole when we were
at the back and vice versa.

"As we proceeded, stretchers bearing wounded,
and yawning gaps in the mole itself which we had
to scramble across, told the story of what might
have been our lot. The behaviour of the troops
was excellent throughout, and they remained steady
and cheerful. Three destroyers could be seen
nearby. One had been burnt out and another broken
in two by enemy action. On arrival at the end
of the mole we found the boat which we were to
embark on had been hit by shell fire. It was
disabled and low in the water. After a longish
wait we embarked at 0200 hours on the 1st June
on a small auxiliary vessel and arrived at
Ramsgate about 0730 hours without further
incident."

Extract from the war diary of the 2nd Division, which had sustained heavy casualties
keeping the escape corridor to the sea open, before its survivors were themselves ordered to fall back on Dunkirk for evacuation.

By 30th May, there remained in the area, at an estimate, 80,000 British troops for evacuation and I had now to complete the plans for the final withdrawal of the Force. I had received a telegram from the Secretary of State, which read as follows :—

" Continue to defend present perimeter to the utmost in order to cover maximum evacuation now proceeding well. . . . If we can still communicate with you we shall send you an order to return to England with such officers as you may choose at the moment when we deem your command so reduced that it can be handed to a Corps Commander. You should now nominate this commander. If communications are broken you are to hand over and return as specified when your effective fighting force does not exceed equivalent of three divisions. This is in accordance with correct military procedure and no personal discretion is left to you in the matter. . . . The Corps Commander chosen by you should be ordered to carry on defence and evacuation with French whether from Dunkirk or beaches. . . ."

The problem was to thin out the troops, while maintaining a proper defence of the perimeter, yet at the same time not to retain a larger number of men than could be embarked in one lift.

I had received orders from home that French and British troops were to embark in equal proportions. Thus it looked at one time as if the British would have to continue holding a perimeter, either the existing one or something smaller, at least another four or five days, to enable all the troops to embark. Yet the enemy pressure was increasing and there was no depth in our position. A line on the dunes could only be held during the hours of darkness to cover the final phase of the withdrawal.

I discussed the situation with the Commanders of 1st and 2nd Corps on 30th May. Embarkation had gone well that day, especially from Dunkirk, but enemy pressure had increased at Furnes and Bergues and it was plain that the eastern end of the perimeter could not be held much longer. The enemy had begun to shell the beach at La Panne. I was still concerned lest the arrangements for embarking the French should for any reason prove inadequate. I therefore motored to Dunkirk to inform Admiral Abrial of my views and to assure myself that the arrangements for embarking British and French troops in equal proportions were working smoothly.

The Admiral assured me of his agreement about the evacuation of the sector, and we then

Extract from the report on the experiences of
the British Expeditionary Force submitted by
Lord Gort to the War Office after the conclusion of Operation Dynamo.

Prime Minister to General Weygand

most immediate

Crisis in evacuation now reached. (Stop)
Five Fighter Squadrons acting almost continuously
is most we can do, but six ships several filled with
troops sunk by bombing this morning. (Stop) Artillery
fire menacing only practicable channel. (Stop) Enemy
closing in on ~~bridge~~ reduced bridgehead. (Stop) By
trying to hold on till to-morrow we may lose all.(Stop)
By going to-night, much may certainly be saved, though
much will be lost. (Stop) Situation cannot be ~~fully~~ judged
by Admiral Abrial *at the front*, nor by you or us here.
~~(Stop) We have therefore ordered Alexander commanding~~
~~Bridgehead to decide for himself whether to stay try~~
~~stay over to-morrow or not. (Stop)~~ Nothing like numbers
of French troops you mention in Bridgehead now, and
we doubt whether such large numbers remain in area.
(Stop) We have therefore ordered General Alexander
Commanding Bridgehead to judge ~~for himself~~ whether to
try to stay over to-morrow or not.
Trust you will agree.

Original draft of the message sent by Prime
Minister Churchill to General Weygand on
June 1. Churchill had been trying to persuade
the French that Britain had not abandoned
France in its effort to avoid disaster at Dunkirk.

Day Three—the Long Retreat

The capitulation of the Belgian army during the night posed a possibly terminal problem for the BEF. By the terms of their surrender, Belgian troops were obliged to allow the Germans to proceed unhindered through what had been their sector of the front, the twenty miles to the sea guarding the British left flank. The pummeled, demoralized Belgians had no intention of doing otherwise. Their soldiers displayed white handkerchiefs to show they were finished with the war even before the Germans moved up. Whatever obstacles to the German advance they had set were removed or left unguarded. If the enemy plunged through in force before the gap was sealed and raced down the coast toward Dunkirk, the perimeter defense for the city, not yet fully established, would prove as useless as the Maginot Line had been. Whatever chance Operation Dynamo had of bringing even a comparatively small number of troops home would be quickly lost. That twenty-mile gap had to be covered immediately.

The task fell to General Brooke's II Corps. Though his troops were hard pressed elsewhere on the front, Brooke patched together an assortment of units to rush into key positions vacated by the Belgians. General headquarters troops were hastily dispatched to do the same. At Nieuport on the coast, the Germans were only just kept from bursting through after they captured a bridge and established a small foothold on the Dunkirk side. At Dixmude, to which a patrol of the 12th Lancers dashed, a Belgian officer—now no longer an ally—had to be forced at gunpoint to reveal how a crucial bridge had earlier been prepared for destruction. The Lancers blew it up only minutes before a strong force of Germans raced up from the east to try to rush across. To Gort's relief, by nightfall, the gap had been sealed and the Germans blocked for the moment from hurtling down toward Dunkirk.

News of the Belgian capitulation came as a shattering blow to French morale. Sanitized official pronouncements had shielded most French people from understanding the desperation of the Allied position. Many had been persuaded by government pronouncements and their newspapers that with General Weygand and Marshal Pétain back in harness, German advances in the north would be checked and the invaders would be thrown back or wiped out. For them, the capitulation of Belgium was more than a betrayal, as Premier Reynaud told them it was in a doom-laden radio address that morning. It was evidence that catastrophe for France was also imminent.

The British government was, of course, also dismayed by the Belgian surrender. With characteristic hyperbole, former Prime Minister David Lloyd George told Parliament, "You can rummage in vain through the black annals of the most reprobate kings of the earth to find a blacker and more squalid example of perfidy and poltroonery than that perpetrated by the King of the Belgians." However, some in London attempted to extract signs of advantage from French fury at being let down by Leopold. It was suggested that if the French were genuinely appalled by Belgium's "treachery," perhaps defeatists among them, advocating a similar capitulation to Hitler, would be silenced. "They must now stand by us to the end," Spears hopefully maintained, "however weak and vacillating some ministers may be," and Churchill believed it "might sting the French to anger in which case they would be very much more formidable opponents to the Germans than in their present stunned and bewildered state." It was clutching at straws.

The withdrawal of the BEF's forward troops was gathering momentum, but not without complications. Lieutenant Colonel A.D.L. Cazenove, commander of the 1st Battalion, Coldstream Guards, which began heading for the coast before dawn that morning, later recalled the difficulties caused by road congestion: "The move back was extremely trying to the nerves. Endless delays took place, and we stood still for hours on end, not really knowing whether we should be cut off by the enemy or not.''

The 1st Battalion of the Welsh Guards withdrew in single file up both sides of the road as a precaution against air attack and "because the middle of the road was filled with other troops, both British and French, mostly without any apparent orders, or under any particular control, and frequently without any visible weapons for their own defence, but all with the cry on their lips 'which is the road to Dunkirk?'"

At Dunkirk, the navy personnel who had arrived and been assigned the previous night to serve as beach patrols and beach masters had set about trying to impose order on the crowds and clusters of men who were converging on the beaches. A single officer, accompanied by a small contingent of seamen, was posted at intervals along the main beaches—at Malo adjoining Dunkirk city, at Bray six miles farther along, and at La Panne, the farthest reach of the planned operation. These officers soon discovered that they were effectively on their own. They had no means of communicating either with other beach masters elsewhere along the sands, with their superiors at navy headquarters at Dunkirk, or with ships offshore to which they were supposed to dispatch the troops congregated on their miniature domains of sand and mud. What was more, there appeared to be little discipline or organization among those troops; nor was there any sign of any organized effort by the army command to establish order or evacuation procedure on the beaches or the dunes. Without giving the matter much thought, the army, concentrating on the intricacies of the withdrawal, had concluded that it was primarily the navy's job to take over once the men got to the shore. Now growing numbers of men were there but the vessels to get them off were still few and far between. Neither the troops nor the navy beach masters had any way of knowing that Dynamo plans were being changed and that the major emphasis would now be on evacuation not from the beaches but from Dunkirk harbor.

When the *Queen of the Channel* had managed to tie up at the eastern breakwater in Dunkirk harbor the previous night, it appeared evident that many more men could after all be embarked there than from the beaches. The vessel, loaded with 950 troops packed into every space on its decks and below, slipped away from the pier as dawn broke, eased out of the harbor, and made for Dover. It didn't get far before a near miss from bombs dropped by a German aircraft damaged it so severely that it sank, though not before most of the men aboard had been rescued by other vessels.

Despite this loss, it was clear that the harbor would have to be the primary avenue of rescue for the great numbers of men to be evacuated. Tennant signaled the destroyers which had been ordered during the night to take up positions off the beaches for loading there from small craft—the *Mackay, Montrose, Vimy, Worcester, Sabre,* and *Anthony*—to go instead to the harbor and make fast at the breakwater, where the pickings would be far better. At the same time, Dynamo headquarters in Dover was advised that many of the other ships coming over should do the same.

Commander J. C. Clouston, appointed pier master at the breakwater, set up a tight control system for the troops to be boarded from the breakwater. He posted men to maintain discipline at the foot of the pier and at access points to it. The troops were organized in groups of up to fifty so that they could quickly scamper along in orderly fashion and be boarded as soon as rescue vessels were properly secured. However, though the emphasis of the operation shifted to the breakwater, there was no intention of abandoning the simultaneous lift-off from the beaches, for which small craft remained in desperately short supply.

The small craft which had been requisitioned and rounded up on the Thames and along the southeast coast of England the previous day had begun turning up at Dover early in the morning. Some had been found to be unfit for Channel service and were sent back to their owners, and some had gone to the wrong assembly points. Having no radios, they could not easily be redirected. The others were stripped of all unnecessary equipment, fueled, and made ready for the Channel crossing.

There being a shortage of naval personnel to man those craft, some of the civilian crews which had delivered them were asked to volunteer for a month's duty with the Royal Navy and given some idea of what would be expected of them and their vessels. Most signed on, some with misgivings, never having imagined their pleasure, fishing, or ferry boats going to war. Others chose not to.

Then, and not until then, we were told, not without a certain amount of lurid detail, of the "stunt" on hand. . . . A cold hard lump formed in my stomach and . . . my "tummy" felt it had dropped to the region of my knees. I dared not look at the others and remembered that I had not even told my wife and the kiddies that I had left London, let alone "joined up" with the Navy. . . . At this point the crew of the "Queen Boadicea" which had joined our convoy . . . said something about having families and not receiving danger money, whatever that is. . . . The three men climbed ashore with their gear amidst complete silence from the other craft and went off. I was glad then that I had not had the pluck myself to make excuses for not going.

Charts were distributed and arrangements were made for the craft to form up in convoys for the crossing as the troops beginning to throng the Dunkirk beaches looked out to sea for rescue.

Since the previous night, Lord Gort had been trying to find General Blanchard, who was still supposed to be coordinating the operations of the Allied armies in the north. He wanted to work out joint British-French action in view of the Belgian capitulation. Also trying to remain on top of the situation, Blanchard had been scurrying from one frontline command post to another, without leaving word of his movements. Not till eleven in the morning did they make contact, when Blanchard arrived at the BEF's new headquarters at Houtkerque.

He was exhausted in body and mind but not too tired to be horrified when Gort, assuming the French had similar instructions, told him that the BEF had been ordered by London to proceed to the coast for evacuation. It was the first Blanchard had heard of Operation Dynamo. Weygand hadn't told him, nor had Admiral Abrial. It was wrong, Blanchard insisted, and why hadn't the British informed him earlier? Gort was, in turn, astounded that the information came as a surprise to Blanchard and that the French forces under his command had not yet also been instructed by Paris to make for Dunkirk to be lifted off. Gort assumed, however, that—evacuation or not—the French and the BEF would synchronize their phased fallback toward the coast during the coming night so that there would be no break in the defensive line.

Blanchard wouldn't hear of it. He did not intend for the

French to retreat further. He believed it was important to keep the Germans engaged to delay their inevitable drive against Paris. He would thus give Weygand's forces south of the Somme additional time to establish a strong line of defense to repel the enemy assault. Every day saved for that purpose, every hour, could prove valuable for the survival of French liberty. Besides, Blanchard said, his troops were exhausted. They had been under attack and on the move without a break for two weeks and were in no condition to keep going. Even if they did withdraw to Dunkirk, evacuation for them was not an option. Perhaps the Royal Navy had worked out procedures for embarking the BEF. But not informed of the French-British naval consultations in Dover the previous morning, he was certain the French Admiralty planned no such evacuation for French troops.

Though not known for his powers of persuasion, Gort tried to convince Blanchard that nothing was to be saved and much was to be lost in standing fast, locked in a closing trap by superior enemy forces. Aside from recognizing the absurdity of such a course, he did not want to be put in the position of ordering his troops to abandon their French fellow soldiers while they fought on, gallantly covering what would look like an ignominious unilateral withdrawal by the British forces.

As Gort and Blanchard debated what was to be done, word came from General Prioux, new commander of what remained of the French First Army (effectively all that was left under Blanchard's command), that his troops were exhausted. No matter what the best course might be, they were in no shape to withdraw. Gort wanted to know how, if they were in no fit condition to withdraw, would they be able to tie down the enemy? The BEF commander pleaded with Blanchard to reconsider his decision.

> I . . . begged General Blanchard, for the sake of France, the French Army and the Allied Cause to order General Prioux back. Surely, I said, his troops were not all so tired as to be incapable of moving. The French Government would be able to provide ships at least for some of his troops, and the chance of saving a part of his trained soldiers was preferable to the certainty of losing them all. I could not move him.

Unable to shift Blanchard, Gort told him that whatever the French did, the British would be pulling back toward Dunkirk to be evacuated. (They were doing so already.) Those were his orders from London and he was obliged to obey them. Besides, he insisted, it would be insane to let his troops be lost to the enemy when an operation to save them was already underway.

Right through the day, fighting on both flanks of the escape corridor remained heavy, as did the casualty levels, inflated that day by an act of murder over and beyond the call of battle. More than eighty men of the Royal Warwickshire Regiment, surrounded near the town of Wormhout, surrendered to the Adolf Hitler SS Regiment only to be herded at gunpoint into a small barn into which hand grenades were then tossed. Machinegun and rifle fire cut down most of those who were not immediately killed.

Communications between Allied command positions and the shifting front continued to deteriorate. Remaining radio and telephone links were breaking down, and contact had to rely increasingly on motorcycle dispatch riders, who tried to make their way through choked traffic to deliver their orders and reports to recipients who often were not to be found where they were expected to be. Aware of the consequences of orders not being received or being received too late, Gort gave his corps commanders a general idea of the fallback defense line for the coming night and authorized them to use their discretion in shifting as many of their fighting units as they safely could back into the Dunkirk perimeter.

The troops withdrew through a landscape of defeat.

> From every house in the villages, from church steeples, farms, cottages, from everywhere where people lived there flapped a white flag, and if not a real flag, a white tablecloth, sheet, towel or handkerchief . . . tokens of surrender which the inhabitants were in a great hurry to have on display by the time the Germans arrived.

Rumors filtered back from the coast of hundreds dead on the Dunkirk beaches and of rescue vessels loaded with evacuees sunk by submarines or Stukas. The routed troops were continually aware of the devastation of which the dive-bombers were capable. Under attack, they dove for cover into ditches, "crawled underneath the wreckage of vehicles, flattened themselves down between the very grass blades in the fields, and stood up to their necks in the water of the canal. In the space of a few seconds . . . not a soul was in sight."

It wasn't only a matter of making for the coast. The men were ordered to travel light. As they approached the Dunkirk perimeter, they were instructed to make certain their equipment would not fall into the hands of the advancing enemy. An officer recalled, "We kept enough transport to get us within a mile or two of Dunkirk. Then we finally destroyed everything except one car, which I kept in case of emergency. All along the road our troops were having an orgy of smashing up. Under a clear blue sky, on a quiet country road, it was perhaps the most astonishing sight of all in this queer war." Vast quantities of equipment were demolished. Men who had been responsible for the care, upkeep, and distribution of costly military hardware were appalled by the waste.

> New wireless sets . . . were placed in rows in the fields, twenty in a row, sometimes, while a soldier with a pick-axe proceeded up and down knocking them to pieces. Trucks were dealt with just as drastically. Radiators and engines were smashed with sledgehammers; tyres slashed and sawn after they had been deflated. Vehicles that were near canals were finally pushed in. Some of the canals were choked with wrecks, all piled on top of each other.

Inevitably, there were mistakes, some of them of monumental proportions given the situation. Spare gunners in the antiaircraft unit which was drawn back to defend the perimeter at La Panne were instructed to take up rifles and join the ground defense of the area. However, the order was misunderstood to apply to *all* gunners in the unit. To prevent their abandoned guns—which were desperately needed to defend the perimeter from air attack—from falling into the hands of the advancing Germans, they destroyed them too before the misunderstanding could be sorted out, to the astonishment, despair, and fury of senior commanders.

Despite the road congestion, by the afternoon a vast multitude of British troops had reached the coast and were sprawled on the dunes and along the ten miles of beaches stretching east of Dunkirk, where, in more agreeable times, children built sand castles and people frolicked on the shore. To men on the ships arriving to take them home, the troops looked "like thousands of sticks."

> The beach was an extraordinary sight. As far as the eye could see it stretched away into the distance, the firm sand of the shore stretching farther back into the dunes where the surface was no more than a thin yellow powder interspersed with parched tussocks of coarse grass. And covering this vast expanse, like some mighty antheap upturned by a giant's foot, were the remains of the British Expeditionary Force, some standing in black clusters at the water's edge, waiting for the boats that were to take them to the two or three ships lying off-shore, while others, whose turn had not yet come, or who were too tired to care whether it was their turn or not, lay huddled together in a disorderly and exhausted multitude.

Queues stretched the entire width of the beaches and into the water. Some of the men had arrived in organized units under command of junior officers and remained as such. Directed into lines for embarkation, they held assigned positions while waiting to be signaled forward to be boarded. But many of the men were from units which had been demolished in battle or fragmented in retreat. Some of these, having been told it was every man for himself, had previously had no idea what was going on—except that things were going badly—and had just "followed the crowd" back toward Dunkirk.

Survival was the only priority. One officer later wrote, "We all had one idea now, one impulse—we only wanted to reach the water's edge and be rowed away quietly into the night like King Arthur." Whether in organized units or "odds and sods" in small ragtag groups, the troops to be lifted off were exhausted, thirsty, and hungry. Some had not eaten for a day or more. On the sand, many were absorbed into organized units, which seemed to offer a greater opportunity for survival. Others who tried to join such groups were told, "You don't belong to us. Get out of here," by men who feared hangers-on would make their own evacuation more difficult. There was nothing for these rejects to do but wander down the beach toward Dunkirk in the hopes of leaving from the harbor or tag on to less exclusive queues from which they might be lifted off home more quickly.

> It would start off as a queue, but if you thought you could get to a boat before the others, you were out there in the water. It wasn't really panic but it wasn't a queue anymore. You waded out to try to get into a boat. After you failed a few times, you'd get fed up standing in the water and you'd go back and sit on the sand. Then when more boats would come in, you'd try again.

Bodies floated in the water. Most were of men who had been killed by German aircraft strafing and bombing the ships, boats, and waterline. But some troops had drowned after clinging to overloaded boats which they had been unable to board and then losing their grip.

The undulating dunes with their clumps of coarse grass provided somewhat more protection from the bombing raids and the German fighter planes zooming past a hundred feet above the ground, their machine guns blazing. At least they offered an illusion of cover in a situation in which cover was hard to come by. Men had to decide whether they'd wait on the dunes, where they felt safer, for the summons to embark from an officer or a navy beach master, or on the beach, where the chances for speedy evacuation seemed greater. On both the beaches and the dunes, the sand muffled the bomb explosions and kept the spray of shrapnel to a minimum. But there were bodies on the sand, some covered with discarded greatcoats, and there soon would be more.

More men arrived all the time, some expecting to be embarked immediately and transported home once they reached the coast. They were shattered to find thousands ahead of them wanting the same. Even on well-organized queues, under control of navy beach masters, some declined to wait.

> I saw a man suddenly rush past . . . out of turn. Immediately a determined shout went up from the other men who were in front of him in the queue. 'Get out. Get back, you bastard. . . .' There was no mistaking their tone. The man failed to reach the boat which was now putting out to sea. He shrank back, immediately forgotten and unobserved,

into the queue. . . . In our urgency we forgot things as
quickly as animals . . . we had the memories of monkeys.

To complicate matters, the swell of the sea, though moderate, was enough to make it difficult for the small boats to come
in close and take men on board. "Tired, wet and hungry,"
quipped one evacuee, "we decided that Bray as a holiday resort
was much overrated."

The tide was a problem even when the breeze tailed off.
When it raced out, the men tried to move with it so as to be as
close as possible to the boats making their way toward them to
ferry them out to the rescue ships offshore. When the tide raced
in, they were reluctant to back away from the incoming boats,
fearing that others would not and they would lose their places at
the head of the line. They found themselves up to their knees,
their thighs, their shoulders in water.

When they reached a boat, they clambered aboard as best
they could. The navy personnel, merchant seamen, or pastime
sailors manning the boats sometimes had to swing oars at them
to keep them from capsizing their craft. More boats were now
arriving to participate in the ferrying operation. But there were
still far too few to make an appreciable dent in the numbers to
be evacuated. It was apparent before midmorning that the operation directly from the shore could not be expected to achieve
much.

At Dunkirk harbor, along the breakwater, things were
somewhat more hopeful. Rescue vessels were arriving, tying up,
boarding, and departing with increasing frequency. The number
of troops being brought back to England was rising. But at the
harbor too, only just so much could be done, and a few thousand more troops embarked did not make a great deal of difference to the overall picture. Thousands still waited their turn
to be lifted off, and tens of thousands more still were making
their way along the corridor to the coast.

Being rescued from Dunkirk did not necessarily mean getting safely home. In addition to the *Queen of the Channel,* which
had gone down in the morning, the merchant ship *Abukir* was
lost, sunk by a torpedo boat, also after it had set off for England
fully loaded. Two other passenger vessels drummed into service
ran aground at low tide. A French cargo vessel, the *Douaisien,*
one of a small fleet of vessels sent by the French Admiralty to

pick up French specialist troops, hit a mine and went down. The trawler *Thomas Bartlett,* searching for German mines off Calais, ran into a British minefield there and sank. Its entire crew was lost. Most of the men on the other vessels were rescued, but an unknown number of troops were lost that day after they had been evacuated. Records of who boarded, who was rescued from the water when their ships were sunk, and who was lost would have been impossible to keep.

An early cloud cover and the pall of black smoke from Dunkirk's burning oil storage tanks had provided partial aerial protection for the area through much of the morning. But later in the day, a shift in the wind's direction cleared the skies and German attack aircraft were once more active over the area, though they weren't as much in evidence over the coast as they had been the day before. The Luftwaffe that day concentrated instead on the shrinking front of the Allied forces inland. But German artillery, which had been moved up close west of Dunkirk, pounded the harbor area, if not with accuracy, with increasing thoroughness.

The damage inflicted was severe. The potential for even greater damage was great. As the day drew to a close, Dynamo headquarters in Dover ruled that civilian passenger ships participating in the operation should no longer use the harbor breakwater during daylight hours, when they could be sitting targets. Only warships would continue to take that risk. These continued to shuttle in and out of the harbor to evacuate troops. Until nightfall, the civilian vessels taking part in the operation were to concentrate exclusively on boarding men ferried out to them from the beaches. Though exposed to air raids, their anchorages offshore were still out of range of the German guns. For how long, no one dared predict.

Though the story till then had been primarily one of Allied setback, retreat, and confusion, German forces had been sustaining heavy losses and facing serious problems as well. General Guderian reported that the equipment of his armored divisions was "in urgent need of repair." Besides, though an armored breakthrough farther inland would have pinched the Allies off from the sea, fighting closer to the coast called for different tactics. "A tank attack," Guderian said, "is pointless in the marshy country which has been completely soaked by the rain. . . . Infantry forces . . . are more suitable than tanks for fighting in this kind of country." Further tank attacks would, he said, result in "the useless sacrifice of our best troops." The panzer divisions were accordingly withdrawn. Besides, they needed to be rested before turning south for the greater glory of crushing the French forces deployed to keep them from marching on Paris.

Their armies having steamrolled across northern France, the Germans had lost both their momentum and their sense of urgency in the north. The Allied troops in the elongated Dunkirk pocket were trapped against the sea. A mopping-up operation was all that was now required to deal with them. German commanders knew that British troops were being ferried home from Dunkirk, and they weren't happy about that. But they could not imagine that a truly massive evacuation operation was either underway or possible.

Nor could Churchill, his War Cabinet, or the chiefs of staff in London make any accurate forecast of what Operation Dynamo might accomplish. Evacuation figures so far provided grounds for gloom rather than confidence. His mission to the Belgian royal court concluded by the Belgian capitulation, Sir Roger Keyes returned that day across the Channel with word that Gort, with whom he had spoken, still did not rate the chances of saving the BEF very high. It was known that the men—whether on the shore, manning the perimeter defense, trudging back through the escape corridor, or holding the corridor open—were desperately short of food and ammunition. Not much could be done about it. And what chance could there be of responding satisfactorily to the avalanche of pleas for more ships and boats and for greater aerial cover?

There was growing unease in Parliament as unofficial reports circulated about the BEF's plight and about how the navy appeared to be engaged in some sort of extremely desperate emergency operation. But Churchill, though bracing the House of Commons for bad news, still declined to reveal to it the extent of the crisis. He also refused to leave room for speculation that Britain might be driven by military setback to seek an armistice with Germany.

> I expect to make a statement to the House on the general position when the result of the intense struggle now going on can be known and measured. This perhaps may not be until

the beginning of next week. Meanwhile, the House must
prepare itself for hard and heavy tidings. I have only to add
that nothing which can happen in this battle can in any way
relieve us of our duty to defend the world cause to which we
have bound ourselves, nor can it destroy our confidence in
our power to make our way—as on former occasions in our
history—through disaster and grief to ultimate defeat of our
enemy.

The prime minister's refusal even to explore the possibility
that Britain might honorably extract itself without further damage from a war in which the country was heading for disaster
was challenged once more in the War Cabinet by his foreign
secretary. Lord Halifax insisted, "We must not ignore the fact
that we might get better [armistice] terms before France went
out of the war and our aircraft factories were bombed than we
might get in three months' time."

Churchill was not moved. He replied that if Britain agreed
to armistice talks and then found that Germany's peace terms
were unacceptable, the country's war effort would have lost its
momentum. He was certain that any armistice terms Germany
might offer would be designed to put Britain at Hitler's mercy.
By the time Britain then left the negotiating table to get on with
the war, "We should find that all the forces of resolution . . .
now at our disposal would have vanished." Further vexing
Halifax by presuming to preach, Churchill declared that "nations which went down fighting rose again but those which surrendered tamely were finished."

Chamberlain, who was still official leader of the Tory Party
and whose views could not be summarily discounted despite his
recent ouster, continued to back Halifax on the advisability of
exploring chances for honorable peace negotiations. It should be
done, the former prime minister said, if only to discourage
France from seeking a separate peace with Germany. The two
next most senior members of the War Cabinet, men held in high
regard by most of the Tory Party, were doing more than merely
disagreeing with Churchill. Given the circumstances, they were
challenging his leadership. In the history of the war that he
wrote subsequently, Churchill makes little mention of their
views at that critical moment or of the additional pressure they
put him under when the fate of a quarter of a million British

troops was very much in doubt. He wrote only of the tremendous support he received from other government ministers who were not members of the War Cabinet, who he said cheered him and praised his stand at a separate meeting that evening.

> Quite a number seemed to jump up from the table and come running to my chair, shouting and patting me on the back. There is no doubt that had I at this juncture faltered at all in the leading of the nation I should have been hurled out of office.

War Cabinet member Clement Attlee, the Labour Party leader who was Churchill's deputy prime minister and whose backing was essential if the government of national unity was to survive, was particularly supportive. But Attlee warned that when the public became aware of the fate that appeared to await the BEF, it would suffer a severe shock. No one who knew what was happening believed that Britain would emerge from the Dunkirk episode and its aftermath with anything less than tragedy. The extent of the government's forebodings was revealed by its decision to mark the country off into seventeen food areas. Each would come under the "supreme control" of a local official "to ensure distribution of food" if communications broke down in an emergency.

The German propaganda war was stepped up. Gort was said to have offered to surrender and the capitulation of France was reportedly about to be announced. Censorship prevented many such claims from getting through to the British public but couldn't prevent all rumors of impending calamity from circulating and affecting public morale. Steps were taken to deal with any agitation against the war effort that might develop on the home front. A defense regulation was to be introduced in Parliament empowering the government to prohibit the printing, publication, or distribution of any newspaper which systematically published material fomenting opposition to the successful prosecution of the war. A particular target was the Communist Party's *Daily Worker,* which, following the lead of the Soviet Union, dismissed Britain's involvement in the struggle against Hitler as a capitalist conspiracy.

British fighter planes—Spitfires, Hurricanes, and Defiants—had been in action over the Dunkirk pocket from first light, giving and taking punishment. Fighter Command flew 321 sorties that day, with some pilots shuttling two or three times from their airfields in Kent. Seventeen British fighter planes were lost or damaged in operations before nightfall. Several of the pilots shot down were rescued, but seven were killed in action. According to information made available after the war, twenty-two German aircraft were destroyed in combat that day, not all over Dunkirk. But even that total was far fewer than the "kills" claimed by RAF pilots unable to make accurate judgments in the heat of aerial combat about whom they did or did not shoot down while providing an aerial screen for the evacuation.

Later, when the BBC was finally permitted to broadcast news of the Dunkirk evacuation, it announced, "Our men can find no words in which to speak of their gratitude to the Royal Air Force." In fact, the troops on the ground found plenty of words to describe their feelings about the RAF. But few of them would have been acceptable for broadcast, as Flight Lieutenant Alan Deere—whose squadron was almost wiped out over Dunkirk—discovered. When Deere was shot down, he made his way to the beaches and sought to board an evacuation vessel so that he could make his way back to his base and get back into the fight. An army major tried to block his way, snarling, "For all the good you chaps seem to be doing over here you might just as well stay on the ground."

Admiral Ramsay attempted to redress such criticism at the end of the operation. He declared, "I and the Forces under my command who have been engaged on the evacuation of the Allied Armies owe a deep debt of gratitude to the Royal Air Force for the support and protection which they have given to us." But in a subsequent statement on RAF support during the operation, Ramsay was scathing.

Rightly or wrongly, full air protection was expected, but instead, for hours on end the ships off-shore were subjected to a murderous hail of bombs and machine-gun bullets. Required by their duty to remain off-shore waiting for the troops, who themselves were unable to move down to the water for the same reason, it required the greatest determination and sense of duty, amounting in fact to heroism, on the part of the ships' and boats' crews, to enable them to complete their mission. In their reports, the COs of many ships, while giving credit to the RAF personnel for gallantry in such combats as were observed from the ships, at the same time express their sense of disappointment and surprise at the seemingly puny efforts made to provide air protection during the height of this operation.

Captain Tennant, watching from Dunkirk, was reluctant to be so harsh. "The sky is a big place," he said, "and it was often difficult to know if our aircraft were present or not."

Regardless of their inaccuracy, the inflated claims of the RAF pilots did much for morale at home. It gave both the British public and the pilots themselves—if not the troops being blasted by enemy aircraft—the impression that Britain was winning the air war with Germany. Air Chief Marshal Dowding was not at all pleased with the implications. Sensitive to criticism of Fighter Command for not providing more comprehensive cover for the men and ships at Dunkirk, he feared it would now be ordered to do so and that he would then lose more fighters than he could spare before the fight-to-the-finish German assault on the British homeland began.

To neutralize any euphoria that might be generated by the inflated claims of the pilots, Dowding reported that the country's home "fighter defenses were almost at cracking point." He warned that if Fighter Command's effectiveness was sacrificed at Dunkirk, "the situation would be serious." He was saying, in effect, that too much rather than too little aerial cover was being provided for Operation Dynamo—not because less would suffice but because the priority requirement remained keeping aerial home defenses intact.

Churchill had a different catalogue of priorities. For him, getting the troops back from Dunkirk was now the prime necessity. He shared the concern of the Fighter Command chief. But the dour Dowding, nicknamed "Stuffy," had earned a reputation for being constitutionally inclined to issue overly gloomy prophecies. In his diary, Ironside had described him as "a curious old thing." Chief of the Air Staff Newall agreed that the Fighter Command chief was being excessively worried. The RAF would continue to provide as much cover as possible at Dunkirk, with the understanding that under no circumstances were Britain's air defenses to be denuded.

*   *   *

Gort moved to the coast that afternoon from his inland command post and set up his headquarters in a former Belgian royal seaside villa at La Panne, ten miles north of Dunkirk. His new command post was close to the cross-Channel Brussels-London telephone cable, permitting the BEF commander to remain in touch with the British capital. After touring the area, he informed the War Office that there were about twenty thousand men waiting to be evacuated, that they were exposed to ferocious air attack, and that things looked bleak indeed. "There can be no doubt that if air attacks continue at present intensities," he warned, "the area must become a shambles and such a situation could easily arrive in next 48 hours."

The BEF commander asked London to clarify its instructions to him. He feared that the flanks of the escape corridor—or what was left of it as more men withdrew—would collapse before all his troops could reach the coast and that the defense perimeter would be overrun before the evacuation operation got much further. He wanted definite guidance on what was expected of him if bad came to worst. Was he to surrender the BEF to the enemy to prevent a slaughter, or was he to fight to the last bullet? Expecting firm instruction, he had to settle for a pat on the back in the form of a message from Minister of War Eden.

> We have every confidence that you and the gallant troops under your command will continue to the uttermost the grim struggle for our country's safety. . . . All possible assistance is being rendered by Royal Navy, and RAF will give maximum cover in their power during these critical days.

Did that mean he was to fight till the last bullet? He wasn't sure.

The evacuation proceeded in greater safety after nightfall when most of the German planes were grounded and when vessels moved in by turns alongside the eastern breakwater to embark troops while small boats continued to work the beaches. But only 17,804 men were brought back to England that day, about a third of them from the beaches. That was more than twice as many as the day before. But it was hardly enough to point to anything but a resounding failure for Operation Dynamo.

Information Minister Duff Cooper finally received cabinet permission to begin preparing the British public for the worst. In a radio speech that night, he tried to brace people for the trouble ahead.

> It will be necessary to withdraw our army from the positions they now occupy, but it will not be a defeated army. . . . It will be an army whose courage is still high and whose confidence is still unshaken, and every officer and man burning with desire to meet the enemy in combat. . . . We can all remember the dark days of the last war. . . . It seemed that the war was lost. But it never was—and all events which seemed disastrous at the time proved but the prelude to victory. . . . As the danger increases so does our courage to meet it.

Not governed by British censorship regulations, the *New York Herald Tribune* reported much more gloomily from London.

> The British Expeditionary Force . . . was all but given up for lost here tonight. . . . In this epic tragedy the port of Dunkerque was the only hope of escape, and Dunkerque was under such brutal bombing by the numerically superior airmen of Germany that the prospect of removing the French-British force in the north was considered in London to be remote. Thus the cream of the British Army appeared, this sad and uncertain evening, to face extinction or surrender. No one in this country thought for a moment that [Gort] would take the latter course.

Under the circumstances, it was difficult not to wonder whether Gort had made a tragic mistake in withdrawing to the coast. "Poor chap," General Pownall wrote in his diary that night. "He feels his position terribly. The most trivial things have always preyed on his mind and now he has a load that he can never shake off all the days of his life. The Commander of the BEF that was driven into the sea in three weeks! So undeserved a fate."

Day Four—Journey Through Hell

The day opened with tragedy. In the dark early hours of the morning, the destroyer *Wakeful,* carrying 650 evacuees who had been lifted by small boats from the beach at Bray, set sail for Dover taking the longest route to avoid German coastal artillery on the most direct route and the mined middle passage. Before it had gotten far, it was hit amidship by a German torpedo. The explosion broke the vessel in two, and it sank in fifteen seconds. Almost all the men aboard had been asleep below and were lost. The *Wakeful*'s sister ship, the destroyer *Grafton,* with eight hundred evacuees on board, was also torpedoed while searching for survivors. Going down, the *Grafton* opened fire on a small vessel lurking in the nearby darkness which its skipper took to be a German torpedo boat. The *Lydd,* a drifter en route to pick up evacuees, rammed and sank this suspect vessel, which proved to have been not an enemy ship but the British drifter *Comfort,* which had also approached to try to rescue survivors from the *Wakeful.* It was not known how many men were lost in this series of misadventures. Such tragic farce, chaos, and grief had by now become part of the Dunkirk story.

Even before the early-morning losses were known at Dover's Dynamo headquarters, personnel on duty there were stricken with intimations of disaster. During the night, some seventy vessels had crossed over, some to pick up men from the beaches, others to embark troops from the breakwater. Where were those ships? They had been expected to begin streaming back to England by 3:00 A.M., but by 9:00 they had failed to return. It was more than possible that many had been sunk or disabled. And if so many ships had been lost under the comforting cover of darkness, what prospects could there be for carrying on with the operation during daylight hours—or at all?

As anxiety built up at Dover, word from Dunkirk, relayed by a destroyer, calmed fears somewhat. "Personnel vessels . . . were having difficulty in making the entrance of Dunkirk harbour in the face of the navigational difficulties caused by a heavy smoke pall over the entrance and in the face of bombing and shelling encountered en route and whilst alongside." Expectations that passenger vessels would embark great numbers of troops from the breakwater before dawn were as a consequence disappointed. In addition, a strong overnight surf compounded the difficulties of the small craft and of the seamen operating under trying conditions. Any northerly wind whipped up a surf on that stretch of coast. Vessels working the shore had been unable to get on with their appointed tasks until the winds had dropped toward morning light.

Meantime, developments on the eastern sector of the perimeter presented a new threat to the operation. The Germans had moved heavy guns up to the Belgian coast near Nieuport, which they had newly captured, forcing the Allied defenders there back toward La Panne. That brought the nearby Zuydcoote Pass offshore, through which the long sea route back to England ran, within range of their artillery and subject to spasmodic fire. The middle Channel passage was about to become the only usable route to and from Dunkirk during daylight hours. It was pronounced swept of mines and all ships crossing during the day were instructed to use it, "exercising navigational caution" in view of likely congestion.

No matter how diligently practiced, navigational caution could not repel air attacks. The Germans had finally realized that British activity on the coast was far more ambitious than they had thought possible. They had previously assumed that except for a comparatively small number who were getting away, the troops locked against the sea had no alternative but capture or slaughter. But air reconnaissance revealed how determinedly and vigorously the evacuation operation was progressing. Once more the Luftwaffe was instructed to deal energetically with the situation, specifically to step up its assaults on the rescue vessels. An intensive aerial assault was launched against the ships and continued virtually without letup until last light. The toll it took was both huge and portentous.

In addition to the two destroyers which were sent to the bottom of the Channel before daylight, another, the *Gallant,* was damaged and put out of action by a near miss; the *Jaguar,* dead in the water after being hit by a bomb, had to be towed back to Dover; and the *Grenade,* loaded with troops at the breakwater and setting off for Dover when she was hit, was turned into a blazing inferno drifting out of control. She was towed clear of the harbor before she could sink there blocking the entrance and exploded just outside. There were few survivors.

A war sloop and two minesweepers were also sunk, as were four passenger ships. Among ships damaged were three other British destroyers, three French destroyers which had joined in the operation though there was as yet no sign ashore of comprehensive French evacuation plans, two minesweepers, and two passenger vessels. Among these last was the *Mona's Queen,* which had been the first vessel to run the gauntlet bringing troops back from Dunkirk when Operation Dynamo had commenced, a depressing omen, though such grim portents were not in short supply. Many small boats were lost, bombed or strafed while trying to lift men off the beaches. They lay near the water's edge, wrecked, burning, or burned out, evoking premonitions of doom among the troops.

Though badly needed, many of the rowboats, some of which could carry as many as thirty men, were abandoned and permitted to drift out to sea by the men they had ferried out to the vessels offshore. One naval officer reported, "On arrival alongside the men would all jump on board and let their boats drift off on the tide. Paddles were lost, rendering the boats useless." Having waited anxiously for rescue, having so far survived air attacks, and having finally reached a homeward-bound ship, few soldiers were disposed to risk rowing the boats back to the beach for men not yet as lucky as themselves. And sailors from the larger vessels, who sometimes shuttled those small boats to and from the beaches, were normally also the men who manned ships' guns against attacking aircraft. They couldn't comfortably be long spared for boat duty when enemy aircraft might zoom out of the horizon at any moment. Besides, they were exhausted, many of them having been working at full stretch with little time for sleep ever since the evacuation of the "useless mouths" had begun. Many of them, and particularly the crews of the navy vessels, had been in action and under air attack the better part of a week.

Even when men could be spared from the ships to help organize the evacuation on the beaches, they were not always successful. When the sloop *Bideford,* anchored off Bray, sent men ashore "in an endeavor to take charge on the beach . . . this was next to impossible. The men rushed the boats and capsized them in shallow water, and then left the boats without making any attempt to right them and use them again."

Though not an isolated case, such behavior was by no means universal. Right through the operation, the conduct of the troops varied according to training, personal standards of behavior, sense of duty, discipline in the presence of officers and NCOs, and emotional reaction to their plight. Some soldiers did row back to shore to ferry more men out to rescue vessels when they easily could have boarded those vessels themselves the first time out, leaving their boats to drift away as most of the others in that situation appear to have done. As many troops as not, patiently or otherwise, waited their turn in the straggly queues rather than rushing to the waterline to try to be the first away.

Some of the men who returned after waiting long hours for their turn to be embarked reported that they had seen not a single incident of indiscipline on the beaches. Others insisted it had been every man for himself on the shore unless a navy beach master intervened forcefully, often brandishing a weapon, when men could not be dissuaded from rushing into the water and capsizing incoming boats while trying to scramble into them.

> I took my revolver out and fired in front of the leading man in the water. The sound of the shot and the splash startled them. I warned them back. I told them, "If you go on like this no one will get away. Now two of you go out and pull the boat into shallow water and turn it around." A major appeared and asked what was happening. I told him and he asked what I wanted done. I said I wanted two embarkation points with lines back across the beach to the sand hills with the men marked off in blocks of sixty with gaps between them to reduce casualties in case of strafing. In no time, he got it started.

The men—those who were disciplined and those who were
not—were worn down and disoriented by being strafed and
bombed, as well as by their long retreat. They wanted desperately to be on their way home, though most knew from watching
German aircraft in action that a hard-won place on a ship homeward bound was not automatic deliverance. Ships were ablaze
offshore and bodies floated in the water. And indeed the experience of troops as they were being brought home from Dunkirk
and the beaches was often more harrowing than those they had
endured while under aerial attack ashore. Few had ever been on
board a vessel when it was under attack—even worse, below
deck.

> At three this morning there was a terrific explosion as a tor-
> pedo hit the destroyer. I suppose the force must have
> knocked me unconscious. First thing I knew I was stumbling
> about in the dark trying to find the door of the cabin. The
> whole ship was trembling violently. . . . Finding my way out
> on deck was a bit of a nightmare. Everything was pitch
> black. . . . It didn't occur to me for a moment that any of us
> had a chance of escape. The sailors last night had been em-
> phatic that a torpedo meant the end of everything. But
> somehow it didn't matter much. The disaster . . . was still
> trying to penetrate the outer layer of my brain. I remember
> similar situations in American films. Gary Cooper always
> finds a way out.

Many men saved from the German trap on land, and believing they were practically home safe, found themselves swimming for their lives out in the Channel. Fearing a watery grave,
a number of merchant seamen engaged in the operation who
had already made the perilous shuttle more than once left their
ships when they docked at English ports and refused to return.
Some others, their ships newly recruited, also bowed out when
hearing of the dangers. Their places had to be taken by navy
personnel, the reservoir of which was running very dry. Land-
based personnel and naval cadets were rushed into service.
   A half century after the events, the Ministry of Defense in
London declines to release for public inspection documents concerning men and vessels who chose not to take part in the operation and who could not be obliged to. But those days were

marked more by extraordinary acts of heroism and selflessness by civilian mariners as well as by navy personnel. Ceaselessly in danger of being torpedoed, or strafed and bombed by enemy aircraft, which appeared with heart-jolting suddenness, their vessels scurried back and forth ferrying troops out of the enemy trap, often dauntlessly rushing to the assistance of other vessels when they were hit. When the paddle steamer *Gracie Fields* was bombed after embarking 750 troops from the beach at La Panne, her upper deck was engulfed in steam from broken pipes and her rudder jammed, forcing her to circle endlessly. Ignoring the danger to themselves and their craft, the masters of two barges tied up tight alongside the vessel to take off its human cargo. The minesweeper *Pangbourne,* already damaged by near misses which had claimed the lives of thirteen men on board, and its compass out of kilter, also went alongside the stricken and sinking vessel to lift off the rest of its men and try in vain to tow it back to England.

Just being there had the dimensions of a mythic journey through hell. The armed boarding vessel *King Orry,* arriving at Dunkirk around 6:00 that evening, found all the other vessels in the harbor ablaze. It was itself attacked by dive-bombers. Hit and badly damaged, it was in danger of sinking in the harbor entrance, blocking further rescue traffic there. But its crew managed to keep it afloat long enough to limp clear of the harbor before it too went down.

Despite intensified Luftwaffe operations, RAF Fighter Command stuck to its policy of carefully husbanding its squadrons for the expected massive German air assault on British cities and aircraft factories. But 11 Group commander Park had been persistently and urgently pleading for a change in aerial cover tactics which prevented his fighters from challenging the Luftwaffe more effectively. Now able to assess the situation more realistically, the War Cabinet reluctantly accepted that Fighter Command resources were insufficient to provide anything like continuous cover, which, in any case, had been ordered when it was believed Operation Dynamo would last only two days. It was agreed now that the operation would "dispense with full cover at less important periods."

For the men on the beaches and the vessels lifting them off, there were no "less important periods," except perhaps at night, when aerial activity was sharply limited. But it meant that Fighter Command could start sending out larger patrols, up to four squadrons at a time, to cope more effectively with the big formations of attacking German aircraft. The result was longer intervals—sometimes an agonizing hour or more—between patrols when there were no British fighters over Dunkirk. Two of the five concentrated German air attacks on shipping that day between noon and night met no opposition at all in the air. Nevertheless, the RAF claimed to have shot down sixty-seven German aircraft over the Dunkirk area that day against a loss of nineteen of their fighters. It was a vast exaggeration. The Luftwaffe lost a total of eighteen planes over all of France and Belgium that day, and some of those were brought down over Dunkirk by naval antiaircraft fire.

However, in flying in larger patrols, when in action in the area the Spitfires and Hurricanes were more effective in disrupting German aerial attacks on the troops and ships. What was more, the stronger British fighter presence had a damaging affect on the morale, confidence, and skills of German pilots and air crews. They had been in almost ceaseless action for almost three weeks, ever since the launching of the offensive. Though verging on total physical exhaustion, they were now required to face much stronger aerial opposition than they had so far met in the war. But the troops on the beaches, seeing ships that had come to rescue them blown out of the water, and those on vessels blasted from the air as they crossed back to England, were increasingly bitter about what they believed was the RAF's inadequacy. Few of them knew that the RAF fighters were breaking up German raids which could have inflicted far greater havoc on the beaches and at sea and that RAF bombers were blasting enemy positions, supply lines, and communications farther back, making it difficult for the Germans to coordinate their attempt to slam shut the Dunkirk escape hatch. Back in England, RAF personnel were cursed out and beaten up in pubs by men newly rescued from France and angrily convinced that the Royal Air Force had disgracefully let them down.

As the day wore on, the beaches and the dunes behind them grew increasingly jammed. British troops were pouring into the perimeter strip by the thousands, and then the tens of thousands.

On our way to the coast, we thought the navy would have some sense and not make such a balls-up as the army seemed to have made of the war. I was under the impression that the navy was out there with heavy guns and they were laying down a barrage behind us and that was protecting us. That was reassuring.

Mostly men arrived in the perimeter on foot, but many vehicles of various descriptions came as well. There were ambulances and trucks carrying needed supplies and equipment, but other vehicles found their way to the beaches too, slipping past military police posted to stop them from congesting the area. With the emphasis on maintaining a strong perimeter defense, few troops could be spared by perimeter command for traffic control. Some men arrived clinging to the sides and tops of trucks, some in abandoned cars they had commandeered. Others used less conventional transport: some on bicycles they found en route, one man driving a Belgian garbage truck, a few on horses they had liberated from other military tasks or from much drearier employment on farms or in the villages they had passed through.

French troops were beginning to pour back through the perimeter line in greater numbers too. When they passed through sectors of the line where the British had established effective traffic control, they were also required to abandon their vehicles and proceed on foot. They did not appreciate being ordered about by foreigners in their own country. Strong feelings were aroused and disagreeable scenes took place in which warnings were exchanged and guns were pointed threateningly. French troops who had been on the run from the moment the enemy had crossed their borders but who were still determined to fight on saw the forced destruction of their equipment as another humiliating sign of their impotence.

Friction had built up en route to the beaches. The British repeatedly complained that the French were constitutionally incapable of maintaining essential road discipline, barging through in their vehicles no matter what the circumstances or previous agreements on who was to travel along which routes. Most of them unaware of or scorning top-level route agreements, French troops protested against what they considered British high-handedness in trying to impose rules and regulations as if it were their country. A French officer recorded in his diary, "A fresh traffic block, a mile long . . . where the British have barricaded all exits so that their columns can pass through with greater ease. The French are wild. Some gunners talk of training their guns on them and shooting."

When they finally did reach the coast, exhausted *poilus* were enraged to discover that the British had organized the evacuation with consideration only for their own safety. French officers protested to Paris about the way they and their men were treated by the British on the beaches, and the French government complained to London. To many of the French, it seemed that not only had the British made a mad rush to the sea when confronted with adversity but that, as if by right, they had taken possession of the beachfront property as well. A French colonel who angrily refused to listen when told which beach he might or might not enter was unceremoniously ordered away at gunpoint. Though, remarkably, there were virtually no incidents in which weapons were fired to enforce beach discipline, a British soldier recorded in his diary, "A party of about twenty French troops, not used to the British habit of queueing, made a rush for the shore and grabbed a rowing boat. They clambered aboard and started to row. They did not get far for a burst of fire from a Bren gun manned by a naval rating stopped them immediately and we saw the boat floating upside down and some more bodies in the sea."

Though it was undeniably a British operation, individual French troops or small groups of them (as well as some Belgians and Dutch) waiting on embarkation queues were neither ordered away nor kept from boarding ships or boats when their turn came. But the French command was expected to make arrangements for the greater numbers, the ones in organized units which had fallen back to the coast. Their arrival, beginning that day, caused acute problems for the Royal Navy beach personnel trying against the odds to keep the evacuation process from disintegrating into chaos. To prevent that from happening, part of the beach at Malo was given over for sole French use and the British urged the French to send more ships for their men.

That French officers and troops were outraged by British seizure of French beaches was understandable. But none except a handful of French senior officers knew that Gort had been trying for two and a half days to coordinate British-French withdrawal and evacuation procedures only to be informed that the French had no intention of being evacuated. That very morning, Admiral Abrial made "a big fuss" because the British were proceeding with more than a limited embarkation of selected personnel despite the fact that he, the senior Allied commander in the region, still had received no orders from Paris that there was to be a mass evacuation. Abrial still intended "to hold on to Dunkirk till the last man and the last round." He believed the British should help in that task.

Gort was both exasperated and baffled. Time was running out. The Germans could not be held back much longer. Yet, while confused instructions from London indicated that every consideration was to be extended to French troops seeking to be evacuated, Abrial, the senior French officer in the region, a man who rarely ventured from his underground bastion, was acting as if the Allied plan was to stand fast and go bravely down to bloody disaster.

Gort asked London for clarification on how he was to deal with the situation. He particularly wanted a clear reply to the delicate question of whether to embark French troops on British rescue vessels, not something he was anxious to promote. He pointed out that "every Frenchman embarked is in the place of one Englishman." The response he received from the War Office was pretty much what he wanted.

> While it is eminently desirable that nothing should be done which might suggest lack of cooperation with French, your instructions that safety of BEF is primary consideration stand. We have every reason to believe that French Admiralty are taking steps to provide shipping for evacuation of French troops. When they have done so, facilities should . . . be shared equally between British and French personnel. Until French ships materialize, however, you are authorized to use British ships for British personnel.

It sounded straightforward. But nothing was without complications during that turbulent operation. The French command that day finally authorized the evacuation. Trying to bolster French resistance, Churchill sent Reynaud a message of solidarity. He told the French premier, "We wish French troops to share in evacuation to the fullest extent. . . . We do not know how many will be forced to capitulate, but we must share this loss together as best we can and above all bear it without reproaches arising from inevitable confusion, stresses and strains." Even with the six French navy vessels that arrived to assist in the evacuation, that wouldn't be easy.

As a result of the communications breakdown, the British had little knowledge of the spirited defense the French were putting up on the right of the perimeter defense line. Their commanders had no reason to revise their conviction that French incompetence was responsible for the Allied predicament. General Brooke, who was about to hand over command of II Corps and return home from Dunkirk, wrote in his diary that the French army had become "a rabble . . . panicking every time German planes come over."

Spears in Paris continued to report the increasing inroads of defeatist sentiment there. Among other things, mobilization of French able-bodied men not yet called to the colors to meet the enemy threat was considered pointless because the quartermaster had no reserves of rifles or uniforms for them—an "absurd state of affairs," Reynaud snarled. Weygand urged that "the British government should be informed that the moment may come when France, against her will, may find herself unable to carry on the struggle in such a manner as to protect her soil." It was hardly the stuff from which renewed confidence could be extracted.

But surprisingly in view of developments, Reynaud suddenly exhibited a resurgence of hope. Rising from the depths of despair, the French leader now seemed to project the belief that the battle, lost in the north, could still be won in the south. He called for the British forces being evacuated from Dunkirk to be quickly reconstituted as fighting units and shipped back to France to tangle with the enemy, together with three British divisions that had been in training for dispatch across the English Channel when the Germans had launched their offensive. Reynaud further urged that the RAF, both Bomber Command and Fighter Command, commit more of its resources to the Battle of France. Orders, he said, had been given for French airfields to be put at the disposal of British aircraft.

Whatever the reason for Reynaud's suddenly lifted spirits, Churchill had by now been forced to accept that France's capitula-

tion was only a matter of time and that a government prepared to cooperate with Hitler might take over from Reynaud when that happened. He wanted France to hold out as long as possible, but he signaled Spears in Paris to be less than completely forthcoming when he informed French leaders about details of Britain's plans for continuing to fight on when France went under.

Emergency preparations were, for example, being made to maintain the flow to Britain from abroad of supplies upon which the country's survival as an independent nation depended. More than half of the country's food and much of its raw materials were imported. Ways had to be found to make certain the convoys continued to get through. The plan was to divert all shipping to Britain's west-coast ports, farthest from Nazi-occupied Europe. German U-boats were a menace on the high seas, which made the use of so many Royal Navy destroyers in Operation Dynamo a great gamble. But it was believed that if 60 percent of import levels could be maintained, Britain "should be able to obtain enough food to feed the population and enough raw materials for essential armament production." Nonessential imports, "such as bananas and children's toys," would have to be reduced.

More immediately pressing were preparations to repel a German invasion. Some of the ideas put forward at meetings of the War Cabinet were bizarre, revealing the limits of Britain's home defense resources. The prime minister suggested, for example, that old German artillery pieces kept in Britain as trophies of past wars might be reconditioned to be used as antitank guns on the country's beaches. In view of the shortage of rifles, thought was given to raiding museums to equip Home Guard personnel with pikes and other primitive weapons, if only to give men something with which to drill.

Nagging anxiety persisted about the new weapons the Germans might have devised. Each day produced a new crop of rumors. One told of an insidious form of biological warfare— the creation by German scientists of an omnivorous strain of grasshopper which was to be released in hordes over British farms to starve the British into surrender. Another rumor told of German bombs the size of ostrich eggs with tremendous destructive power and of a mysterious device which could put guns out of action and which, it was said, hastened the Belgian surrender.

Home defense forces were alerted to the possibility that the invasion attempt might come in the form of a massive seaborne raid in which up to two hundred fast motorboats, each carrying one hundred heavily armed men, would attack simultaneously at various points along the British coast. Those boats, newly designed, might be able to run right up onto the beaches before disgorging the troops they carried. Such an onslaught might be made to coincide with airborne enemy raids inland so that home defense forces would be hard pressed to cope with both at the same time. The Chiefs of Staff Committee ominously noted, "We do not consider that by naval or air action we could prevent such a landing."

Aware of this and other perils, Churchill remained determined to prevent defeatism from sapping British spirits, as it easily could if the wretched news from Dunkirk did not get better. He knew how contagious panic would be if an image of German invincibility took hold of the British imagination. As a directive he issued that day demonstrated, he considered the moods and attitudes of government officials vitally important.

> In these dark days, the Prime Minister would be grateful if all his colleagues in the Government, as well as high officials, would maintain a high morale in their circles; not minimising the gravity of events, but showing confidence in our ability and inflexible resolve to continue the war till we have broken the will of the enemy to bring all Europe under his domination. . . . Whatever may happen on the Continent, we cannot doubt our duty and we shall certainly use all our power to defend the Island, the Empire and our Cause.

The war effort was to be intensified. Not only were workers in war factories to be encouraged to increase their efforts but the country was to be scoured for all possible war materials. Antique cannon, pointing out over the Thames at the Tower of London and no longer salvageable as effective weapons, were to be melted down to make bombs and shells. Railings around parks and squares in many cities were torn out and also dispatched to the furnace, as was metal from park bandstands. At the same time, officials thought it was time to make plans to ship Britain's art treasures in the National Gallery and the Royal Collection off to Canada for safekeeping.

*   *   *

At his command post at La Panne, Gort still didn't know what London expected of him if the Germans broke through the perimeter defenses, possibly at any moment. At the War Office, Chief of Staff General Dill was worried that the BEF commander might mistakenly interpret the ambiguous message of confidence sent to him the previous evening as meaning that he was to continue fighting to the bitter end, regardless of casualties. Lord Halifax proposed that Gort be told instead that it would not be dishonorable for him to "relinquish the struggle"—that meant surrender—if the alternative was a massacre of his men.

Churchill disagreed. He said such instructions would only make matters more difficult for the BEF commander. It would be wrong to complicate his understanding of his position by appearing to offer him a difficult choice before it was necessary for him to make one. The prime minister maintained that in the absence of precise orders, any brave man was entitled to use his own discretion in a desperate situation. That was the position Gort was in. Churchill insisted that there was nothing in the message of confidence sent to him that conveyed the impression that if the troops were left without food, water, ammunition, or hope of rescue, they should keep on fighting. Indulging once more in what seemed at that stage to be unwarranted optimism, the prime minister said that a day saved at Dunkirk by not prematurely suggesting to Gort that he might surrender could mean an additional forty thousand men brought home. The decision was to be left entirely to the BEF commander. Churchill told him as much in a personal message that evening.

> If you are cut from all communication from us and all evacuation from Dunkirk and beaches had in your judgement been finally prevented after every attempt to re-open it had failed, you would become the sole judge of when it was impossible to inflict further damage upon the enemy. HMG [His Majesty's Government] are sure that the repute of the British Army is safe in your hands.

This additional message of confidence was appreciated. After commanding one of the most momentous routs in British military history, Gort badly needed it. But his instructions with regard to fighting on to the last were no clearer than they had been before. Why was the emphasis placed on "the repute" of the army? Was its honor to take precedence over the lives of the men?

The way to the coast was packed with British troops. "Every road scoring the landscape," recalled one among them, "was one thick mass of transport and troops, great long lines of them converging towards the one focus—Dunkirk. Ambulances, lorries, trucks, Bren-gun carriers, artillery columns—everything except tanks—all crawling along those roads in well-defined lines over the flat, featureless country. . . . Under their greyish camouflage paint they resembled from a distance a slow-moving river of muddy-coloured lava from some far-off eruption." In the final stage, when they had to destroy their vehicles, almost all of them, thousands upon thousands, though physically exhausted, were walking to the sea.

> Weariness came down like a board on our heads [said a Coldstream Guards officer]. As I marched, my eyes kept closing and I knew that I was walking about like a drunkard. After a little, nausea overcame me, and I fell out for a few minutes. When we halted for a ten minutes' rest, I lay flat on the cold wet road and found a few minutes' relief.

Many units remained intact, some retaining their transport until they reached the perimeter, some elite infantry units marching in columns that were in amazingly good order considering what they had been through and the numbers they had lost. But countless companies and platoons had broken up into smaller groups or had disintegrated altogether. Countless men were on their own or had joined up with a few others, sometimes total strangers, in their trek. Officers, NCOs, and ordinary soldiers trudged forward together. Many had pruned tree branches to use as walking sticks. They all converged on the Dunkirk perimeter.

Even when they passed through the perimeter line, forward momentum was not permitted to flag, even after dark. They had to get to the beaches just a few miles off to be ferried home.

> We continued towards Malo-les-Bains, crossing the railway and marching through the ruined street of Rosendaal whose

skeleton walls stood around us like the ruins of some bygone
civilization. . . . Mysterious shadows flitted about the
streets, in and out of broken doorways, and disappearing
around corners. They were stray inhabitants who had been
cut off by the swift march of events and were living in cellars. And a few looters. And, probably, a few spies.

By nightfall of May 29, three days after its pilgrimage to
the coast had begun, virtually all of the British Expeditionary
Force had completed the trek. Except for stragglers, it had withdrawn into the Dunkirk perimeter. Paying a steep price in casualties, the troops holding the escape corridor open had done
their job, and now the survivors among them had withdrawn as
well. The desperate retreat had been carried out. But for most
of the men, the great escape still appeared to be no more than
a hope.

Men were dismayed by what they saw as they approached
the end of their trek. From a distance, they beheld the pall of
smoke from Dunkirk's burning oil tanks.

[It hung] like Death's hovering wing. Underneath, the tops
of the tall skeletons of wrecked buildings and churches were
silhouetted in black against the horizon and the lower edge
of the dark, threatening wing. Amidst these silhouettes huge
fires raged, the long tongues of orange flame leaping high
into the air. . . . It was a forbidding spectacle. Looked at as
a refuge, a gate of escape, it was anything but inviting. We
seemed to be heading straight for a holocaust.

And then, to bypass this vision of hell to reach the beach,
and see the mass of humanity there, all of them apparently with
prior claim to evacuation, seemed another foretaste of doom.
Those who had just been fighting the Germans knew the enemy
advance guard couldn't be far behind. And all had been under
attack or threat of attack from German aircraft and knew their
safety was still far from assured. For most who were not now
deployed to keep the enemy ground forces from cracking
through the perimeter defense, once they reached the coast
there was nothing to do but find a place on the beach or the
dunes and wait. Some would be there up to forty-eight ex-
cruciating hours; a few even longer.

Along stretches of shoreline, rows of summer houses, now

abandoned by their owners, squatted just behind the dunes. In
some places, they practically fronted on the beaches. Many had
been demolished by bombs; others had suffered only minor
damage. Some troops settled down within their walls, hoping to
be safe there from air raids.

> In the basements of the houses which faced the sea, we took
> shelter. . . . It needed no enticement to make for them. . . .
> There was one man who was so frightened that he had no
> inclination to leave the shelter. I asked him, "Don't you
> want to go home?" His reply was, "No, I'm staying."

When not under attack from the air or in immediate prospect of embarking, to shake the tedium some of the men
scratched together teams to play soccer on the shore, it being
understood that they could always reclaim their established positions in departure queues. Others wandered about if only for a
change of scenery or to stretch their legs. The more adventurous
ambled back into built-up areas beyond the dunes to scavenge
for food and drink in abandoned hotels, stores, and cafés, most
of which had already been thoroughly cleaned out. One soldier
stumbled across some French troops in Bray village huddled
around a fire over which they were engaged in serious culinary
activity. When he came close, they invited him to take part in
their repast, which turned out to be baked beans washed down
with champagne. He was lucky. Some men went without suste-
nance till they were aboard ship, and most till they were back in
England.

When ships and boats were loading, the lines moved forward at a pace that was agonizingly slow for the men who were
farthest from the breakwater or from the waterline. Unnerving
as the air raids were—both the anticipation and the actuality—
for most of the men on the shore they provided the only excitement until their turn for embarkation approached, the only
break from the appalling tedium of just being there.

Despite warnings from Gort that the Germans might break
through at any moment, despite the alarming naval and air
losses, despite the suspension of daylight evacuation from the
breakwater by civilian passenger vessels, it began to dawn on
London and on Dynamo headquarters in Dover during the

course of the day that the operation might not be a complete failure. Far more troops were being brought back to England than had been imagined possible when the operation was launched. In the morning, they had boarded from the break-water at a rate of two thousand an hour.

What was more, despite Gort's forebodings, all reports indicated that the perimeter defense was holding. It was conceivable that it would continue to hold for another day, or even two. During that time, the evacuation could be accelerated. More than half the BEF might be lost—a still daunting prospect. But it might yet be possible to rescue tens of thousands more of those who had fallen back into the perimeter. Tighter, more efficient organization was required on the Dunkirk side of the Channel, where the intricacies of the improvised operation continued to be responsible for mistakes and missed opportunities. Many vessels had been made to wait too long outside the harbor for their turn to enter and tie up at the breakwater. On the long stretch of coastline, some ships were waiting needlessly and dangerously off beaches on which, in contrast to patches farther along, not many men had congregated. As a consequence, some returned to Dover less than fully loaded.

Captain Tennant and his naval shore party had gone with little sleep since arriving two days before. Supervising and controlling the evacuation of an army under battle conditions was a formidable task. Tennant needed help. That afternoon, Rear Admiral Frederic Wake-Walker, a former battleship commander on the staff of the Admiralty in London, was instructed to make for Dunkirk to speed things up. He was not to supersede Tennant, who would remain Senior Naval Officer on land. Instead, Wake-Walker was to command "sea-going ships and vessels off the Belgian coast." He was to instruct them where to go when they arrived from England to embark troops. The "off the Belgian coast" formula was devised so that Wake-Walker would neither come under the command of Admiral Abrial in Dunkirk, who remained the senior Allied officer on the northwest coast of France, nor further ruffle Abrial's already much ruffled feathers when he ignored him as he went about his duties.

Wake-Walker was accompanied by two other senior naval officers who would be in charge off the La Panne and Bray beaches, respectively, and a team of officers and men who were to help maintain discipline on the beaches. Though disciplinary

problems remained and would remain till the operation was concluded, they would have an easier time of it than the navy beach
masters already ashore. The disorganized crowds of troops
which had earlier congregated on the beaches had mostly either
already been lifted off or brought to order. The more recent
arrivals from inland were for the most part disciplined fighting
troops and related units. What was more, officers were increasingly inclined to enforce their authority in unmistakable
ways.

> Just as it would have been our rightful turn to board the next
> returning rowing boat, an officer, with drawn revolver, leapt
> into the water and ordered our party to the back of the
> queue, stating we had jumped the queue. . . . My party be-
> gan to argue vigorously against this injustice. The officer
> threatened to shoot us. I think he meant it, so did the oth-
> ers. In despair, we left the water and tramped wearily up the
> crowded beach.

More small craft began arriving to lift the troops off, including the first of anxiously awaited landing craft, only eight as yet
but a promise of more to come. In London, the Admiralty, responding to anguished pleas from across the Channel, ordered
the Small Vessels Pool to requisition more "suitable motor
boats" for immediate service from ports farther along England's
southern and eastern coasts, from Portsmouth to Yarmouth.

As hopes rose for getting ever greater numbers of troops
home, the Admiralty made a decision during the day that sent
them plummeting again. Of all types of vessels involved in the
operation, destroyers were rescuing most of the men being
brought back to England. In addition, of all the vessels involved, they were by far the best equipped to repel German air
and sea attacks while scurrying between Dover and Dunkirk.
Nevertheless, late that day, the Admiralty decreed that the most
modern destroyers in the operation would be withdrawn from
evacuation duty.

With a total of ten destroyers sunk or otherwise put out of
action in the operation before nightfall that day, the possibilities
were frightening for the defense of Britain. If that rate of loss
was sustained, Britain's fleet of modern destroyers would be

decimated. It was similar to the reasoning that limited the number of RAF fighters committed to battle over Dunkirk. Britain could not be left without adequate naval resources to repel an enemy invasion attempt and to guard maritime sea-lanes, which had to be kept open if the nation were to survive.

Admiral Ramsay was informed that he could continue to employ his fifteen remaining older destroyers as well as whatever other vessels he could muster. But the modern destroyers would not be permitted to shuttle ceaselessly through the danger zone; nor could they be anchored in place off Dunkirk as troops embarked, sitting targets for the enemy. It was regrettable, but, said the Admiralty, it had to be done.

What could not be so easily regulated by decree was the danger of mistake or miscalculation by hard-pressed embarkation control officers. That evening, an officer of the naval shore party whose judgment "had been affected by the events of the day" sent word back to England from La Panne BEF headquarters, via the War Office and the Admiralty, that because of the tremendous enemy aerial bombardment, Dunkirk harbor was blocked. As a result, further embarkation from the breakwater was impossible.

It wasn't true. The harbor was littered with wreckage and dotted with burning ships but it was not blocked. The breakwater was as usable as it had been before. But direct communications between Dover and embarkation personnel at Dunkirk left much to be desired. Radio contact with the Dunkirk end could be made only through destroyers when they were tied up at the breakwater. Unable to get either confirmation or denial from Dunkirk or other sources and never imagining that so important a message could be mistaken, particularly if channeled through the War Office and the Admiralty, Dynamo headquarters had no option but to order that no further ships should try to enter the harbor. Instead they were again limited to the less effective and more time-consuming process of squatting offshore and sending their small boats to ferry men from the beaches. As a consequence, for the rest of that day and during the following night only five small ships entered the harbor to evacuate not the many thousands who might have been boarded from the breakwater but only a few hundred.

The accelerated morning embarkations from the harbor had raised hopes that fifty to sixty thousand troops would be evacuated that day. Instead, because of the mistaken report, only 47,310 men were brought back to England that day—33,558 from the harbor, 13,752 from the beaches. That made a total of 72,783 evacuated since the operation began, many more than had at first been expected but still leaving much to be done in the little time believed remaining before enemy action closed the operation down.

The rescued men were received as heroes as they came ashore in England, if only for having survived and returned. Cheered as they disembarked at Dover, Ramsgate, Sheerness, and other ports in southeastern England, they were handed sandwiches, tea, beer, and cigarettes and bundled into waiting trains. They were cheered again at stops along the route to collecting centers all over the country where they were to be reclothed, fed, and sorted out for dispatch to camps where their units would be reformed.

Churchill passed word to Reynaud, "As soon as we have reorganized our evacuated troops and prepared forces necessary to safeguard our life against threatened and perhaps imminent invasion, we shall build up a new BEF" to be sent to France. That process would take far longer than the British leader seemed to suggest—more than four years.

Day Five—Armada in Miniature

Ships out there were sinking. Airplanes were dive-bombing. Soldiers were streaming in and down to the water. Two arrived carrying a stretcher between them upon which was the body of a third soldier. They stopped where the sand sloped down to the beach, lowered the stretcher to the ground, and, with the butts of their rifles, they scooped out a grave. Then they buried the dead comrade they had carried goodness knows how many miles, as near to England as they could get him. They covered him with sand and made their farewells to him, standing at attention and saluting. Then they went down the beach to take their place on a queue.

The British public still had only a vague idea of what was occurring on the other side of the English Channel. Comfort was drawn from a French report that two thousand German aircraft had been shot down since the start of the battle. That appeared to confirm exaggerated RAF kill claims publicized at street-corner newsstands throughout the land. But it was known that things were grim, that Boulogne and Calais had fallen to the enemy, that Belgium had capitulated, and that Royal Navy warships had been sunk. And though it was not commonly understood that the British Expeditionary Force was being driven into the sea—the BBC announced only that a number of troops "not immediately engaged" had been evacuated from France—it was known that the troops had fallen back to the coast, and word was spreading of the large numbers of ragged soldiers arriving at Dover and other ports along the coast of southern England.

Censorship blocked press publication of accounts of the rescue operation. But reports in local newspapers printed when censorship was eased immediately after Operation Dynamo was terminated described what onlookers saw during the days of Dunkirk when the defeated troops were being shuttled home. "It was a dirty, tired army that tramped to the waiting 'buses [in Dover] that took them to the station and the waiting trains. . . ." Florid prose sometimes conveyed the picture more vividly.

> Saturated with sea water, grimed with battle smoke, hungry, thirsty and unspeakably weary, they dragged their tired, war-stained limbs to the sanctuary of the land whose institutions they had given so much to preserve. With brains numbed by incessant bombing, nerves wracked by the inferno of noise which modern warfare brings, and senses crushed by the fearful scenes through which they had passed, there were but two things they craved—comfort and rest.

Unrestrained by censorship, the American press didn't have to wait to publish what its reporters and a lot of other people at Dover saw—that "dog-tired, wounded and unkempt Allied troops floundered sleepily home from the death trap of Flanders in bomb-raked ships" and that the "shattered remnants of the BEF—blood-stained, muddy and walking like men asleep" had begun arriving at British ports.

The British public at large was spared the realization that a good part of the BEF might be left on the beaches at Dunkirk when the Germans broke through the perimeter defense. Instead, in the columns of the *Manchester Guardian,* Harold Nicolson, parliamentary secretary to the minister of information, who a few days earlier had advised his wife that she, like he, should keep a suicide pill handy, urged the people of Britain not to be dejected:

> The news is bad. We must expect worse news in the days that follow. . . . Let us not be down-hearted. . . . Sorrow is inevitable but hope is also inevitable. The resources of our Empire far exceed anything which Germany can com-

mand. . . . It may well be that by employment of methods
which did not exist in previous wars [the Germans] may be
able to land in Great Britain some thousands of their
troops. . . . [But] the whole country will rise as a man to
resist such invasion and whatever confusion or destruction
may momentarily occur the ultimate issue is beyond doubt.

The correspondent of the Associated Press very likely was
taking journalistic liberties when he reported to America, "Invasion of England itself was described by Britain's leaders tonight
as really imminent." But while they were unlikely to have said
anything of the sort to a reporter, that was what British leaders
feared. The possibility of a German invasion had become an ob-
session in the upper reaches of the government and the military.
Intelligence services reported that the Germans had intensified
their naval activity on the Norwegian coast and were gathering a
fleet of motorboats at North Sea ports. And though they had
been busily laying mines in British waters, they were also reported to have ominously left a stretch of water off the British
coast clear of mines. Admiral of the Fleet Sir Dudley Pound
reported to the War Cabinet that he was confident the Royal
Navy could deal with a major attacking armada, but he thought
it conceivable that some enemy invading craft could slip through
the net. They might have to be dealt with on land, though it was
impossible to say where along the coast they might arrive.

The failure until then to install antitank mines on British
beaches where the Germans might try to storm ashore aroused
both alarm and dismay. Production of those mines was not expected to start until the following week. The War Cabinet and
the chiefs of staff were tormented by how inadequate available
coastal defenses appeared to be. In desperation, Churchill suggested that if the enemy did manage to land on British shores,
poison gas should be used against them. Though it was banned
by international law, he felt that Britain "had the right to do
what it liked with our own territory."

Some twenty-five thousand children who had been evacuated from London and other cities considered prime targets for
German bombers were to be shifted again. They had been sent
to places of refuge on the south and east coasts of England,
where German landings were now considered most likely. The
children were to be moved elsewhere, to the English Midlands
and Wales.

Fear of saboteurs and fifth columnists led to a curfew being imposed on all aliens over the age of sixteen who had not already been interned. In addition, unless authorized by the police, no alien was permitted to have use of a bicycle or motor vehicle that might assist him or her in subversive activities.

Civil defense measures were tightened. The authorities began cracking down on people who had neglected to erect miniature air raid shelters of corrugated iron, more than two million of which had been distributed to the public free of charge for erection in their homes or back gardens. A regulation was issued requiring individuals who had been given those shelters either to put them up properly or explain to the authorities why they had not done so.

The day had begun at Dunkirk with Captain Tennant wondering about the whereabouts of ships which should already have arrived at Dunkirk harbor. Unaware that Dynamo headquarters had been mistakenly informed that the harbor was blocked, he had made arrangements to evacuate thousands of troops from the breakwater before dawn. Troops on the adjoining road and beach had been readied to hurry along the pier and clamber aboard for the homeward journey as soon as vessels tied up.

The failure of the ships to appear deepened the sense of nightmare dread for the naval personnel at the breakwater and the waiting troops. Tennant and his staff feared that the vessels might have been sunk or crippled en route, that a replay of the heavy losses of the previous day was in the making. They did not know that Dynamo headquarters, informed that the harbor entrance was blocked, had instructed the vessels which streamed across from Dover under the cover of darkness to make instead for positions off the coast to service boats working the beaches.

For Rear Admiral Wake-Walker, who had arrived off the coast after dark the previous night to make sense of offshore arrangements, the first daylight view of his task was not encouraging. The sloop HMS *Bideford*, with forty feet of her stern blown off, was aground nearby. The paddle steamer *Crested Eagle* lay burned-out on the beach not far away. Other vessels of various sizes and in various states of damage, some still burning, were abandoned in the shallows. Clusters of huddled men were at the water's edge, some of them wading out in search of rescue. Large groups of troops were on the beach. Others were on the dunes. Ships may have been diverted from Dunkirk harbor to stand offshore, but few were in sight and few boats appeared to be working the beaches.

A team of navy signals personnel was supposed to be ashore with Aldis lamps to signal the ships to send in their boats and make ready to receive evacuees, but not one was to be found on the beaches that morning or at any time during the entire operation. Nor were communications between Dunkirk and Bray and elsewhere along the beach ever established. As a consequence, beach patrols, trying to accelerate the evacuation, at no time knew whether it was or was not advisable to march waiting troops the few miles along the shore to be embarked at the harbor on vessels that might be waiting at the breakwater there.

In many places along the shore, embarkation control procedures remained totally haphazard. "Any organization for forming groups for the next boat," one naval officer later reported, "was constantly ruined by streams of stragglers coming down to the water's edge. . . . Stragglers were continually arriving and forming batches out of their turn."

Gort's La Panne headquarters called for more boats, and again for more; men under air attack were waiting and had to be lifted off. London was again told that the perimeter defense would not be able to hold the Germans back much longer and that great numbers of troops would be lost when they broke through. Such warnings were now a regular refrain in communications from La Panne to the War Office. With wide patches of beach jammed with weary, hungry men under repeated air attack, the sense of urgency in the Dunkirk pocket was never in danger of wearing thin. German guns found the range of the beaches during the day. They as well as the harbor were being bombarded by artillery, without great accuracy and with limited effect, but some men were wounded and killed and a growing number of bodies lay on the beaches, some covered, others not.

Worse was the news that though the Germans didn't seem to be suffering supply difficulties, some of the troops holding them back at the perimeter defense line were running perilously short of ammunition. It was not inconceivable that positions would be overrun because the defenders did not have enough shells and bullets to fight off the enemy.

Gort's hope was that before that happened, the beaches would be cleared of most of the men already there. Then the perimeter defenses would be thinned and the troops withdrawn from the line evacuated, leaving only enough men on the line to hold back the enemy. That final rearguard would then be pulled back under the cover of darkness and lifted off in one carefully prepared swoop. One look at the swarms of men still on the shore made it seem a pipe dream.

At Dover that morning, Admiral Ramsay had no more reason than Gort to be hopeful. With Dunkirk harbor reportedly blocked, without the modern destroyers which had been removed from the rescue operation the day before, with civilian passenger vessels restricted to nighttime operations because of concentrated enemy activity, and with several of his larger ships already sunk or otherwise put out of action, there seemed little possibility of doing more than was already being done—except perhaps discover whether the harbor remained blocked and the breakwater remained unusable. The continued loss of the breakwater for embarkation purposes would be a great blow. Tennant calculated, "A destroyer going full out with her boats to the beaches could only embark 600 men in 12 hours, whereas this could be done in 20 minutes at the Pier." It was a matter of the safety of the ships and their crews as well as the speed of the evacuation.

Direct communications between Dunkirk and Dover still unavailable, Ramsay dispatched a destroyer, the *Vanquisher,* to take a close look at the harbor soon after sunrise. It reported back that while it had sustained serious damage, it was in fact not blocked at all! Vessels could, without difficulty, enter and leave, something Ramsay might have learned from the five small ships which had done exactly that during the night had arrangements on the England side of the operation allowed such information to percolate upward from the bustle at the debarkation ports.

After a tour of the harbor area, Wake-Walker confirmed that the breakwater remained usable despite German shelling and that it remained a far better point than the beaches for rapid boarding of troops. Navy vessels—though not civilian passenger ships—were again instructed to make for the pier to start loading. There was such a scramble aboard each and every ship by men who had thought they had been abandoned that when a freighter tied up with provisions for the men in the perimeter, unloading of cargo had to be stopped when it was only half completed.

An extraordinary explosion of activity was taking place on the beaches as well. A vast flotilla of small ships and boats, far more than had been there before, appeared off the coast. The methodical work of the Admiralty's Small Vessels Pool and the requisitioning teams Ramsay had sent out was proving its worth. It was an extraordinary sight. All manner of small and medium-sized craft appeared—barges, train ferries, car ferries, passenger ferries, RAF launches, fishing smacks, tugs, motor-powered lifeboats, oar-propelled lifeboats, wherries, cockle boats, eel boats, picket boats, seaplane tenders. There were yachts and pleasure vessels of all kinds, some very expensive craft, some modest do-it-yourself conversions of ship's lifeboats. There were Thames River excursion launches with rows of slatted seats and even a Thames River fire float.

They came from Portsmouth, Newhaven, Sheerness, Tilbury, Gravesend, Ramsgate, from all along England's southern and southeastern coast, from ports big and small, from shipping towns and yachting harbors. Some, from upriver, had never been in the open sea before. They were manned mostly by volunteers, men who, without being given the details, had been told that they and their vessels were urgently needed to bring back soldiers from France. Most were experienced sailors—professional or otherwise—but many were fledglings who knew nothing about maritime hazards. Had the weather been bad, some would not have risked going; neither their experience nor their craft would have been up to it. Some mariners would forever be convinced that the extraordinary uncharacteristic calm which ruled the sea during most of the ten days of Dunkirk, permitting the evacuation to proceed—"the water was like a millpond"—was literally heaven-sent because "God had work for the British nation to do."

Some of the vessels which had been requisitioned were manned by naval sublieutenants straight from training school. Most who set out had charts to guide them past the shallows and sandbars of the Channel, but some of their compasses were of doubtful accuracy, which led a few to the now dangerous waters off Calais within range of German guns. One sailor went ashore at a desolate spot to find out where he was, ran into two astonished German soldiers, and had to shoot them with his pistol to make his getaway.

Not knowing what to expect when they got to the Dunkirk beaches, these hastily recruited crews were astounded by what they saw—the long lines of bedraggled men winding across the sands and stretching out into the water, looking anxiously, expectantly out to sea. Men who had been standing in the water for long periods of time to guard their places in the queues could barely move. Their waterlogged boots had become deadweights.

A breeze blew intermittently, tossing boats about and making their approach to the shore difficult and sometimes impossible. When that happened, some of the troops grew fearful that rescue, though so near, might never come. At one point, at Malo, a horde of men broke from the lines on the sand and surged to the water's edge, infected by a fantasy that despite the sea swell, the boats were managing to move in close enough to pick them up. After peering vainly out at craft much too far offshore for them to reach, they turned in frustration sullenly back to resume their places in the straggly queues.

When the winds permitted, the smallest of the boats came practically up onto the beach so that the men only had to get their feet wet. But for most of these craft, the men had to wade out into deeper water and hope they would be dragged aboard. The master of one rescue boat said, "The snag was that when a rope was thrown to a man, about six grabbed it and just hung on looking up blankly with the water breaking over their shoulders and it was a hell of a job getting any of them to let go so that the rest could be pulled aboard."

Some of the men seemed incapable of understanding that boats capsized when too many men tried to board them. Other boats were swamped by the loads they were carrying and the men who had piled on board had to wade or swim back to shore to try their luck again. Some men grabbed planks of wood or bits of wreckage, anything that would float, and, kicking their legs, tried to propel themselves out to meet the incoming craft. Some men found collapsible dinghies, inflated them, and tried to row out to the ships offshore, using their rifles as paddles. Others improvised rafts. Some stripped off their clothes and swam out to be picked up. The crew of a yacht, newly arrived offshore, was amazed to see a man stark naked swim up to them. Other troops tried to swim out fully dressed.

These new arrivals from England quickly learned the chief hazard with which they would have to contend. The sky would be clear and seconds later a Messerschmitt 109 would roar out of the distance, its machine guns spitting, or a Stuka would scream down to unload its cargo of death. There were other worries as well. Clothes the men discarded, rope, and sometimes bodies fouled screws and rudders, and crew members had to go over the side to free them. Most of the vessels, never having been worked so heavily, and some having been laid up for long periods prior to the operation, suffered mechanical and other difficulties which teams of maritime engineers back in southern British ports stood ready to tackle. During the operation, at the port of Ramsgate alone, repair work had to be done on 170 vessels stricken with engine, electrical, or hull problems which had nothing to do with enemy action.

The problem of getting the men on the beaches to the ships offshore was never satisfactorily resolved. There just weren't enough boats. Motorized craft were finally employed retrieving abandoned rowboats and getting them to the water's edge. But the boats remained in short supply and men continued to wade out as far as they dared to be picked up by small craft, which couldn't come in close for fear of beaching.

At places along the shore, engineer troops, among the comparatively few kept busy during their time on the beaches, improvised piers—built mostly of heavy-duty vehicles—to permit men to reach boats unable to come close enough to the shore. Considerable ingenuity and muscle power went into their construction.

Fifteen or more lorries, to a length of approximately 150 yards, were driven or manhandled through soft sand and positioned whilst the tide was out nose to tail on hard sand thus enabling dinghies and other small craft to be loaded from either side. To "anchor" the jetty all tyres were punctured, generally by firing bullets through them and when this was completed the backs of the lorries were filled with sand. . . . The walkway was made up of decking panels taken from a bridging lorry and the gaps between the roofs of the three tonners were covered by planks "borrowed" from a timber yard. . . . The military police controlled the numbers embarking at any one time usually 50 servicemen. . . . During our long spells of duty [maintaining this jetty] we were more often than not up to our shoulders in the sea and frequently covered in oil seeping from the chain of lorries.

Efforts to find more small craft to dispatch to Dunkirk continued unabated back in England. The crew of the Margate lifeboat *Lord Southborough* that morning volunteered en masse to go to the Dunkirk beaches. They were provided only with helmets and left "in the very best spirits." The Ramsgate lifeboat *Prudential* crossed over with eight small boats in tow. In all, nineteen coastal lifeboats went to Dunkirk, but not with the consent of all their crews. The coxswains of three of the lifeboats, summoned to participate in Dynamo and told they were expected to run their craft onto the beach to embark men, said they were too heavy for that kind of operation and declined to go. The navy then commandeered their craft, putting its own personnel on board. Seven other lifeboats were then commandeered as well, to the anger of some of the crews, which, though the navy didn't know it, had been prepared to take part. Members of one lifeboat crew had even bought steel helmets for the occasion. Finally realizing that these men were not the recalcitrants they had previously encountered but having already assigned men to the craft, the navy said it would be happy to take along the motor mechanics among those crews. But the offended lifeboat men replied that it was all of them or none. None it was. Under pressure, overburdened, the navy had no time for niceties or even to fully appreciate the situation. As a result, the operation was denied the services of some useful mariners.

Nevertheless, the search for small craft was pursued with unrelieved vigor. Individuals whose names were on file with the Small Vessels Pool were personally contacted. For Charles Hunt, the owner of the yacht *My Quest,* it was a visit from two naval officers at his Putney home.

He was told to consider himself and his boat at the disposal of the Naval authorities, given a brief outline of the situation and told to keep it "under his hat." His instructions were to get underway as soon as possible. He mentioned the affair to a friend, Mr. Ted Avery, who volunteered at once. . . . Naval crew took over at Sheerness.

The little ships and boats were doing far better work than had been thought possible when the operation began, or seemed likely even that morning. Now that they were there in profusion, they were able to ferry thousands of men from the shore. But it remained a cumbersome, inefficient procedure. The sinister likelihood remained that unless more large vessels were immediately available to board great numbers of troops from the breakwater, the operation, for all its achievements so far, would fail and long columns of bedraggled British troops would be marched off into captivity.

Admiral Ramsay contacted the Admiralty to plead for the urgent return of the modern destroyers removed from evacuation duty the day before. He understood that those fighting ships were needed to guard Britain's lifelines but insisted that the country's lifeblood might depend on the safe return of the men from the sands of Dunkirk. If Dynamo failed, the future of the country would be very bleak indeed. Ramsay was persuasive, and within hours six of the modern destroyers—*Harvester, Havant, Ivanhoe, Impulsive, Icarus,* and *Intrepid*—were back on rescue duty, dodging bombs, boarding men from the breakwater, and ferrying them to England.

Gort's chief of staff, General Pownall, had returned from Dunkirk overnight to report to Churchill, military service ministers, and the chiefs of staff. He said some sixty thousand British troops—his rough guess—had still not been evacuated and pressed for efforts to be intensified to bring them home as soon as possible. Churchill once more asserted that it was important to embark French as well as British troops. Pownall told him he thought the French should be responsible for saving their own men. He was bitter about the blunderings of the French command, which he held exclusively responsible for the BEF's predicament. Ignorant of the fact that French ships had begun participating in the evacuation, though not in great numbers, he repeated to Churchill the refrain that so long as the French failed to provide ships to carry their men to safety, "every Frenchman embarked [on a British ship] meant one more Englishman lost." This was an inconvenient truth which Churchill, stung by French charges that Britain had turned tail, was not happy to hear. He conceded that embarking French soldiers might reduce the number of British who would be saved but insisted that "for the good of the common cause, this must be accepted."

Convinced that Churchill still failed to grasp what had happened and what was still happening on the far side of the Channel, Pownall tried to convey to the prime minister a picture of the confused conditions with which Gort had to contend in the Dunkirk perimeter. Aside from the British troops, he said, the entire area had become a "congested mass of disorganized Frenchmen, refugees and Belgians." The difficulty of maintaining discipline under such conditions had not been resolved. At one point, he said, it looked as though about fifteen hundred Frenchmen were going to try to storm the boats on the shore instead of queuing up to wait their turn. After a beach area had been allotted to the French at Malo, the situation on the shore had eased. But problems persisted and the defense line remained under pressure.

The British did not know that the Germans were withdrawing their tanks from the assault on the Dunkirk perimeter. They were haunted by a vision of the panzers crashing through to the troop-congested shore. No one at the meeting believed that it would be possible to bring many more men home "if the German armored divisions supported by the Luftwaffe pressed their attack." It seemed inevitable, Pownall said, that "the perimeter would be broken as it thinned out and there would be carnage on the beaches." It was a terrifying prospect, and an awkward one for a prime minister, new to his job, who might have to explain to Parliament and the British people how so much of the British army had been lost.

A renewed plea from General Weygand that the men evacuated from Dunkirk be shipped straight back to bolster French forces preparing to repel the expected German drive against Paris couldn't be treated seriously in London, even if Britain could rely on a home defense force larger and better trained than the one available. The men brought back had no guns, no tanks, no transport. All they had was their rifles, and many not even those. Britain no longer possessed a fighting army of any significance. It had to be rebuilt, rearmed, and reinforced. Besides, no one knew how many men would finally be rescued. The War Office in London, accepting Pownall's estimate of sixty thousand still to be evacuated, hoped that forty-five thousand might be disengaged from the perimeter line that night and ferried home before dawn, the remainder to be lifted off the following day. In fact there were still more than one hundred thousand British troops in the Dunkirk pocket.

Conferring later that day with Admiral Ramsay, Pownall advised him to consider the dark early hours of Saturday, June 1, the morning after next, as being the last "reasonable date" by which the rearguard could be expected to hold back the enemy. That did not rule out the possibility that the Germans might break through before then. But by 1:30 A.M. on Saturday it was hoped to have reduced British forces ashore to four thousand men of the final rearguard, all the others having by then been disengaged, marched back to the beaches or the pier, and brought back to England. Special attention was to be paid to assembling and holding ready ships, boats, and tugs for the climax of the operation, lifting off that last four thousand troops between 1:30 and 3:30 A.M. on Saturday. Special effort had already been made to separate senior sergeants and other experienced cadre from most other units to bring them back to England to start rebuilding the British army. But these last troops were elite fighting men. They had to be brought home!

Final plans for closing down Operation Dynamo would be reviewed the next afternoon, Friday, May 31, in the light of conditions prevailing at that time. But at that moment, said Pownall, the Royal Navy was not doing enough to bring the troops home. He warmly praised the navy's efforts and achievements but expressed doubts about whether the Admiralty had initially fully understood the magnitude of the task to which it had been assigned. He was in fact saying that it had still not caught up with events—it was essential to get still more ships and more boats over to Dunkirk at once!

For operational and morale reasons, Churchill had earlier been reluctant to tell Gort what to do when the final moment at Dunkirk approached. But he now agreed that specific instructions had to be issued to the BEF commander. A brave man, and mortified to have led an army that was being driven into the sea, Gort had indicated that he intended to stay with his troops till the end. But his capture would be a propaganda coup for the Germans. Churchill accordingly told him to forget any notions he might have of superintending a heroic last stand by the BEF and ordered him to prepare to return to England.

Continue to defend the present perimeter to the utmost in order to cover maximum evacuation now proceeding well. Report every three hours through La Panne. If we can still communicate we shall send you an order to return to England with such officers as you may choose at the moment when we deem your command so reduced that it can be handed over to a Corps Commander. You should now nominate this Commander. If communications are broken you are to hand over and return as specified when your effective fighting force does not exceed the equivalent of three divisions. This is in accordance with correct military procedure and no personal discretion is left you in the matter. On political grounds, it would be a needless triumph to the enemy to capture you when only a small force remained under your orders. The Corps Commander chosen by you should be ordered to carry on the defense in conjunction with the French and evacuation whether from Dunkirk or the beaches, but when in his judgment no further organized evacuation is possible and no further proportionate damage can be inflicted on the enemy he is authorized in consultation with the senior French Commander to capitulate formally to avoid useless slaughter.

The BEF's III Corps had already been mostly evacuated, and II Corps had begun to embark. Their commanders—Generals Brooke and Adam—were departing for England that day, handing over their commands to subordinates. That left General Michael Barker as the only original BEF corps commander remaining in France. Gort told Barker he was to stay behind to oversee the closing act of the Dunkirk defense and evacuation. He was to be expendable. His instructions were to hold out as long as he could. When no other option remained, he was to surrender.

The appointment of Barker for this endgame assignment raised objections from General Montgomery, who, having succeeded Brooke as III Corps commander, was himself being evacuated. Never one to hold his opinions of others to himself, Montgomery told Gort that the appointment of Barker, a high-strung man given to bouts of anxiety, was a serious mistake. He said that Barker "was in an unfit state to be left in final command," that 1st Division commander Major General Harold Alexander, though junior to Barker, would be a more appropriate choice, and that Barker should be evacuated back to England. Alexander was much respected for his cool, methodical approach to problem solving. Montgomery suggested that such a man might even be capable of performing the miracle of keeping the enemy at bay till everyone could be evacuated.

Like many who came in contact with Montgomery, Gort found his arrogance irritating. But he realized that he was right about Barker, an aging soldier no longer up to the strain of combat, and agreed that Alexander should take final command of the rearguard instead. When Barker was informed by Alexander the following day, he broke down and wept.

Developments in the war threatened to complicate further the perpetually fragile relations between Britain and Ireland. It was realized in London that the Germans would be pleased to use Ireland for backdoor entry into Britain. It was believed German intelligence had established an espionage network in the country. A report by Sir Charles Tegart, a counterinsurgency specialist, claimed that Ireland was crawling with German agents and that the Germans had a detailed plan for taking over the country. The week before, the Dublin police had raided the home of an Irish businessman of German ancestry and had found details of Irish airfields, harbors, bridges, and military installations, as well as a radio transmitter and receiver. German submarines were active in Irish waters, and it was believed that they were used to make contact with agents on the shore and to supply them with the paraphernalia of espionage.

A quasi-fascist Irish "Blueshirts" movement, which had never had much of a following, had largely fizzled out by the time the war had started. But the violently anti-British Irish Republican Army, though believed by London to be a greater threat than it actually proved to be, was very much in evidence. The previous Christmas the IRA had demonstrated its daring and capacity for action when it had subdued the sentries and garrison at an Irish army arms warehouse near Dublin and made off with a million rounds of ammunition. Contacts between the IRA and German intelligence had long been established; indeed, they had existed even in the First World War. There could be no doubt that the organization was ready and willing to help the Germans conquer Britain. The fear in London was of an IRA-assisted German landing in Ireland as a prelude to an assault on Northern Ireland, which then as now was a province of the United Kingdom. An attack on the British mainland could well follow.

The previous day, Churchill had received intelligence reports that "the Germans have concerted detailed plans with the IRA and that everything is now ready for an immediate descent upon the country." Chamberlain maintained that the IRA was almost strong enough to overwhelm the Irish army, which had as its core only seventy-five hundred regular troops. The former prime minister urged that British forces be readied to be sent to Ireland to help suppress internal subversion and repel external aggression. In fact, a column of British troops based in Northern Ireland had already been secretly alerted to cross the border into Ireland when given the order. But it was recognized as likely to be counterproductive to take any action until a German attack on Ireland actually materialized.

Thousands of Irishmen had enlisted in the British armed forces, and many were at Dunkirk. But the legacy of anti-British feeling remained so strongly implanted in their country that Irishmen in the British armed forces were advised to wear civilian clothes when they went home on leave. No government in Dublin could have survived permitting British troops to deploy on Irish soil until a German assault had been launched. Prime Minister Eamon De Valera informed the British that Ireland would fight if attacked by Germany and would call for British assistance if that became necessary. But if British forces arrived without being invited, the Irish government would not be held responsible for the consequences.

London was told that the government in Dublin was confident it could deal with the IRA without outside help. Nevertheless, a top-secret two-man official mission—Joseph Walshe of the Irish Department of External Affairs and Colonel Liam Archer, chief of staff of the Irish army's intelligence branch—had been dispatched to Britain a few days earlier to seek specialist military advice for preparing for the possibility of a German invasion attempt. When they returned to Dublin, they were accompanied by a British army defense expert—in mufti—assigned to offer on-the-spot advice on defense precautions. Word of his presence in Ireland was a nervously guarded secret.

The chiefs of staff remained anxious about Ireland. They believed that "until [Ireland] abandons her attitude of neutrality she cannot fully safeguard herself against danger of enemy activities within her territory, nor obtain the full cooperation of our forces to anticipate and resist attack. Unless this security can be achieved, Eire will remain a serious weakness in the defense of these islands." Churchill shared those misgivings, but, always probing to pluck advantage from adversity, he said that if the Germans tried to move against Ireland, Britain would "have the greater part of the [Irish] population on our own side for the first time in history." He also maintained that if the Germans did seek a backdoor entrance to Britain through Ireland, it would not necessarily be a bad thing for Britain. He pointed out that the RAF would then be able to take on the Luftwaffe in an air war over Ireland "under conditions specially favorable to us and costly to them." The suggestion must have shocked Fighter Command chief Dowding, whose squadrons were already spread frighteningly thin covering Dunkirk while preparing for the expected onslaught against Britain from newly seized forward Luftwaffe bases in Europe.

With the British army, navy, and air force all actively engaged in the evacuation, interservice rivalry and recriminations were inevitable. Criticism of the RAF for the limited aerial cover it provided was persistent. But the Royal Navy, which was also paying heavily for its part in the operation, did not escape censure either, despite the remarkable feat of improvisation in which it was engaged. When Admiral Wake-Walker met with Gort at La Panne that evening to review the situation, he was surprised to be called upon to answer for the navy's performance, something which he had assumed to be worthy of nothing but praise. It was made clear to him that the army felt it had done its job in bringing the BEF back to the coast; now it was up to the Royal Navy to bring the men back to England, but, in view of the persisting congestion on the beaches, it didn't seem to be doing too well. Caught by surprise, Wake-Walker made no reference to the failure of the army to plan for or provide adequate beach organization or control or, for that matter, to maintain greater discipline in the ranks. He explained that much of the navy's performance depended on weather conditions, which hadn't been unrelievedly favorable, and on the intensity of enemy action. But to his exasperation, he could not dispel mutterings about the "ineptitude of the navy."

German generals were also muttering about ineptitude—
that of their own forces in failing to close down the Dunkirk
bridgehead. Halder complained about standing by and watching
"countless thousands of the enemy get away to England right
under our noses." Brauchitsch moaned that the "effects of the
blunders forced upon us by OKW [Armed Forces High Com-
mand] . . . are beginning to be felt now. We lost time and so the
pocket with the French and British in it was sealed later than it
could have been. Worse, the pocket would have been closed at
the coast if only our armor had not been held back." Everyone
was busy blaming someone or something else—the Luftwaffe
for failing to wipe out the bridgehead, the order to halt for preventing the tanks from doing the job, the diversion of troops
and equipment to knock France out of the war.

That day Army Group A, which had made the running all
the way from Sedan, was withdrawn from involvement in the
Dunkirk episode. Its armor, which was useless anyway in canal-
laced terrain that was being flooded after the French opened
protective floodgates, was to be regrouped, repaired, and rested
for the attack south to bring France to its knees. The operations
officer at army headquarters insisted that it was necessary to in-
tensify efforts to disrupt the evacuation but complained that "no
one is now interested in Dunkirk anymore."

That wasn't true. The bridgehead had become a serious embarrassment to the commanders still assigned to wiping it out.
So anguished did they become at their failure to do so that they
considered landing troops from the sea to accomplish the task.
They also contemplated pulling their forward units back from
contact with the perimeter line to give the Luftwaffe a free field
of attack against the defenders. But finally it was the ground
troops, pressing against the perimeter, who remained responsible for trying to break through, and they found the defenders
"fighting back very stubbornly."

Like the Allies, the Germans were plagued with communications problems and had difficulty coordinating their attacks.
Their commanders worried about the danger that their troops
would be firing at each other. To add to their frustration, they
were intercepting British radio communications which indicated
that, despite Gort's repeated urgent pleas for more boats, the
evacuation operation was proceeding with considerable success
and was even being stepped up.

By midnight, 53,823 troops had been brought back to England that day, most of them from the beaches. Many more would have been evacuated had embarkation from the breakwater resumed earlier in the day once the report that the harbor was blocked was proved to be mistaken. But a total of 126,606 troops had now been brought home since the start of Operation Dynamo.

Hope began to percolate through the War Command in London that the unbelievable was taking place. It looked as if far fewer troops would be left to the Germans at Dunkirk than had seemed likely even the night before. But this surge of cautious optimism was balanced by a growing flood of demoralizing rumors circulating among the public. It was said that German saboteurs were being caught all over Britain, indicating that the enemy was readying a major assault on the homeland. It was said that the Irish government had signed a secret alliance with Germany that would expose Britain to attack from across the Irish Sea. Most worrying of all for morale purposes, it was rumored that the War Office was offering the public such limited information on what was happening across the Channel because British troop losses there were devastatingly huge. The British public finally had to be told what actually was happening.

Day Six—the People Are Told

On the morning of May 31, the people of Britain were finally told by the BBC and their newspapers about the desperate operation to evacuate their army from France. "Under the guns of the Allied navies," the London *Daily Express* reported, "under the wings of the Royal Air Force, a large proportion of the BEF who for three days had been fighting their way back to the Flanders coast have now been brought safely back to England."

"Eyes hollow from lack of sleep," the London *Daily Mirror* said, "days' growth of beard on their chins, some without food for forty-eight hours, they were utterly weary as they stumbled into train after train." A newspaper cartoon described BEF as standing for Bravery, Endurance, and Fortitude.

There was no mention of how many casualties had been sustained by the forces which had kept open the retreat corridor for almost a week or of the men killed or wounded on the Dunkirk beaches and while being ferried home. Making a rough estimate, Pownall had told Churchill the previous day that the casualties amounted to a very substantial number—between sixty thousand and eighty thousand men. But that morning's news, as released by the Ministry of Information, was dressed up to generate a mood of relief after all the worrying rumors that had spread about the fate of the men. It was reassuring for the British to hear that so many of their boys were already back home, safe behind their English Channel moat, and that the others were following.

There had been a steady flow homeward during the night. But winds of up to force three blew up from the northwest during the early morning. These were moderate by textbook definition but the strongest since the operation began and fresh enough to disrupt embarkation from the shore. Many of the small boats capsized or were swamped. All the boats, and larger craft as well, were bounced about by the waves. The coxswain of the lifeboat *Lord Southborough,* which tried to get in close to the beach, called it "a nasty surf."

> Troops were rushing out to us from all directions and were being drowned close to us and we could not get to them. . . . It seemed to me we were doing more harm [than good] by drawing the men off the shore, as with their heavy clothing, the surf was knocking them over and they were unable to get up.

Some troops who considered themselves fortunate to have been lifted off despite the surf were thrown back into the water when their boats capsized. They had to wade or swim back to the shore. All along the coast, boats blown ashore or unable to pull back fast enough when the tide raced out were stranded high and dry in the mud.

For the men manning the small craft, endurance had become problematic, as the naval reserve officer put in charge of the motorboat *Triton* recalled soon after.

> My crew and myself were drunk and stupid with exhaustion. My body ached all over and I was almost hoping I would be knocked out to escape my weariness. The lad working the engine was sleeping, the cox was steering anyhow. . . . My arms felt as if they had left their sockets [from hauling men aboard]. . . . I drove [my men] when they were crying with exhaustion. May God forgive me for the hell I put them through.

There was no telling how long the winds would blow. It could be hours before there was a letup, or longer. It was not unusual for the surf along the coast to act up for days without a break. Wake-Walker despairingly reported to Dynamo headquarters from a destroyer offshore that a change in operation procedures was once more essential: "Majority of boats are broached to and have no crews. . . . Consider only hope of em-

barking any number is at Dunkirk." In case that message wasn't
fully appreciated, he followed shortly after with another: "Dunkirk our only real hope." Believing the perimeter defense could
collapse at any moment, Dynamo headquarters at Dover nevertheless insisted it was important to go on trying to use the
beaches as well as the Dunkirk breakwater as long as possible.
Wake-Walker responded curtly, "Dunkirk our only hope," and
acted accordingly, diverting arriving vessels to the harbor.

Men on the beaches were formed up and directed westward
along the sand toward the breakwater, some in military order,
others straggling along in groups or knots, some all alone, trudging wearily to where they hoped rescue could be found. Like
much that happened during the ten days of Dunkirk, it was a
remarkable sight and an even more remarkable experience for
those who took part.

> Long columns of men three or four deep, wandering irreg-
> ularly along like vast serpents—somehow faintly reminiscent
> of the Children of Israel in the wilderness! . . . The move up
> was the most devastating business we ever had. At first we
> moved along fairly quickly, and did as much as 300 yards at
> a time with perhaps ten minutes rest. This got slower and
> slower till in Dunkirk we moved 20 yards and rested for any-
> thing up to half an hour! . . . One had to keep awake to
> avoid losing one's unit at the next move, as well as the risk
> of not being taken on by another if one did lose touch.

Dunkirk remained a dangerous place to be. From their
positions west of the city, the Germans had intensified their artillery bombardments, while the Luftwaffe continued to pay special attention to the harbor as well. At 9:00 that morning,
Tennant reported to Dover, "We have been continuously and
heavily bombed and they are finding the range of our loading
berth." In fact, casualties were already being inflicted on the
breakwater itself.

> Half way along the mole [breakwater], a solitary, khaki-clad
> figure lay on the wooden staging. We could not see his face
> for a great-coat had been spread over him, hiding the stark
> reality with an illusion of sleep. A helmet, pierced with shell
> splinters, lay close by on the edge of a gaping hole of shat-
> tered timbers and concrete below which the sea lapped. Poor

sod! What rotten luck! So near, so very near and he almost
made it. Without pause and without comment we filed
ahead.

Gaps blasted in the pier by shells were quickly spanned by
loose planking, though places remained along its length where
troops had to vault over the holes. Wake-Walker sent messages
to Dover pleading for the enemy guns to be bombed and silenced, and those messages were passed on. But despite RAF
efforts, the shelling was sustained for much of the day. It added
considerably to the pressures not only on the evacuees but also
on the navy pier masters keeping things under control at the
foot of the breakwater, rushing the men along it when vessels
berthed, and getting them aboard quickly so that the turnaround
of the ships could be expedited.

> Why the jetty was not blown [a pier master said] I shall
> never understand; one good bomb at the inshore end would
> have completely held up the embarkation and it is doubtful
> whether we would have got off half the number we eventu-
> ally did.

Gort reported from La Panne to the War Office by telephone that morning that the Germans appeared to be preparing
a major attack to crack through the perimeter defenses and descend on the harbor and the beaches. In view of that, the question of how to deal with French evacuees came up once more. In
an extraordinary phone call at midnight the previous night,
Churchill had personally ordered Gort to accelerate the evacuation of French troops. Now the BEF commander wanted clarification.

He had earlier been told how important it was for elite British fighting troops mounting the rearguard to be brought home;
indeed, Dynamo headquarters was making special arrangements
to get them away. Now Gort wanted to know from London
whether, when it seemed unsafe to delay any longer, he should
order those troops to fall back for speedy evacuation, even if
such a move would expose great numbers of French soldiers to
capture. The alternative was for the British rearguard to hold
their positions till the last possible moment, exposing themselves
to even greater dangers than they already faced, in order to

cover the evacuation of many more French troops than might otherwise be lifted off. Put that way, the question left London with no real choice. Secretary of War Eden told Gort that if it came to that, his main concern had to be getting the British rearguard to safety.

Departure arrangements for Gort himself were now finalized. His request that, contrary to the orders he had received the previous day, he be permitted to remain with his troops till the end was turned down. He thereupon called on Admiral Abrial at his Bastion headquarters near the harbor to coordinate the remainder of the evacuation process, to inform him that he was leaving later that day, and to report that General Alexander would be assuming command of what was left of the BEF in the area. He offered to take senior French officers back to England with him, but that offer was declined. Only a pretense remained that the BEF was under Abrial's command, so it was not an overly agreeable leavetaking. Though increasing numbers of French troops were being evacuated, Abrial could not be shaken from the conviction that to save their own skins, the British were abandoning France in indecent haste.

In Paris, it appeared that the mills of fate were grinding inexorably toward catastrophe. In his desperation, Reynaud urgently renewed his earlier pleas to Churchill for troops to help block the impending German drive against the French capital. The French premier also again asked for increased RAF involvement on the continent and for joint appeals for American help of the kind Washington had already made clear would be rejected. Aware of Churchill's Francophile inclinations, King George felt inclined to remind him that he was prime minister of Britain, not of France. But it wasn't necessary. Churchill had no intention of agreeing to any of Reynaud's requests.

He feared, however, that blunt rejection would be seized upon by defeatists in Paris as reason to press for immediate armistice terms. To boost French spirits, he flew to the French capital that morning to attend a meeting of the War Council there. His plane and its fighter escort had to take a roundabout approach to avoid German fighters, but he arrived looking "as fresh as a daisy" and glowing with confidence.

The French leaders made no such pretense. National calamity seemed around the corner, and they were bitter about it.

They were openly resentful of what most considered Britain's puny contribution to the struggle. And they were angry about how the Dunkirk evacuation was proceeding. When Churchill boasted that the evacuation was turning into a historic success, that far more men had been evacuated than had been thought possible, Weygand asked acerbically, "But how many French? The French," he charged, "are being left behind." It was said this would cause much ill feeling in France if it came to the attention of the public. Churchill tried to tone down French bitterness. "We are companions in misfortune," he said. "There is nothing to be gained from recrimination over our common miseries."

Weygand was not easily soothed. Reynaud, upon whom Churchill was counting to keep France in the war as long as possible, was also bitter about evacuation statistics. He extracted from Churchill the estimate that of 220,000 British troops, 150,000 had so far been evacuated, while of 200,000 French troops, only a mere 15,000 had been taken off. Churchill maintained that much responsibility for the disparity rested with the French. He said that the French forces in the north still appeared not to have received orders to be evacuated. He suggested that Weygand immediately rectify that situation.

Speaking with deep feeling of the common sufferings of France and Britain, the British leader then declared that his troops would not receive priority treatment in the evacuation but that the troops of the two countries would leave Dunkirk "arm in arm." What was more, he said that it would be the British who would constitute the final rearguard for the evacuation, even though they would inevitably suffer heavy losses as a result. That would permit the French rearguard to disengage and be evacuated first. "I will not," the British leader declared grandly, "accept further sacrifices from the French."

Churchill's princely gestures and backbone-stiffening oratory partially mollified the French, but not everyone in the prime minister's own party was pleased with his performance. Spears, for one, objected to Churchill's magnanimity.

> His emotions were leading him too far, I thought. He was being too generous. After all, if we were in such dire jeopardy, it was due to colossal French incompetence and, steeped as I was in the French atmosphere, I knew that in

French eyes we only came into the picture in so far as we
could help France. Perfectly natural perhaps, but we, on the
other hand, ought not to sacrifice our chance of survival to
the French, who certainly would not do so for us. The idea
that we might be invaded because we had absolutely no
troops to resist even a weak landing was unbearable.

Churchill appeared to have no such qualms. On the verge
of tears, he told the assembled French leaders how deeply he
felt the suffering and loss of the men in the north. He declared
that Britain was determined to fight on to the end. "England did
not fear invasion," he said, "and would resist it most fiercely in
every village and hamlet. It would be better . . . that the civilization of Western Europe, with all its achievements, should
come to a tragic but splendid end, than that the two great democracies should linger on [under Nazi domination], stripped of
all that made life worth living."

His voice breaking with emotion, Churchill said that in
order to make certain that as many combat-ready men as possible would be brought back from Dunkirk to be reorganized immediately into new fighting units to continue the struggle against
the enemy, he had ordered that the British wounded be lifted
off last, which probably meant leaving them to be taken prisoner. The neutral Americans would be asked to try to see to the
well-being of the casualties that had to be left behind. Churchill
declared that his country would never accept slavery and that "if
one of the two comrades fell during the course of the struggle,
the other would not lay down his arms until his friend was on his
feet again."

This declaration of undying friendship did not have the intended effect. Some found it considerably less than encouraging.
War Council secretary Baudouin felt that it implied that "England has already coolly assumed that [France] should succumb
in this struggle. . . . England has already put on mourning for
us." Not for the first time, Baudouin was led to wonder whether
France should continue to fight a war that was as good as lost, as
Churchill seemed to indicate, as well as expensive in lives and
money.

His doubts were reinforced by Churchill's refusal to be
shaken from his insistence that he could not immediately send
additional troops to help France fight off Hitler's armies when

they turned toward Paris. The prime minister explained that the men being brought back from Dunkirk could not be regrouped and reequipped overnight and he had no other forces which might be sent at once. Besides, at that moment, there were no more than five hundred heavy guns in all of Britain. That was not enough to mount a nationwide defense against a German invasion, much less adequately arm a new expeditionary force.

Churchill insisted that Britain had not been remiss in its contribution to the common struggle against the enemy. He pointed out that ten of its precious squadrons of fighter air-craft—of which a great many had been lost—had been sent to France. Its remaining twenty-nine squadrons were barely enough to guard Britain's cities and aircraft factories against German attack.

There was a tense moment at the Paris meeting when Spears responded sharply to the suggestion of a French official that continuing military setbacks might force France to modify its foreign policy. The implication was that it might find coming to terms with Hitler the only suitable way out of the impasse. Aware that some of Reynaud's ministers were already advising such a course of action, Spears warned that if the suggested pol-icy change meant what he thought it meant, Britain not only would feel obliged to blockade France but also to bomb strategic French centers which came under German control. The two Al-lies would, in fact, become enemies.

Despite the differences of views and emphasis of those pres-ent, it seemed to the British delegation that Churchill's strength of will had in the last analysis done its magic. By the time the meeting had concluded, the senior French figures in attendance appeared to agree with the British prime minister that the strug-gle with the enemy not only should be maintained unflinchingly but that it would lead to ultimate victory.

However, this transfusion of hope, if it actually occurred, proved short-lived. Once mutual assurances of fighting on to vic-tory had been exchanged, the French leaders were compelled once more to come to terms with the unpalatable facts being created on the battlefield, as Churchill soon discovered. He overnighted in Paris, and at dinner at the British embassy, Rey-naud and the prime minister's other French guests seemed much more subdued than they had been at the conclusion of that af-ternoon's War Council conclave. After his French guests left,

Churchill "realized in his heart that the French were beaten,
that they knew it, and were resigned to defeat."

It had been easy enough for Churchill to promise that the
British and French would leave Dunkirk "arm in arm." But
Gort, preparing to leave for home, realized that the pressure of
events might not permit him—or General Alexander when he
took over from him—to be so generously disposed, even if they
wanted to. Greatly increased numbers of French troops had received evacuation orders and were pouring into Dunkirk and
onto the beaches. Though reliable signal communications had
finally been established between Dunkirk and Dover, neither
Tennant on the shore nor Wake-Walker coordinating from offshore had been given any idea of how many there would be. It
was therefore impossible for them to provide information to Dynamo headquarters on the size of the rescue fleet that was
needed, an important consideration in view of the continuing
hazards involved. Nor was information available on how many
French vessels, of what capacity, would be available to take part
in the operation.

The weather, which had caused difficulties for the little
ships and boats that morning, improved considerably during the
afternoon. The wind dropped off and a high tide refloated boats
driven aground earlier. Wake-Walker was again able to direct
vessels to positions off the beaches, and the boats resumed ferrying troops out to them. But no matter where Wake-Walker
instructed the ships to position themselves, many dropped anchor as soon as they spotted lines of men on the shore and boats
picking them up to be ferried out, so that some vessels which
had been sent farthest east to stand off Bray and La Panne
didn't get that far. Troops on the beaches farthest from Dunkirk
waited in vain until German artillery bombardment sent them
scurrying over the sand toward greater safety on beaches nearer
to the harbor.

The result was that some ships that did go as far up the coast
as instructed infuriatingly found few men waiting there to be
picked up. Wake-Walker began receiving bewildering messages
from ships that there were no troops on the shore when, in fact,
there were thousands. At the same time, he was receiving messages from the shore that not enough boats were coming in to
pick up the troops, when farther along boats were turning back

empty from the beaches. The absence of direct ship-to-shore communications meant that much effort was wasted that day.

The weariness of ship's crews, the intermittent congestion, the floating wreckage and sunken ships, and the need often to swerve quickly in the offshore waters produced increasing numbers of accidents at sea. At midday, the destroyers *Icarus* and *Scimitar* collided, and the latter had to be ordered back to Dover for repairs. Other vessels in collision, either in the harbor or off the beaches, were less lucky. Some had to be towed back to England; others sank to add to the litter of sea wreckage.

A particular danger to small craft and the men they lifted off the beaches was the need for larger vessels to take quick evasive action when they came under sudden air attack.

> Our motor yacht went alongside a destroyer. They had scrambling nets down the side. Our chaps were scrambling up when all of a sudden she shot ahead. We were tied up to her so she towed us with her. A lot of the soldiers fell from the nets into the water. They were shouting for help but we couldn't do anything about it. We were being pulled along. A few seconds later we knew why. They'd seen a dive bomber coming down. The bombs fell just astern of where she'd been. We never saw those men who fell into the water again.

During the day, the situation at the La Panne beach aroused new concern. The Germans had moved their guns closer around Nieuport and, resorting to a primitive but effective device, had sent up a manned observation balloon to direct artillery fire. Wake-Walker signaled Dover for aircraft to shoot the balloon down. But the Germans kept raising and lowering it and it reappeared through much of the day, enabling German gunners to zero in more accurately on targets in the La Panne area. The beach there, crowded with troops, was getting to be a serious liability to the British. Men were being hit, but still few facilities existed anywhere along the beach for caring for the wounded and no facilities at all for properly interring the dead.

> A horrible stench of blood and mutilated flesh pervaded the place. There was no escape from it. Not a breath of air was blowing to dissipate the appalling odour that arose from the

dead bodies that had been lying on the sand, in some cases,
for several days. We might have been walking through a
slaughter house on a hot day.

British intelligence reported to the War Office that day that
the Germans were building amphibious tanks capable of rolling
up from the sea onto the beaches of England. It deepened the
anxiety felt in London at the continuing loss in the Dunkirk operation of warships and planes needed to repel the expected invasion. Senior figures—newly baptized in the murky, chill pond
of realism—were not reassured by accounts of trouble in Germany, where shortages in consumer goods and raw materials
were said to be causing widespread resentment, where news of
heavy casualties on the western front was said to be arousing
alarm, and where the Nazi command was said to be terrified that
it would not be able to fulfill promises made to the German
people that the war would be brought to a rapid conclusion. All
of that sounded encouraging, but so had prebattle assurances
about Allied might.

In fact, to an observer on the spot in Berlin the German
people appeared to be largely untroubled by the war. Correspondent William Shirer noted in his diary, "The Kurfuerstendamm
jammed with people meandering along pleasantly. The great side-
walk cafés on this broad, tree-lined avenue were filled with thousands, chatting quietly over ersatz coffee or their ice-cream. . . .
The war has not been brought home to the people of Berlin."

It had, however, been brought agonizingly home to Wake-
Walker watching his rescue ships blasted and sunk, pleading
with Dover for more vessels and still more, and pursuing his
methodical way of dealing with problems frustrated by the chaos
in which he found himself.

It was always impossible for me to do more than deal with
the situation of the moment. I did not know what ships were
coming or when. . . . Nor was it possible for Dover to give
me much information. Ships got back there, unloaded, and
were off again, the stream was constant but irregular and it
was not possible to see any way ahead.

When Gort left for England that evening and General Alexander took charge of British troops remaining in the perimeter,

he, like Gort before him, officially came directly under the command of Admiral Abrial. Like Gort, he was given the escape option of appealing to London if any of Abrial's orders were likely, in his opinion, "to imperil the safety of the Force under your command." No matter what Churchill had promised the French, Alexander's primary task was to wind up the evacuation of remaining BEF troops in France as expeditiously as possible. He was, however, authorized, in consultation with Abrial, to capitulate to the Germans to avoid useless slaughter if it appeared that "no further organized evacuation was possible and no further proportionate damage could be inflicted on the enemy."

No sooner had Alexander taken over for Gort than Anglo-French differences about evacuation procedures resurfaced. It was now accepted that the deadline for completing the BEF evacuation early the following morning as planned could not be met. There were still too many troops on the beaches and dunes, and, amazingly, the defense line was still holding. But Alexander told Abrial that he believed it was unlikely that the operation could be sustained more than one more day and night. He urged a concentrated effort during the coming night to lift off the troops already awaiting embarkation and to disengage and evacuate the rearguard during the night after. The plan now would be for the curtain to come down on Operation Dynamo by first light on June 2, twenty-four hours later than planned earlier.

Abrial did not approve. He thought such a deadline would be a total miscalculation. He did not believe French troops holding rearguard positions could disengage so quickly. He maintained that the Dunkirk bridgehead had to be held until all troops could be embarked.

> His idea [Colonel William Morgan, Alexander's chief of staff, later recalled] was that . . . the troops were to remain and, as far as we could see, were to remain for some time. Of course, we knew this was impossible. The British troops were absolutely finished. They could not go on much longer. . . .

Outraged by British haste to abandon France, Abrial threatened to use his authority as commander to close Dunkirk harbor, though it is unlikely that he was serious. "General," he scolded Alexander, "you must stay. It is a matter of England's honor. French soldiers have let themselves be killed to protect the embarkation of the British army. Now your last troops must take part in the defense of Dunkirk to permit the evacuation of the greater part of our troops."

What he was asking was, in fact, less than Churchill had offered the French in Paris earlier that day. He wanted the British only to share final rearguard duties, not take on all of them. He did not know of Churchill's offer but he did know that when taking leave of him, Gort had promised—in the confusion which attended his departure—that the British rearguard would continue to hold its sector of the perimeter line so that the evacuation of French troops could continue.

Alexander had heard nothing of that promise. Gort had neglected to inform him. The new British commander focused on what he considered his primary duty as spelled out in his orders—to do nothing to imperil the safety of his troops. If that meant letting the French down, that was regrettable. He told Abrial that in his opinion, any plan to delay final evacuation past first light of June 2 "did not take into account the true military or naval situation." Abrial conceded that the perimeter defense line was unlikely to be able to hold where it was. He proposed drawing it a mile or two closer to the coast (in fact less than four miles from the beaches) and reconstituting it there to stand fast.

Alexander thought that was nonsense. He protested that such a new stop line would be so near the coast that close-range enemy artillery fire on the harbor and the beaches would rapidly render further evacuation impossible. It was not simply a matter of differences of opinion. The British commander had no confidence whatever in Abrial's judgment. He believed that his continuing reluctance to venture forth from the protection of his subterranean fortress headquarters to see for himself what was happening colored his understanding of what was possible and what was not. When Abrial insisted on having his way, Alexander said he would have to invoke the escape clause of his instructions and refer the matter to London.

Hurrying back to BEF headquarters at La Panne, he was relieved to see the telephone connection with London was still intact despite enemy bombing. He quickly contacted Secretary of War Eden by phone—the last call that could be put through. He told Eden that the delay Abrial had in mind would lead to the loss of some of Britain's finest fighting troops. Eden—who had not yet heard of Churchill's offer in Paris to have the British rearguard take last honors at Dunkirk—agreed. He authorized Alexander to proceed as he had proposed, aiming to wind up the evacuation of British troops by dawn the day after next.

But the formula wasn't to be as simple as that. Alexander was instructed to embark Britain's remaining troops at Dunkirk "as rapidly as possible *on a 50-50 basis* with the French army." "50-50" could be interpreted in two ways—current or retrospective. But "as rapidly as possible" had only one meaning as far as Alexander was concerned. His intention was to get the British troops out by then no matter what. He returned to Abrial's headquarters to tell him as much. He said he hoped that the French commander would have his troops also work toward the new deadline so that the final evacuation could be even-handed. But he made it clear that the last of the British would have left by then even if they did not.

Abrial resented being confronted with an ultimatum, especially one handed him by a subordinate. But all he could do was complain to Paris. To make things personally awkward, it was already night and Alexander did not want to risk trying to get to his new headquarters, now moved closer to Dunkirk city, in the dark. He and his aide overnighted at Abrial's Bastion, stretched out on a cold concrete floor.

Instead of the expected forty-eight hours, Operation Dynamo had now lasted almost three times that long. But the incessant fears that the perimeter defense line would not be able to hold the enemy back much longer now appeared on the point of being justified. It was time to wind the operation down quickly, starting with the tricky task of shortening the perimeter line.

The plan was for the left of the line, just inside Belgium on and near the coast, to be shortened and reestablished by a rearguard farther back toward Dunkirk, on the French-Belgian border. La Panne and its beach were to be evacuated of troops. First the troops abandoning the far left of the perimeter in Belgium were to disengage after last light and fall back on La Panne beach, from which, they were told, they would be speed-

ily evacuated. Speed was essential because, as the Germans
would soon realize, the area was about to become no-man's-
land.

But traversing La Panne to the beach had become a perilous undertaking despite the cover of darkness. Much of it now
in ruins, La Panne had been a prosperous, modern city, its main
streets lined with new buildings of concrete and glass. It was a
strange place for the ragged remains of an army to be trudging
through.

> The streets of La Panne were an amazing sight. The roads
> were nearly blocked . . . with every conceivable type of ve-
> hicle. . . . Houses were crashing down and tramway cables
> and standards all over the place. The civilians were rightly in
> the cellars.

German spotter planes dropped flares to light up the scene.
Soon after came "the thump of distant guns followed by the
whine of approaching shells." Being out the open seemed dis-
tinctly hazardous to well-being and orders were shouted to get
the men under cover.

> "Off the streets! Into the shops!" came the orders, shouted
> along the street, and no one required second bidding. Great
> plate-glass windows, still intact in our part of the street, shat-
> tered under the impact of rifle butts, heavy glass clanging
> tunefully to the pavement. Soldiers hastened through. . . .
> One little cameo of the moment was the abrupt appearance
> behind his glass of a restaurateur, gesticulating excitedly to
> the troops to desist. Such is the inherent respect for prop-
> erty, that several [men] paused, butts poised, while the
> owner hastily unlocked his glass door; and in they streamed,
> plate glass still intact.

For those troops and for thousands of others, as the day
drew to an end, rescue back to England still seemed a long way
off. But despite the difficulties and delays, the anguish and the
casualties, by midnight on May 31, the sixth day of Dunkirk,
68,014 more men had been brought back to England, more than
on any day so far—45,072 from Dunkirk harbor, 22,942 from
the beaches. Most of the BEF was home again, accompanied by
thousands of French and some Belgian troops. Almost two hun-

dred thousand troops had been rescued since Operation Dynamo had been launched.

Satisfaction in London at 10 Downing Street and the War Office was severely blunted by the realization that tens of thousands of men were still to be brought home and that the chances of saving them were growing slimmer by the hour. Concern about the fate of those troops was heightened by German press allegations of cruel treatment of German soldiers who had escaped or had been liberated after having been captured by the British. It was charged in German newspapers that British officers and men had acted as if their German prisoners were "cannibals or murderers."

> They were subjected to vile insults, beaten, threatened with death and robbed of all personal possessions. Chained hand and foot and thrown into a corner or left out in the street to be exposed mercilessly to artillery fire. On the march, those who could not keep up with the column because of wounds or fatigue were driven with big clubs in the hands of sadistic officers. When questioned, they were subjected to blinding light to weaken their resistance when asked for military secrets. Germany will not forget nor allow such conduct to go unpunished.

With perhaps sixty thousand British troops still stranded across the Channel facing capture or death, such allegations and threats were alarming. For the War Cabinet, the possibility that those men were about to become hostages of Hitler, perhaps a bargaining factor, remained chilling.

Day Seven—Death from the Skies

For men manning the vessels fully engaged in the operation from the beginning, the strain was approaching breaking point. Many aboard destroyers which had so far not been put out of action by enemy attack had been on duty, except for brief snatches of sleep, for five straight days or more and were reaching the limits of their endurance. For those who had briefly been rested while their vessels underwent quick repairs, the prospect of a return to Operation Dynamo was agonizing. For all, going back to Dunkirk meant venturing once more into an inferno in which their senses would be stretched to the limit and from which the chances were they would not return.

There was no letup in the hazards the vessels had to face on each crossing—shelling, bombing, strafing, German submarines and torpedo boats on the prowl—and while squatting at anchor exposed to the enemy for long periods of time while troops boarded at the breakwater or off the beaches. None of this was made easier for ships' personnel by the crush on board during each trip home, with evacuees crammed into every possible cranny and cubbyhole.

Crews grew anxious and jittery, and some men suffered mysterious afflictions as a result of their efforts and experiences. The chief officer of the Channel steamer *St. Seriol*, working his ship's remaining lifeboat, frantically rescuing men from a sinking vessel before they drowned, pulling survivors from the water, was stricken with a form of nervous paralysis from the waist downward which made him incapable of standing for any length of time for some time afterward.

A growing number of reports were filed about men losing control. Ships began returning to English ports carrying their cargoes of evacuees with almost every crew member, including most officers, fast asleep. In warship wardrooms as vessels crossed the Channel to get on with the job, hands shook as men lifted glasses and cups to their mouths. Aboard the destroyer *Whitshed,* two seamen who had been "jocular, robust men" were reported to have turned "sullen, morose, depressed, hard-faced and silent. Occasionally they wrung their hands." They said they would jump over the side rather than face another night at Dunkirk. The minesweeper *Hussar* had to be removed temporarily from the operation when a bout of weeping broke out among the crew. Thirty crew, including officers, of the minesweeper *Hebe* had to be put ashore for treatment after an outburst of what was described as "mass hysterical epilepsy." Dynamo headquarters had anticipated problems. Spare naval personnel had already been rushed to Dover to fill in for men incapacitated by the horrors of Dunkirk.

For the civilian crews of the passenger vessels which had been committed to the operation, the hazards were somewhat less. Now crossing only by night, they were no longer exposed to enemy targeting. But these men were not trained for battle nor under any official obligation to keep returning to a war zone. Like warships, their vessels still risked being shelled by enemy guns firing at random at Dunkirk harbor while tied up at the breakwater, and they risked being sunk by torpedoes while traversing the Channel. Collisions remained a constant danger, particularly in the dark. And though doing a reasonably thorough job, Admiral Ramsay's minesweepers were unable to clear away all the mines German planes continued to lay in the Channel and off the English coast each night. The crews of small, fragile passenger ships which had never ventured far from the English coast were undertaking journeys that were trying the nerves of personnel aboard heavily armed warships. The master of the *Malines* explained why he was withdrawing his vessel from the operation.

> It was evident that my crew was on the edge of revolt. . . . I considered the odds against a successful prosecution of an-

other voyage too enormous and the outcome too unprofitable to risk the ship. My draught does not permit me to reach the beaches at Dunkirk, and the quay appears to be untenable.

For the little ships, the strain was severe as well. Most were new to the operation. Indeed, Ramsay's scavenging parties were still out along the south coast of England rounding up more small craft to send across. But the pressure was mounting sharply on those working the beaches. The perils of navigation in waters that were often congested compounded the dangers of enemy attack. Smaller ships were continually exposed to buffeting when caught in the wash of larger, faster craft and repeatedly had to swerve sharply to avoid being swamped.

The effect of the consequent plunging on the troops below in a stinking atmosphere with all ports closed can well be imagined. They were literally packed like the proverbial sardines—even one in the bath and another perched on the W.C., so that all the poor devils could do was just sit and be sick.

Some of the civilian-manned craft which had volunteered or been drummed into service, their engines groaning under the strain of the operation, the nerves of their crews shot, now slipped quietly away to their home ports after unloading the men they had rescued. The masters of others simply announced that they had done their bit, were dog-tired, and would not cross the Channel again. In several cases, Royal Navy vessels were instructed to "force them back to their duty." Increasing numbers of naval officers and seamen, many drawn from other commands, were put aboard civilian vessels, either to take charge of them or to stiffen the morale of the civilian seamen reeling under the Dunkirk experience.

That night some ships were spotted returning empty from France under the mistaken impression—which their masters and crews had formed with gratitude and relief—that the operation had been concluded.

We were running this RAF launch in and out from the beach. Night came and day came and night came and day came. One evening things seemed to quieten down. Somehow the bustle and banging had eased off. We got the impression that this was the end of the road. We were tired out. We thought we'd done our bit. There didn't seem much more to do. We thought, "Let's go home." We didn't discuss it. It just came to the three of us. We were so bloody tired, we didn't have the sense to pick up another dozen soldiers to bring back with us. But we didn't even know if we'd be able to get back. It was getting dark. We had no compass, no charts, no weapons, no lights, no food, no nothing. We didn't even know if we had enough fuel to get home.

The tide on the coast continued to prove dangerously mischievous to sailors unfamiliar with its fast-in-fast-out perversities. With scores of small ships and boats crewed by inexperienced mariners, many beached at each low tide. Tugs and other vessels capable of towing them free were in great demand. Spotting a tug making for Dover with a cargo of evacuees, Wake-Walker called on it to turn back to tow off a minesweeper which was stranded deep in the mud off Bray. Paying no attention, the tug's master continued on his course back to England. He had volunteered for his vessel to serve as a transport to bring back the troops, and he intended to abide by that understanding. But with so many men still to be evacuated, Wake-Walker was determined to maintain as much control of the situation as he could. He had a gun trained on the tug and instructed a naval reserve sublieutenant aboard the vessel to take charge of it and go to the assistance of the beached minesweeper. The tug captain was outraged to be treated that way, but he was not the only man in the operation who found that far more was demanded of him during the Dunkirk days than he imagined would be.

Despite assurances to the contrary from their officers, forward troops who had fallen back after dark the previous night toward La Panne beach from the now shortened perimeter line in Belgium were to have no easy passage home. They discovered that no quick evacuation awaited them. They and other troops making their way through the debris-strewn streets of La Panne found nothing but muddled hopelessness on the beach. Hordes of men were already congregated there, but not many were being lifted off—no more than three hundred an hour—by the few boats working the shore in that sector. A mood of despair and dread prevailed, compounded by the effects of the random shelling of the beach by German guns and by the virtual absence of beach masters and beach patrols to explain what should be done.

Navy personnel on the shore had been ordered under no circumstances to allow themselves to be captured by the enemy, and most had by now been evacuated, some reluctantly in view of how much there was still to do. Confusion and bewilderment reigned as newly arrived troops proceeded along the beach in search of rescue, shells falling around them claiming dead and wounded, most of whom were left untended where they were hit. Recollection of the horror stayed with many of the men for long after the fact.

> To my right and left lay three still figures; a fourth, propped on one hand, spoke. His voice carried an entreating note of despair. . . . "Help me. Help me," was all he said, face indistinguishable except in outline in the darkness, a stranger whose voice has ever since accused—because I slogged on without pause. Those were the orders. But the main drive was that of self preservation, and whether the medics ever found him alive I could never know.

Senior officers on the spot decided that there was no alternative to marching troops down the beach toward Dunkirk. They might find transport while on the way to Bray or at Bray beach itself. But the supply of boats appeared to have dried up all along that stretch of the shoreline as well, as demonstrated by the sequence of messages that flowed across the Channel in the early-morning hours:

0243—Minesweeper Gossamer *to Admiral Ramsay: "We must have more boats west of La Panne."*

0324—Ramsay *to* Gossamer: *"It is now impracticable to send more boats. You must do your utmost with yours."*

0341—Tanker Niger *to Ramsay and Wake-Walker: "Situation on beaches is critical. . . . More boats urgently required."*

0358—Gossamer *to Ramsay: "Thousands more (? moving) from La Panne westward. No boats."*

0430—General Whitaker, 7th Guards Brigade, *to General Dill at the War Office: "Absolutely essential provide many more small boats with motor boats to tow if grave losses are to be avoided and remainder BEF cleared. Matter utmost urgency."*

0611—Wake-Walker to Ramsay: "All craft used for towing boats have returned in the night. They must be sent back."

The troops who had converged on La Panne beach after dark the previous night, mostly disciplined infantrymen, had formed up and made off toward Dunkirk along the soft sand under command of their remaining officers. They picked up stragglers on the way. Men who had been separated from their units shouted out in the dark, trying to find them again: "A-Company, Green Howards!" "C-Company, East Yorks!" Most finally found rescue from the breakwater at Dunkirk harbor, though some were lifted off the beaches before dawn by small craft which had worked right through the night.

> I saw what appeared to be a causeway about eight feet wide leading out into the water, so [my ship] made for it and hoped to find the men at the end of it. Imagine my surprise when I found that it was a perfectly straight formation of men standing in line about six deep as if they were on the Guards Parade! When I came right up to them and not before did a sergeant step out to say, "Yes, sir, sixty men." He walked down the line, the straight unmoved line . . . and told off sixty men to follow me out.

In desperation, in frustration, some men stripped down, discarded their weapons, and tried to swim out to ships they spotted offshore. Some succeeded. Some were lucky enough to be picked up by boats heading in toward the beach. But many were never seen again. At one point thirty soldiers making their way along the beach swam out toward a warship when an officer accompanying them said anyone who thought he could reach it could "have a go." It was early-morning light by then—4:30 A.M.—and soon after they set off, German fighters swooped low out of the horizon to strafe them and the ship they were heading for, the minesweeper HMS *Halcyon*. The *Halcyon* managed to avoid damage, but of the thirty swimmers, only four were saved, and two of those had been wounded in the water.

Right through the dark earliest hours of day, men had filed steadily along the breakwater at Dunkirk harbor onto vessels which had tied up there. At one point during the night, ten thousand British and twenty thousand French troops waited to load at the pier. "A solid block of troops" jammed the pier and access to it and extended onto the beach for about two miles. Some of the men had been waiting most of the previous day; some since the previous night. Here too the Germans continued to lob shells at random. Aside from the casualties they claimed, the damage they did, and the fear they generated, they served to magnify the eeriness of a mass embarkation of ragged, weary men illuminated by a backdrop of the still-blazing Dunkirk oil storage tanks, Dunkirk ablaze, and an occasional German flare.

French troops arriving in great numbers complicated matters on the beaches for cultural as well as language reasons. Either by experience or by heritage, many of the French were farmers from far inland for whom the sea and seagoing craft were impenetrable mysteries. Having reached the coast, many declined to go farther even when given a chance and just milled about aimlessly, adding to the congestion on the shore. Others, like many of the British troops, piled into boats at the water's edge, paying little heed to space or weight limitations. Some of those craft just settled deep into the mud and were stuck there. Having found sanctuary of a sort, those aboard just settled in and waited. Some sat there long enough for the tide to come in and lift them away.

Even along patches where great numbers of troops were not congregated, the shore stretching up the coast from Dunkirk was no longer the tidy seaside playground it had been a few days earlier.

The litter on the beach was indescribable: rifles, Bren guns, kits, everything lying all over the place. Destroyers and large and small boats of every description were lying on the bottom quite close to the shore, with masts, bridges, and funnels standing right out of the water. One destroyer was actually beached, cut completely in two by the bombs.

Dawn of June 1, the seventh day of Dunkirk, had risen clear and bright, and not long after came the first of the German bombing raids of the day. A second wave was mounted about an hour later and a third about an hour after that. Again and again right through the day, flocks of bombers, dive-bombers, and fighter planes roared in to attack the rescue vessels as they arrived from across the Channel, as they loaded, and as they headed back to England, their holds and decks crammed with evacuees. Once more the Luftwaffe shifted priority attention to the task of pounding the ships and disrupting the rescue of the Allied troops remaining in the perimeter strip, now some one hundred thousand French and forty thousand British—a course of action which, if systematically pursued from the start, would have wrecked Operation Dynamo days earlier. Some of the men saw the specific ships they expected to be ferried out to from the beach—and to which men before them on queues had already been carried—hit, set ablaze, and sinking.

> The troops on the shore were watching the Navy being bombed [recalled a civilian volunteer yachtsman]. . . . The really astonishing thing was that there was or appeared to be nothing . . . happening to the troops. I thought that this was an excellent bit of German terror-psychology . . . bombing the Navy, letting the troops watch the "might" of the Waffe, making them think twice before being sure that was the way they wanted to go home.

For the men on the beaches it must indeed have looked like Armageddon out at sea, with the forces of evil prevailing. It must have seemed that way to many British mariners as well. As if being dragged to his doom, the captain of the destroyer *Ivanhoe,* damaged and under attack, shouted out to the destroyer *Havant,* which had come close to render assistance, "Get out of here or you'll end up the same as us!" The *Havant* was soon also hit and went to the bottom near the entrance of the harbor. Out of control, the *Ivanhoe* was taken in tow and managed to be hauled back to England.

The destroyer *Basilisk* was hit off La Panne and sank while struggling home. The minesweeper *Skipjack* had picked up between 250 and 300 men off La Panne when a bomb struck her amidships. Before the order to abandon ship could be obeyed, "she turned turtle" and sank. Most of the evacuees aboard were below and were lost. Those who were flung into the water or managed to jump overboard were machine-gunned.

The French destroyer *Foudroyant* was sunk, as was the gunboat *Mosquito*. Ship after ship was sunk, crippled, or damaged. Once again, in the midst of this deadly turmoil, hundreds of men were saved from certain death by ships which, despite the danger to themselves, moved in close for evacuees and crew to transfer from stricken vessels.

The German onslaught from the air continued right through the day. During intervals between attacks, hasty emergency repair work on damaged vessels was undertaken, men were transferred from stricken ships, survivors were fished out of the water, and the wounded were treated. Those intervals also were periods of dread expectation, because no one doubted that the Stukas, Dorniers, Heinkels, and Messerschmitts would soon be back. The waters off Dunkirk had been turned into a special kind of maritime Hades, dotted with vessels ablaze or burned out, some beached, some half sunk, their bows pointing skyward, with bodies and wreckage flowing in and out with the tide.

As before, bitter complaints were voiced at the failure of the RAF to provide anything like adequate aerial cover. But RAF Fighter Command was at a fundamental disadvantage. The Germans could pick time and place for their ferocious aerial forays. By keeping the intervals between patrols as brief as possible and through sheer luck in timing, British fighters were able to challenge and disrupt some of the enemy raids. But though the RAF lost thirty-one aircraft that day (to twenty-nine for the Germans), more than once it was conspicuous by its total absence, leaving the enemy unchallenged mastery of the skies over Dunkirk.

When not challenged by British fighters, German attack planes had to contend only with antiaircraft fire, mostly from British destroyers. The planes came over low and fast, too fast for the gunners to distinguish Spitfires from Messerschmitts. They fired at both, usually with little effect, but kept firing nevertheless. Under the exposed circumstances in which they found themselves, there could be no holding back, no husbanding of resources. HMS *Keith*, like other destroyers in the operation, had turned around so quickly at Dover to get on with the job after unloading its complement of evacuees that it arrived back at Dunkirk down to its last thirty antiaircraft shells. Attacked from the air, it twisted and turned at speed but was hit, crippled, and sunk. It was turning into one of the most tragic days in the history of the Royal Navy.

*   *   *

Resentment and humiliation must have colored Gort's feelings when, back in London that morning, he arrived to attend a meeting of the War Cabinet. He had reason to believe that much of the guidance and instructions he had received from the War Office and Churchill himself over the previous two weeks had been ill-informed and confused. At the same time, being commander of an army which had done little more than retreat and which was being driven into the sea was not likely to reflect credit on his abilities, regardless of circumstances. But so greatly had the evacuation already exceeded expectations that despite the numbers of men still locked in the German trap on the northwest coast of France, Gort was warmly received at the meeting. Had the national security situation not been so grave, he probably would have been given a hero's welcome, if only for the sake of public morale.

The War Cabinet was anxious to hear the latest about conditions prevailing in the Dunkirk perimeter and the prospects for the continued evacuation of fighting troops. Gort told the assembled ministers and service chiefs that the defense line probably would hold till the following morning but it might be a near thing. Every effort should be made to complete the evacuation that night. Churchill's unceasing insistence that as many French troops as possible should be rescued, even if it might entail British losses, still did not impress him. Unaware of the heroism and determination displayed by the French rearguard, now keeping the Germans at bay as it took responsibility for ever longer stretches of the Dunkirk defense line, Gort doubted if many French troops of fighting quality remained in the area. He could not refrain from voicing his conviction that the French command had been massively and overwhelmingly responsible for the dilemma in which the BEF had found itself and implied that, therefore, French troops were unworthy of any additional perilous effort by the Royal Navy to save them.

Gort's belief that Dynamo would have to be wound up that night was echoed by the service chiefs. Profoundly alarmed by the punishment the Royal Navy was continuing to sustain, Sir Dudley Pound, chief of the naval staff, had no doubt that there was little chance of embarking any men after sunrise the following day. Pound reported that nearly all the destroyers engaged in the operation had suffered at least some degree of damage.

What was more, the Germans had now moved guns into position to shell the last Channel route through which ships had been able to reach Dunkirk with a measure of safety. Few of the one hundred fishing vessels which the French had offered for participation in the operation had appeared, and some of the French vessels which had been taking part were heading for Le Havre down the coast with the troops they had embarked, to unload there rather than making for England.

The RAF, also reeling from its accumulating losses, supported the navy's urgings that the operation be brought rapidly to a halt. Britain's fighter plane strength was said to be "already considerably below the minimum essential" for the defense of the country. The War Cabinet was told that for the previous three weeks, Fighter Command had been operating at a rate far in excess of its ability to replace lost pilots and aircraft. In addition, sending the Spitfires and Hurricanes aloft might soon prove a futile gesture. Machine-gun ammunition for the aircraft was being used up faster than new supplies were becoming available. A serious shortage was looming.

Having returned that morning from Paris, where he had the previous day assured French leaders of Britain's everlasting camaraderie, Churchill was reluctant to be swayed by the arguments and warnings of his military chiefs into downgrading the importance of evacuating French troops. He maintained that it was essential to hold on at Dunkirk as long as possible, even at the cost of naval and military losses, so that the French might be disabused of their belief that the British were abandoning them. The prime minister was, however, persuaded that General Alexander, as British commander on the spot, was best situated to know what the possibilities were and that the decision on when to wind up the evacuation should be left to him.

Alexander had no doubts about the timing. That morning, he had met with Abrial at the Bastion to confirm that the reduced British rearguard would hold what remained of its portion of the defense line only till nightfall, after which maintenance of the line would be completely in French hands. Informed of the decision, senior officials and officers in Paris were enraged. It confirmed the belief of many of them that, having rescued its own troops, perfidious Albion couldn't care less what happened to those of its ally. To soften the blow, Churchill cabled Reynaud and Weygand to explain the factors influencing British actions.

The critical point of the evacuation has now been reached. Five fighter squadrons are practically continously in action. This is all we can provide [to cover the evacuation]. Six ships, several of which were packed with troops, were sunk this morning. The only practicable channel is under artillery fire. The enemy's grip is tightening, and the bridgehead is narrowing. By attempting to hold on till tomorrow we may lose everything. If we close down tonight much will certainly be saved, although much may be lost. The situation cannot be assessed as a whole by Admiral Abrial, alone in the depth of his fortress, nor can it be by you, nor by us here. We have therefore ordered General Alexander, commanding the British sector of the bridgehead, to examine with Admiral Abrial the best line to follow. We are relying on your agreement.

The original draft of the Churchill message to Reynaud and Weygand said that Alexander had been ordered "to judge for himself" exclusively on how to proceed. But even when toned down, the message did nothing to mollify Reynaud. The French premier icily informed General Spears that it seemed that Churchill's assurances the previous day that Britain would not act unilaterally had lapsed with remarkable rapidity. His anger was fueled also by reports that French officers were being grossly abused by the British at Dunkirk. He had heard that a French general and his aide had been manhandled away from a rescue ship and told that if they embarked, it would mean that two less British soldiers would be evacuated and that could not be tolerated.

Spears had by now stopped trying to smooth over differences between Paris and London. The Allies had developed fundamental differences. While Dunkirk appeared to be turning into something of a triumph for the British, it was a symbol of defeat and disgrace for France. Instead of trying to explain things away, Spears was now answering charge with countercharge. As for the French general allegedly mistreated at Dunkirk, he suggested that by trying to flee France alone, he had been using his rank to save his own skin, and not the lives of the troops under his command, and that was wrong. Spears also firmly rejected criticism by Reynaud of Gort's performance as BEF commander. He asserted that Gort's failing, if he had one, had been not to complain about "the abysmal collapse of the French Staff and French generals."

The matter of Admiral Abrial's jurisdiction and judgment remained a delicate issue. The British—first Gort and now Alexander, with Tennant acting for the Royal Navy—had repeatedly consulted Abrial as they went about running the Dunkirk end of the operation on land. However, those consultations had for the most part been mere gestures in recognition of Abrial's rank as Dunkirk commander. Abrial and the French in general were keenly aware it was largely only a formality, devoid of substance, and they were not at all happy about it. But the British—as Churchill made plain in his cable to Paris—were convinced that Abrial couldn't manage events if he chose never to emerge from the seclusion of his Bastion fortress. It was, of course, also a convenient excuse, permitting them to continue acting in accordance with Britain's own needs, which, at that moment, were thought to involve national survival.

The end of the road appeared to be fast approaching for British troops still holding rearguard positions. Aside from running low on ammunition, they knew they had been reduced to comparatively few in number and that the Germans could not be held back much longer. Orders and instructions were sometimes neither clear nor consistent. Under intense enemy pressure, some officers understood that they were to pull their men back to the coast at their discretion when it seemed to them that the situation was hopeless. Others understood they were to hold fast no matter what until specifically ordered back. An officer of the 5th Borderers was shot dead by command of a Coldstream Guards major when, following superior orders, he defied the major's command not to withdraw his unit from the line. It was a futile gesture because the unit soon had to pull back anyway.

During the day, the rearguard was forced from several previously secure positions, taking heavy casualties in the process. A serious German penetration which developed on the eastern rim of the perimeter, near the Belgian-French border, cut sharply into beach embarkation possibilities. Easternmost beaches had to be abandoned, and evacuation of men directly from the shore was restricted to the sands extending only for about a mile and a half up the coast from the base of the breakwater. Beyond that, beaches from which thousands had been evacuated over the previous days were now no-man's-land. The few reserves available were thrown into the battle to stop a German breakthrough that appeared to be developing. By evening that enemy advance had been checked. That meant the elaborate embarkation plans for the coming night had not been in vain, though they so easily could have been. The great escape was still in progress. However, men still on the line were hardly confident that they would get away.

Stories filtered back to them of hundreds lying dead on the sands and of ships fully loaded blasted out of the water. They were close enough to the coast to hear the explosions and gunfire off the coast. Some doubted whether they'd even get the chance to be embarked. From experience, from limited knowledge of what was happening elsewhere on the line, and from ingrained prejudice, they had little faith in the French soldiers who were assuming ever wider responsibility for defense of the shrinking perimeter.

But the French were fighting with unflagging spirit and determination. Each breach the enemy was able to force in their positions was quickly sealed, though General Alexander remained cynical about the new defense line they were trying to establish closer to the remaining evacuation areas, little more than three miles in from the coast. The remaining British rearguard would withdraw to the beaches through that line after dark, but Alexander believed it would crumble under the first serious German assault, probably early the next day, after which Dunkirk itself would quickly fall, city, harbor, beaches, and all.

Nevertheless, the British commander was instructed by London that evening to "hold on as long as possible in order that the maximum number of French and British may be evacuated. Impossible from here to judge local situation. In close cooperation with Admiral Abrial, you must act in this matter on your own judgment." The last of the British were still due to be lifted off before dawn, but clearly London was prepared to continue Operation Dynamo as long as there was any reasonable chance of saving more French troops. If that was the case, the new deadline Alexander had set for ending the evacuation by the coming sunrise was also no longer valid. Now it was up to the French to prove he was wrong to doubt their ability to hold back the Germans.

As reports of the day's enormous naval and maritime casualties accumulated at Dynamo headquarters in Dover, Admiral

Ramsay realized that the operation could not be sensibly sustained along the lines it had been following. The pace of the evacuation had not diminished. The one remaining cross-Channel route used by the rescue vessels was kept busy.

> It was almost like a motorway with ships going up and down in both directions, with different lanes for faster ships and slower ships. That's where the Spitfires were [said an evacuee who hadn't seen much of them before]. It was a protected line.

But the price was mounting frighteningly. Before nightfall, thirty-one rescue ships, including six destroyers, had been sunk or otherwise put out of action that day.

> In these circumstances [Ramsay later reported] it was apparent that continuation of the operation by day must cause losses of ships and personnel out of all proportion to the number of troops evacuated, and if persisted in, the momentum of evacuation would automatically and rapidly decrease.

He decided therefore that starting the following morning, the operation would be suspended during daylight hours for all larger vessels, including warships. Big-ship embarkations still to take place before Operation Dynamo ran its course would be confined to hours of darkness. Little ships, the loss of which would neither damage British defense capabilities nor take great numbers of troops down with them if they were sunk, could continue working the beaches by day.

As darkness settled again over Dunkirk, ships once more began entering the harbor to tie up and load. As many as seven vessels at a time made their way into the harbor, gingerly trying to navigate paths clear of the debris to which so much had been added that long, savage day. There was no dawdling on the pier. The waiting troops were rushed along it and onto the ships as soon as vessels were made fast. They quickly loaded and made off again, leaving berthing space for other vessels. Ships berthed two or three deep at the pier. Many evacuees used some of those up against the breakwater, as well as burned-out wrecks, as pontoons to scramble over to get to the vessels that would carry them to England.

By midnight, 64,429 more men—almost half of them French—had been brought back that day, 47,081 from the harbor, 17,348 from the beaches; a total of 259,049 since the operation had begun. And more were already en route. Word of this remarkable exploit was spreading quickly to other parts of the world. Across the Atlantic, the *New York Herald Tribune* paid its tribute.

There have been trapped armies, terrible retreats, perilous embarkations, and heroic rearguard actions in the past, but no combination of them on a scale like this. Defeat sustained with such fortitude is no disaster. . . . These are soldiers of civilization, enrolling themselves imperishably among those who will save by suffering everything that makes civilized life of value.

The *New York Times* added its acclaim with Churchillian grandiloquence.

So long as the English tongue survives, the word Dunkirk will be spoken with reverence. For in that harbor, in such a hell as never blazed on earth before, at the end of a lost battle, the rages and blemishes that have hidden the soul of democracy fell away. There, beaten but unconquered, in shining splendor, she faced the enemy.

Day Eight—Thwarted Hopes

A decision had to be made about the wounded fortunate enough to be under medical care in the perimeter. Most were at Rosendaël just inland from Malo, where the single remaining casualty clearing station in the bridgehead was located. Churchill had assured the French that wounded British personnel would not be evacuated so that only men able to return immediately to battle could be saved. But no orders to that effect had been passed down, and many wounded troops had been lifted from the breakwater and rushed to hospitals when they had been brought back to England. However, the intensity of German bombardment of the harbor had led to a decision to embark only casualties who could walk and could therefore be evacuated quickly and without difficulty.

An effort was now made to bring home the more seriously wounded before the Germans overran the area. Two British hospital ships, clearly identified as such, were sent across by daylight after an uncoded radio message, meant to be intercepted by the Germans, was transmitted announcing their mission. Both vessels were attacked. One was sunk; the other was badly damaged and had to turn back. The 230 remaining stretcher cases at Rosendaël would have to stay behind.

However, they were not to be abandoned. Medical staff consisting of one officer and ten men for every one hundred nonambulatory casualties were to remain behind to care for them. A ballot was taken. The first names out of the hat left for home by way of the breakwater. Three officers and thirty men stayed on to care for the wounded and be captured by the Germans.

The wounded that had to be left behind at La Panne when it was abandoned to the enemy appear not to have been so fortunate. Four American army officers, neutral military attachés based in Berlin, were taken by the Germans on a tour of La Panne early that day. Their report to Washington indicated that because of the frenzy during the last hours before the area was abandoned, the casualties there had been left to their own devices.

> We entered the town [La Panne] a few hours after the British forces had completed their attempt to evacuate by sea. . . . German troops . . . were still in the process of mopping up. The British had left some of their dead unburied (we saw approximately 100 bodies on the beach and the beach boulevard) and had left no medical personnel with their wounded. The latter were reported to number 700 of which 50 died almost immediately after the town was captured. The Germans report that no British medical officer had remained behind.

The postbattle scene beheld by the American officers at La Panne was one of death and destruction.

> That the British put up a desperate and stubborn fight is admitted by the Germans. Most of the British dead were found in small groups beside trucks or guns. . . . Some bodies of drowned soldiers were seen. All had overcoats on and are believed to be from wrecked transports. Large numbers of British transports and some anti-aircraft guns of all calibre as well as abandoned equipment and ammunition were found scattered on the beach and in the town in great disorder. . . . A single British destroyer was lying broadside on the beach. The Germans claim she was put out of action earlier in the day by a Stuka attack. . . . German artillery was firing over us . . . in the direction of Dunkirchen. The combined fire of German artillery and air bombing on the town was terrific. . . . [A] rate of about 100 explosions per minute . . . was still being maintained.

Boarding had been brisk from the breakwater in the harbor in the darkness of early morning. Troops, both British and French, proceeded down it in a seemingly endless flow. Rescue vessels had arrived in goodly number and continued to do so until just before dawn. Columns of men moved along the pier four abreast, two columns of British troops, two of French, boarding in good order. Despite the great numbers of men and ships in motion and the hasty overloading of the vessels, there was not a great deal of noise. The men were too weary for chatter and too pleased finally to be homeward bound in the seeming safety of comparative darkness to grumble. Ship's engines rumbled as, full up, the vessels headed out to sea. Ships' sirens hooted, though not as often as the heavy traffic seemed to warrant. Shells bursting sporadically in the harbor during the night were now part of the Dunkirk scene and caused no special excitement, except when one exploded close to the breakwater or a vessel, after which it was soon as if it had never happened.

But a problem arose. Though the road and beach approaches to the breakwater, and the breakwater itself, had been jammed with men when the previous night had fallen, those waiting were boarded and gotten away well before dawn. Suddenly a strange lull interrupted the brisk pace and mood of the operation. The breakwater was empty except for a few ships' officers and men, aware that they could be blasted to smithereens at any moment, nervously peering down the pier for more men to board.

Inadequate communications prevented word of passage availability at the harbor from reaching the throngs of troops farther along the sands who were hoping to be lifted off there before the imminent German arrival. Officers from destroyers which tied up at the pier during the night scoured nearby beach and dunes to find evacuees, without great success. Equally unsuccessfully, the navigator from the destroyer *Malcolm* wandered through the streets of Dunkirk playing the bagpipes to lure troops out of cellars in the devastated city in which they might have hidden for safety.

The last four thousand British troops of the rearguard had disengaged from the line after dark the night before, but they had miles to go, most of them on foot, before reaching embarkation areas. As they headed, tired and hungry, for the coast, they passed through the new French stop line which Abrial said would hold the Germans back when ground fighting resumed come the morning. For many of them, the rescue was to be totally haphazard.

A still close dark night, lit dimly by a steady glow from Dunkirk . . . and intermittently by the gun flashes of French artillery firing lots of ammunition. French sentries kept
challenging from the darkness; we were none too certain we
were on the right road, when suddenly we reached the beach
and turned left toward the Mole. Into the final straight at
last, but the finishing post—the Mole—a most unpleasant
looking place seen from a mile or so. Apparently blazing like
Hell from end to end (this was really the oil tanks behind it);
crashes and bangs near the shore told us that it was being
steadily bombed and shelled. Pick up the step there, chaps—
left, right, left right. Suddenly a young Staff Officer was
reached: "Take your party down to the beach and get away
in boats; lots are coming in." Order obeyed with alacrity.
Not so good when one paddled in, found many others pad-
dling, no boats in and nobody knowing anything. Like a traffic jam this muddle sorted itself out eventually, and before
dawn most of the Regiment [18th Field Regiment, Royal Ar-
tillery] were aboard some small craft or other.

Troops who still had transport, or were able to commandeer
abandoned vehicles, were spared the footslog. Despite the attempt to prevent vehicle congestion within the perimeter, Dunkirk and Malo village were packed with vehicles, and countless
others littered the dunes and beaches. At 1:00 in the morning, the
remaining few tanks and carriers of regimental headquarters,
46th Division, drew up on the mud along the water's edge at
Malo. The tank crews got out and spiked their guns and smashed
the engines of all the vehicles. "After which everyone waded out
to sea and was sooner or later picked up by a boat."
    Twenty-four men of the 27th Field Regiment, Royal Artil-
lery, were separated from the rest of their unit, who had managed to be embarked from the breakwater. Unable to force their
way onto the pier when it was crowded, the twenty-four waded
out to a Thames River barge which had run aground on the
beach nearby and which had been abandoned by its crew, who
presumably had found alternative transport home. When the
barge rose with the tide, the men managed to get a sail up and
headed across the Channel.
    But most of the rearguard troops heading, as instructed, for
the breakwater to be embarked weren't so lucky. Word had finally spread to would-be evacuees that the pier was the place to

be, and suddenly there was again no shortage of men jamming
its approaches, anxious to be boarded and carried away. Among
them was a milling multitude of French troops, belatedly aware
of the breakwater embarkations. They cut into the flow of British rearguard troops, for whom priority embarkation, now
thwarted, had been planned.

As predawn light began to poke over the horizon, Wake-
Walker, aboard a motorboat inside the harbor, gazed about,
waiting for the moment when embarkation for the day would
have to be suspended and men left behind, with no guarantee
that it would be resumed when darkness again fell.

> Looking shoreward, the whole town and harbor were shut in
> by a pall of smoke overhead, which was lit up by the glare of
> fires in several places inland. Against the glare, the piers,
> harbour and town were sharply silhouetted, and on the piers
> and quays an endless line of helmeted men in serried ranks,
> sometimes moving, sometimes stationary. The funnels and
> masts of ships showed clear as they lay alongside or went in and
> out of harbour, their hulls hidden and dark and invisible.

Some men had made their way well along the pier in sight
of rescue when, with light creeping across the sky, the last vessel, fully loaded, departed. Word was passed along the breakwater that it had to be cleared at once because German planes
were likely soon to come roaring in from the distance, their machine guns blazing, their bombs plummeting down. The men farthest along the pier, most exposed, tried to get back to the
beach as instructed. But those closer to the foot of the pier
wouldn't believe embarkation had been suspended. They had
waited too long to give ground easily. There was much jostling
and griping until the pier was finally cleared.

Informed as dawn rose that embarkation would not be resumed until nightfall, stranded rearguard troops were marched
back to the dunes to dig in, scrounge for food and water, and
hope the French troops manning the new defense line would
hold fast during the long day ahead. They had expected no such
delay and were bitter about it.

> We had been told [a Coldstream Guards colonel said] that
> embarkation would continue until such time as the BEF was

evacuated or enemy action made it impossible. It was a poor
prospect for us, with eighteen hours to wait through the day.
We had little faith in the resistance which the French were
likely to put up, and we had only rifles and Brens to fight
with. . . . A gunner major came to me and asked for orders,
but apart from the necessity for dispersion, I had nothing to
tell him. It was humiliating.

Their departure blocked, some rearguard troops were summoned from the dunes, where they had hoped to sleep the day
away, and despite their weariness and limited firepower, were
deployed as emergency backup for the nearby front line. They
were to cover the approaches to the harbor in case the Germans
broke through French defenses.

Now that La Panne had fallen, it appeared that the Germans were most likely to advance down the coast. The dozen
remaining British antitank guns were positioned to block them if
they came that way—a meager display against the resources at
the disposal of the enemy. Seven remaining British antiaircraft
guns were deployed on the beaches as well, but they were short
of ammunition. There was little they could do against enemy
aircraft when they resumed their raids at dawn. A British army
chaplain celebrated Holy Communion on the dunes east of Dunkirk soon after sunrise, but he and the men attending were scattered by enemy aircraft swooping low. With no large ships at sea
or in the harbor during daylight hours, the Luftwaffe could concentrate on the French defense line and on troops awaiting rescue. That they did, adding to the toll of bodies on the beach.

The final evacuation [Admiral Ramsay signaled warships still
involved in the operation] is staged for tonight, and the Nation looks to the Navy to see this through. I want every ship
to report as soon as possible whether she is fit and ready to
meet the call which has been made on our courage and endurance.

Drained of energy, many of the men who were called upon
to reply and who had repeatedly risked death shuttling back and
forth to Dunkirk would have preferred to bow out. But all ships
reported either that they were "fit and ready" or that their crews
were prepared to serve in any capacity. Though not under or-

ders or military obligation, many of the civilians who had volunteered or otherwise been drawn into the operation were equally willing to get on with the job. Indeed, some continued by choice to operate off the beaches during the day while the navy waited until nightfall. But some, like others before them, decided they had done enough and removed themselves from the operation. Armed guards were posted on some vessels to keep crewmen from abandoning ship in the harbors of southeastern England before they could be replaced by navy personnel and to make certain that once they reached Dunkirk after dark, they did not hang back from entering the harbor because of German shelling.

That night's evacuation procedures were more meticulously planned than at any time since the full dimensions of the evacuation came to be appreciated. The suspension of daytime sailings provided a respite in which Ramsay and Dynamo headquarters personnel could examine the situation clearly. The eleven destroyers still at Ramsay's disposal were scheduled to reach Dunkirk at half-hour intervals starting at 9:00 at night. The timing for the other vessels—thirteen passenger ships, two cargo carriers, fourteen minesweepers, and an assortment of other ships—was also plotted with greater thoroughness than had been possible before. Navy motorboats were to take up positions in Dunkirk harbor to guide the ships to their berths. Special ladders were constructed to speed along the embarkation of the troops. Liaison with RAF Fighter Command arranged for strong patrols over the evacuation area for the hour prior to darkness to warn the Luftwaffe away from the night operation. In the best tradition of the Royal Navy, Operation Dynamo was to be wrapped up before dawn with calm, meticulous efficiency.

Confusion on the numbers still to be evacuated was inevitable. It was thought there were between four thousand and six thousand British troops left, including stragglers from virtually every unit in the BEF. During the day, almost all were organized for rapid embarkation and were not expected to present much of a rescue problem if the defense line held. Assuming the Germans did not break through, the problem would be the French troops. There could be anywhere between twenty-five thousand and sixty thousand of them. Despite the careful planning, the calculations involved a great deal of guesswork.

The suspension of activity at the breakwater that morning gave Commander Clouston, the piermaster at Dunkirk, who had been superintending the frantic evacuation from the harbor for five days, an opportunity to leave the area for a few hours. He sped by motorboat back to Dover to participate in the planning for the night's operations, as well as for some sleep, a bath, and a meal. Somewhat refreshed, he headed back to Dunkirk that afternoon to oversee the coming night's activity at the breakwater. En route, his motorboat—one that was to help guide ships to their berths in the harbor that night—was attacked and sunk by German dive-bombers. Clouston and the party accompanying him were thrown into the water. A second motorboat which had been accompanying theirs turned to rescue them, but Clouston, aware of the danger to any boat that stopped in those waters when enemy aircraft were in attendance, signaled it off. Instead, he and the men with him started swimming toward ship's wreckage some distance away. His body was later spotted floating in the water. His death would have a bearing on the Dunkirk proceedings that night.

Now that restrictions on the publication of news about the Dunkirk evacuation had been eased, Britain's newspapers were full of accounts of the heroism of the men involved in the operation and of the great numbers of men brought back from France. But rumors continued to circulate in many parts of the country that the losses across the Channel had been frighteningly heavy. It couldn't be otherwise with more and more families receiving War Office regrets about men killed or wounded in France. Despite the reports of the magnificent exodus from the continent, a great many others waited in vain to hear that their kin had safely returned to the bosom of the motherland. Minister of War Eden went on the radio to boost morale and give assurances that Britain remained strong.

> The British Expeditionary Force still exists, not as a handful of fugitives, but as a body of seasoned veterans. . . . [Our spirit] has been tried and tempered in the furnace. It has not been found wanting.

Though he never showed it, among those who had needed reassurance was the prime minister. From the moment Churchill had heard of Gort's decision to fall back to the coast, he had imagined great numbers of British troops dead and wounded in and around the "bomb trap" at Dunkirk, and "long, dreary processions [of captured British troops] making their way to prison camps and starvation in Germany." He had also known how precarious his political position would have become if, as he and his advisers expected, only a small fraction of the BEF was rescued. Now, though deeply saddened by casualty levels and anxious about the naval and RAF losses in the operation, the prime minister, referring to the loss of most of the British army's heavy equipment, was able to quip that though the men had been brought home, "we lost the luggage."

The British leader pressed relentlessly ahead with his campaign to prevent any sense of defeat or gloom from permeating both the senior counsels of war, which had access to details of the serious losses sustained, and the public imagination. He told the chiefs of staff, who knew better, that "the armed forces in Great Britain are now far stronger than they have ever been" and that German invaders would meet not "half-trained formations, but the men whose mettle they have already tested, and from whom they have recoiled, not daring seriously to molest their departure." Had they heard the prime minister's words, men whose departure from Dunkirk had been "seriously molested" might have shaken their heads in wonder.

Meantime, the armed forces increased their vigilance along the coasts of England. In a dispatch which heightened invasion fever, an American reporter covering the war from the German side reported that correspondents had seen "certain 'specialized troops' whose nature they were pledged not to reveal." "MYSTERY NAZIS MASS AT CHANNEL" is the way a Chicago newspaper headlined that story, a danger with which the War Office was already trying to cope. Preparations were made for demolishing bridges on all roads in Britain going inland from the shore all the way from Kent to Scotland.

The War Office also considered organizing a campaign of guerrilla warfare against the German invader if that became necessary. All commands had been issued with instructions for making Molotov cocktails. Ironside noted in his diary that General Orde Wingate suggested the formation of the kind of organization he had established in Palestine when he was on special duty with the British administration there before the war and had formed squads of Jewish irregulars to guard a crucial oil pipeline against raids by Arab insurgents.

*   *   *

At Galway in Ireland, an evacuation of a different kind had taken place that day. The liner *President Roosevelt* had arrived from the United States to transport Americans who had been visiting or resident in Britain out of war's danger. The vessel normally carried 460 passengers. But for this journey, 725 passengers, some with their pet dogs, plus 375 ship's company, all wearing lifebelts, were accommodated. Though many of these passengers were not accustomed to traveling anything but first class, the liner was so crowded that some were assigned to makeshift berths in the ship's post office and baggage compartments. To leave no doubt about the vessel's identity, large American flags had been painted on its sides. It was lit up like a Christmas tree, and the Germans as well as the British had been informed of its route so that no mistakes would be made by their submarines. From Berlin came the suggestion that the British might attack the ship and then blame Germany, hoping to draw America into the war on the side of the Allies.

The publicity given this emergency evacuation assured the presence of a large crowd of onlookers as the ship set sail from Galway to carry its passengers far from the blackouts, shortages, and uncertainties of the European conflict. The *Manchester Guardian* reported, "Very few friends [of the passengers] had been able to get to Galway to say goodby to the Americans returning to a land where there are still lighted streets."

As evening gave way to night at Dunkirk, everything was ready for the final act of Operation Dynamo. A picket of men from the 5th Green Howards, who had withdrawn from the defense line but failed to be embarked the night before, formed up from the base of the breakwater along the adjoining beach. They were positioned fifty yards in from the water line for a distance of five hundred yards to keep the embarkation procession moving along quickly when the rescue ships began berthing at the pier.

It worked well. Without interruption, the troops tramped from the beach onto the access road to the breakwater, then along the pier to the vessels to which they were directed, and they clambered quickly aboard. The operation proceeded so smoothly that within a few hours, it was hard to find more men to embark. Except for the nonambulatory wounded, those caring for them, and a number of stragglers, all British troops in the perimeter had been boarded. What had seemed beyond the realm of possibility had been accomplished. Just before midnight, Captain Tennant signaled Dynamo headquarters, "Operation completed." The BEF—which so many had given up as doomed—had been evacuated.

That day, 26,256 men had been embarked—19,561 from the harbor, 6,695 from the beaches. That made a total of 285,305 troops ferried to England since the operation had been launched eight days earlier. It had been an extraordinary achievement. But the belief of ships' crews that Dynamo was now to be declared concluded and that they need not return again to the horrors of Dunkirk would, to their anguish, prove premature.

Day Nine—Save the French

The evacuation of the BEF having been completed by the previous midnight, a strange stillness had fallen over Dunkirk harbor. The oil tanks in the backdrop were still on fire and shells still fell intermittently. But it appeared as though the area—only recently clogged with men—had been vacated.

At half past midnight, a bewildered Wake-Walker reported to Dover that vessels were berthed at the breakwater but the thousands of French troops thought to be ready for embarkation were nowhere to be found. An hour later, he again signaled Dover, "Plenty of ships. Cannot get troops." There was no sign in the wharves of the harbor, on the breakwater, or on the adjoining beach of the expected multitude of evacuees. Most troubling, there was no sign of the French rearguard troops who had manned the defense line the last two days, enabling the last of the BEF to be lifted off.

It was pointless and dangerous to keep vessels at the pier for evacuees who did not show up. The destroyer *Vanquisher* was ordered home from Dunkirk at 2:30 A.M., returning to Dover with only thirty-seven evacuees, picked up from a small boat outside the harbor. The destroyer *Codrington* returned with only forty-four troops. The *Malcolm* returned with no evacuees at all. The crossing had been wasted for all the vessels, including five of Ramsay's destroyers, sent over during the early hours of June 3 for the grand finale. Several ships waited in vain for an hour or more before heading back to England. One vessel stayed tied up in vain at the breakwater for three and a half hours before finally making for home, its crew bitter at being needlessly exposed to danger.

*   *   *

All British troops having been evacuated and the operation seemingly concluded, General Alexander prepared to leave as well. He first boarded a motorboat in the harbor and prowled along the beach eastward for about two miles, as close inshore as the boat's shallow draft permitted, while he repeatedly called in English and French over a megaphone, "Is anyone there?" There was no reply. He returned to the harbor and toured the wrecked wharves, calling out the same question with the same result. Satisfied no one still waited for embarkation, Alexander and his aides boarded a waiting destroyer and set off for England, picking up an RAF escort when they approached the English coast as dawn broke.

But sixty thousand French soldiers were still in the perimeter, more than half of them the rearguard troops who had not yet been able to fall back on the harbor. For tactical reasons, their counterattack, to foil a German attempt to break through the new defense line, had been delayed until late the previous evening, and they were still in the process of disengaging and falling back. As for the others, the absence of Commander Clouston, the pier master who had been killed on his way back from Dover the previous day, was sorely felt. Liaison between remaining British evacuation personnel and makeshift French embarkation control officers was practically nonexistent, leaving thousands waiting in vain near the western rather than the eastern breakwater or in the dunes awaiting instructions to move to the harbor. The opportunity to evacuate thousands more men before sunrise was lost.

Ironically, after this missed chance, just before dawn, the harbor suddenly burst into activity once more. Men who had earlier held back in ignorance of available passage now rushed to the eastern breakwater to be embarked on an assortment of French small craft which showed up in profusion to take them away, lifting them from the west pier and the harbor wharves as well. Rearguard troops now began showing up too.

In the harbor crush, vessels got in one another's way and collided. Some ran aground in shallows of the inner sections of the harbor and had to await high water. Fearing to be left behind, men who advanced along the eastern breakwater tried to board the first vessel they came across, blocking the passage of other troops to ships tied up farther along the pier. Many who could have been taken off were left behind as predawn light broke through the darkness once more and the ships again hastily withdrew. The men left behind retired reluctantly to the dunes and settled in there to await either the enemy or evacuation the next night, whichever came first. Queer, quiet desolation, intermittently punctuated by the burst of shells, descended again on the harbor area.

During the morning, under Admiralty instructions to make another effort to rescue stranded French troops, Ramsay met with his chief aides at Dynamo headquarters in Dover to discuss how to proceed. Soon after, he sent what was almost an apology to the ships under his command:

> I hoped and believed that last night would see us through, but the French who were covering the retirement of the British rearguard had to repel a strong German attack and so were unable to send their troops to the pier in time to be embarked. We cannot leave our Allies in the lurch and I must call on all officers and men detailed for further evacuation tonight to let the world see that we never let down our Ally.

Back from Dunkirk, General Alexander, who would have known as well as anyone in Britain, reported that he had no idea how many French troops were left in the bridgehead. It was therefore impossible to determine the number of ships still needed to evacuate them. The empty return of the vessels which had risked doom to make the journey the night before was infuriating, particularly as it was now possible for Dynamo headquarters personnel to review the situation and grasp how serious were the naval losses so far sustained.

Only nine of the forty destroyers which had been committed to the operation were still available to return to Dunkirk. But Churchill had personally directed that efforts continue to save as many French troops as possible. Ramsay began making arrangements for the coming night, but he warned the Admiralty of problems that would arise if Dynamo was not wound up after the coming night.

> After nine days of operations of a nature unprecedented in naval warfare, which followed two weeks of intense strain,

commanding officers, officers and ships' companies are at the end of their tether. I therefore view a continuance of the demands made by evacuation with utmost concern as likely to strain to breaking-point the endurance of officers and men. I should fail in my duty did I not represent to Their Lordships the existence of this state of affairs in the ships under my command, and I consider it would be unfortunate, after the magnificent manner in which officers and men of the surviving ships have faced heavy loss and responded to every call made upon them, that they should be subjected to a test which I feel may be beyond the limit of endurance. If therefore evacuation has to be continued after tonight, I would emphasise in the strongest possible manner that fresh force should be used for these operations and any consequent delay in their execution should be accepted.

Ramsay was not alone in worrying about what might happen after that night's operations. At a War Cabinet meeting, the determined resistance of the French rearguard aroused concern as well as admiration. It was recalled that Weygand had earlier wanted to defend the Dunkirk bridgehead indefinitely instead of using it only for evacuation purposes. It was possible that the French might after all try to hold the bridgehead despite German military superiority.

The prospect did not please the British High Command. If that happened, Britain would be obliged to lend continuing support, which would impose an ongoing strain on its naval and air resources. A report that only three French fighter planes had been sent airborne when more than two hundred German bombers attacked the suburbs of Paris that day, and that those three had confined themselves to patrolling above their own airfield, never challenging the German attack, did not stimulate a desire in London to commit additional British forces to the defense of Dunkirk.

Forever sounding the alarm, RAF Fighter Command chief Dowding pressed the point home by once more alerting the War Cabinet to the dangers involved in the continued commitment of his fighters to the operation. He reported that he had been forced that very day to withdraw the last three of his squadrons that had not yet taken part in Dynamo from their bases in Scotland to do their bit over Dunkirk. All his other squadrons had already lost precious planes and pilots in the operation. The previous night, it had been necessary to draw from eight different squadrons to patch together enough serviceable aircraft to constitute a strong enough Dunkirk patrol for the morning. Britain couldn't hope to fight a war with such shifting and patching. Dowding warned that if the Germans decided to launch a heavy air assault on Britain at that moment, he could not guarantee air superiority for more than forty-eight hours.

The details he provided from statistics newly gathered were indeed alarming. During the first ten days of the German offensive, 250 Hurricanes had been lost in France. That worked out to twenty-five of Britain's modern fighters each day as compared to only four replacements received each day from the aircraft factories. Justifying his earlier opposition to sending additional fighters to France, he said, "Had this rate continued, we would have lost all our Hurricanes by the end of May." He reported to the chiefs of staff that the number of modern fighters serviceable as of the day before, June 2, was only 280 Spitfires and 244 Hurricanes. But he said even those figures were, in effect, overestimates because some of his pilots, drawn from other flying duties, were still to make their first solo fighter flights.

Dowding was notorious for indulging in gloomy hyperbole in his effort to preserve Britain's home air defenses, but the dangers he harped upon aroused genuine jitters. The lives of many of Britain's comparatively small corps of experienced fighter pilots, who had been counted on to play a key role in the defense of Britain during the expected German invasion, had already been claimed in the Dunkirk operation. Having lost men and planes, many of the fighter squadrons were disorganized, not yet having received aircraft replacements and having no time to assimilate newcomer pilots properly. Chief of the Air Staff Newall, who often attempted to moderate Dowding's unrelieved forebodings, warned that in view of the comparative strengths of the British and German air forces, for Britain to achieve air superiority, it would have to destroy German planes at a rate of eight to one, something that wasn't happening even if, as was the case, the inflated kill scores marked up by Fighter Command pilots were accepted as genuine. Newall pointed out that Britain's fighter defenses had been organized in the buildup to the war to protect the country against bomber attacks from Germany, not to cope with enemy bombers escorted by short-range fighters flying from nearby captured airfields.

The implication of all of this, compounded by the Admiralty's alarm at lost destroyers, was that Operation Dynamo had to be wound up no matter what, and soon. It was a relief to have the army back, with or without its equipment. But it would be unforgivably reckless to continue the Dunkirk episode if it meant hopelessly crippling Britain's naval and air defenses.

The operation had to be concluded that night. There could be no further extension. Churchill passed word of the windup to Reynaud.

> We are coming back for your men tonight. Please ensure that all facilities are used promptly. For three hours last night many ships waited idly at great risk and danger.

Weygand, for whom the Dunkirk evacuation symbolized his failure to lead the Allies back from the brink of shameful defeat, was less than impressed with this gesture. He bitterly recalled Churchill's unfulfilled promise that the British would supply the rearguard at Dunkirk till the end. It was a time for unrestrained recriminations. With the German conquest of France apparently inevitable, the French military commander charged that the British leader had played "a double game and had abandoned France to herself." Still harking back to imaginary might-have-beens, he insisted that Churchill had sabotaged the operation that had been ordered ten days earlier to link up the armies in the north with French forces south of the Somme. He said that operation would have been successful if the English, who "cannot resist the call of the ports," had not been continually looking over their shoulders at the sea.

Such grumbling amounted to little more than a search for a scapegoat for France's monumental military bungling. With the French woefully weak in the south, had the armies of the north turned in that direction—and they might have had the Belgian defense line not cracked, endangering the BEF's left flank—they probably would have put up a strong but brief fight before being overwhelmed by German armored might. There would have been no Dunkirk—no rescue, no great escape, and no British army left.

Late in the day, a report came from the British liaison officer at French naval headquarters at Dunkirk that the number of French troops still to be embarked was thirty thousand. (Once again that figure was no more than a guess.) Among the vessels dispatched in quick succession starting that evening to lift them off were thirteen destroyers (four of them French), nine British passenger ships (the master of another refused to sail), eleven minesweepers, and a flotilla of smaller British, French, and Belgian craft and motorboats.

Much would depend on the Dunkirk embarkation facilities, now even more under threat from forward German artillery positions, and the speed with which men could be boarded. Some of the French troops who clogged the embarkation areas the previous night had still refused to board, fearing the sea or reluctant to leave their homeland. Others had refused to be embarked unless their entire units could board the same ship, and some who had boarded tried to push their way off again when they realized there wasn't enough space for all the men in their units. French naval personnel accompanied the Royal Navy pier party sent back from Dover to help sort out such problems during the final windup.

Questions remained as to whether French troops still holding the line could hold fast. The Germans mounted several concerted attempts to break through during the course of the day. Though the capture of Dunkirk had been downgraded as a priority by the German command, it was obvious that its defenses were about to crumble and that death or capture was the probable fate of surviving French rearguard troops. Nevertheless, they fought for every bit of land, every street, every house. In places they fought till the last man was cut down, and still a line held, farther back now, in Dunkirk itself but far enough away from the harbor as the day drew to a close for the final evacuation operation to proceed as planned once darkness fell. The performance, determination, grit, and soldierly skills of these French troops showed that the battle of France might have followed a totally different course had the country's senior commanders been worthy of such soldiers.

So close to final victory but warned off by the ferocity of French resistance, exhausted from battle, uncertain about the terrain, and confident of an easy triumph the following day, the Germans once more ceased pressing forward when night fell. Taking advantage of the lull, survivors of the rearguard quietly disengaged and slipped back toward the harbor for the ships sent to deliver them from death or capture.

By then, many of the vessels had arrived from England and had begun boarding. They had found the harbor "swarming with French fishing craft and vessels of all sorts." Some of these had tied up at the eastern breakwater. Only with difficulty were they persuaded to move off to pick up men from the west pier and the wharves and thus make room for larger vessels, which couldn't berth anywhere else and which could load far more men. Wake-Walker observed the scene in amazement.

> The congestion was chaotic, ships going astern into others coming ahead. French destroyers shrieking on their sirens, small craft nipping here and there, rendering the exit most dangerous.

Bumpings and collisions abounded. Wrecks piled up in the harbor. Some skoots ran aground at the near end of the west pier and had to wait for the tide to lift them off again. Congestion ruled the breakwater as well, now with only a young British navy sublieutenant acting as pier master, trying to get as many French troops as possible boarded.

> Lord help us! I was grey-haired by the end of the night. First of all whenever a shell came over they all fell flat on their faces, and it took at least three minutes before they started moving again, and as the shells were arriving in salvos every two minutes they hardly moved at all. Next when they came to the first gangway at the first ship they all tried to get on board together. In consequence there was a complete block; all the other ships along the jetty were stranded with no one to go on board. If one tried to point this out to them they merely shouted that as half their regiment was on that particular ship the rest must get in too. . . . In desperation I resorted to guile and force. I stationed the biggest seamen I could find near the first ships and they *threw* the French soldiers along the jetty, thus breaking up the regiments. The other method was to ask them what their regiment was and then through a megaphone to shout *"A moi le dixième,"* and so lead them at the double up the jetty to the end ship and so fill up the whole jetty, which of course was the state of affairs at which we were aiming.

By midnight of June 3, with the Germans halted at nightfall barely two miles away, more than 26,746 men had been evacuated that day despite the congestion and confusion and the suspension of the operation during the daylight hours. That made a total of 312,051 since the commencement of Dynamo, and the operation, which had originally been expected to last forty-eight hours, was going into its tenth day.

Day Ten—Closedown

Not till 2:00 in the morning on June 4, this last day of Operation Dynamo, did the last of the rearguard make its final withdrawal from the suburbs and outskirts of Dunkirk where they had stopped the Germans at last light. There was some machine-gun and rifle fire from the enemy, as there had been ever since nightfall, but it was sporadic and undirected, a gesture from soldiers who were as exhausted as their prey and who knew it would finally be all over come the morning. The French troops stole quietly away through the ruins of Dunkirk toward the harbor and evacuation. An alarm was raised at Dover about German torpedo boats which were reported to have left Ostend not far up the coast and which might attempt to attack the rescue ships, but the troops knew nothing of that—only that they were to be embarked and that ships were standing by to take them on board less than an hour away across town.

However, these men who had held the line so that the last of the British troops as well as thousands of their French fellow soldiers could escape were to be disappointed. As they proceeded through Dunkirk to the eastern breakwater to be lifted off, they found their way blocked by a vast multitude of men previously not taken into account. A horde of thousands of individual French soldiers who had holed up in fear in the cellars and ruins of Dunkirk and Malo for days, having learned that the Germans were about to arrive and acting through herd instinct, now emerged from their hiding places to claim priority embarkation. These were stragglers from all kinds of units, mostly noncombatant support troops who had separated from their units or been separated from them and who had earlier converged on Dunkirk for sanctuary. This vast impromptu ragtag army jammed the approaches to the breakwater, blocking the rearguard troops off from the embarkation they had made possible as effectively as a concrete wall.

They could do nothing but watch in anguish and hope that by some miracle this disorderly throng could be cleared away before daylight and that there would still be room enough for them aboard rescue vessels. But just before morning twilight, most were still waiting as the last of the big ships—the venerable British destroyer *Shikari*—left carrying a thousand troops.

A few smaller vessels continued to pick up small batches of evacuees from the harbor as light began to break through. But the great exodus was effectively over. Some of the men still stranded trooped back into Dunkirk city to await the arrival of the Germans. Others waited where they were.

Under orders from Paris not to be captured by the Germans, Admiral Abrial had left for England before dawn, together with Generals de La Laurencie, Fagalde, and Barthélemy, who, with their troops, had gone some way during the closing phase of the battle in the north to redeem the reputation of the French army. Later that morning, Abrial conferred in Dover with Admiral Ramsay about the advisability of prolonging the operation one more night to try to rescue some of the men left behind. Abrial thought it would be a wasted effort. He said the troops still in Dunkirk were out of ammunition with which to hold back the enemy any longer and that a further attempt at evacuation would needlessly endanger the rescue ships.

In fact, shortly after dawn, both the center of Dunkirk and the beaches east of the breakwater had come under small-arms fire from the enemy.

> . . . by the time we left [said one of the last of the Royal Navy personnel to depart] the Germans had occupied most of the town. . . . The town [was] a mass of flames with huge shell-ridden and gutted buildings standing out black against the flames.

All resistance having ceased, the Germans moved in quickly. They established themselves in key positions in case

further action was needed to ensure their control of the city and
the port. But Dunkirk was finally, unquestionably theirs. A British army ambulance driver who had been kept too busy to be
evacuated and who now waited to be taken prisoner surveyed a
scene of hushed devastation as morning rose and the episode
drew to an end.

> It was quiet now. The ruined buildings sent up only a little
> smoke and in the beautiful clear morning could be seen the
> sunken ships all round the inner harbour, and out to sea as
> well, a Thames barge still floating at anchor untouched—the
> quays, canal sides and beaches crowded with abandoned
> wagons—many dead upon the beach, and the greater deso-
> lation because it was obviously the end. The Navy had gone.
> The AA guns were gone. The wireless van was scuttled, and
> we could hope for nothing more.

At 9:00 that morning, General Beaufrère, who had been
left in command of French troops there, met with a Lieutenant
General Friedrich-Carl Kranz, commanding attacking German
forces, to arrange for the surrender of the thirty thousand to
forty thousand French troops (no one knew how many exactly)
still in the bridgehead. The swastika flag was run up over Dunkirk's town hall. Ironically, some French soldiers still lined the
eastern breakwater when the Germans arrived at its foot to take
them prisoner and run up a swastika banner there as well.

Ships and boats continued to arrive at English south coast
ports right through the morning, their navigation problems having been complicated by fog which also served to protect them
from air attack as they negotiated Channel passage. After unloading their passengers and being authorized by Ramsay at
10:30 that morning to disperse, they made for their home ports
all over southern England for rest and repair, and in the case of
the warships to make ready to repel the expected German attack. The urgency, the pressure, the bombing and shelling, the
navigation through wreckage-strewn waters pockmarked with
shallows, sandbars, and mines was suddenly over. For many
who manned those vessels, the final return must have been, as it
was for Wake-Walker, "like waking from a dream."

At 2:23 that afternoon, the Admiralty in London officially

announced, "Operation Dynamo now completed." The official War Office communiqué said, "The outstanding success of this operation, which must rank as one of the most difficult operations of war ever undertaken, has been due to the magnificent fighting qualities of the Allied troops; to their calmness and discipline in the worst of conditions; to the devotion of the Allied navies; and to the gallantry of the RAF. Although our losses have been considerable, they are small in comparison with those which a few days ago seemed inevitable."

On that last day of Dynamo, 26,175 troops—almost all French—had been ferried to England from Dunkirk. The final total evacuated, including the "useless mouths" lifted off in the days just before Operation Dynamo was launched, was 364,628—224,686 British. Within days, many of the French troops would return to France to try in vain to help stem the total conquest of their nation by Hitler's armies. But to the immense relief of Churchill, the High Command in London, and the people of Britain, the British army, so nearly lost, was home.

Finale

> Had a combined staff been told to investigate the problem of evacuating 300,000 men from a harbor and beaches under the shadow of hostile shore based aircraft and in close contact with the enemy's troops, it is probable that their appreciation would have been very pessimistic. It is even possible that by all known rules the operation could have been summed up as impossible.
>
> —Royal Navy report, June 18, 1940

The impossible may have been accomplished. The British troops brought back from Dunkirk may have been welcomed in England as if they were heroes returning in triumph rather than an army of ragged soldiers who had found themselves in a very tight spot from which they had had to be extracted. Newspapers throughout the land were rhapsodizing about the skill and daring with which the operation had been carried out. But the fact remained that Britain had just suffered a major defeat, acknowledged by Churchill in his refusal to authorize the minting of a Dunkirk medal for the evacuees.

Not a few Britons wondered what the cheering was all about. More than sixty-eight thousand men of the British Expeditionary Force had been killed, captured, or wounded or were missing in action, including at least two thousand killed or wounded by enemy action during the course of Operation Dynamo. The families of casualties already knew that they were dead or wounded or hadn't heard of their safe return and feared the worst.

RAF Fighter Command had lost 106 fighter aircraft and eighty fighter pilots during the operation and was urgently tallying up its resources for the expected enemy aerial assault on the homeland. RAF Bomber Command had lost seventy-seven of its aircraft. Of 693 British ships which had taken part in the operation, 226 had been sunk, including six destroyers. Nineteen other destroyers had been put out of action. Seventeen of 168 ships of the other Allies had also been sunk. The bulk of the British army's heavy equipment—including virtually all its tanks and antitank guns and heavy artillery, as well as sixty-four thousand vehicles, almost all of the army's machine guns, and half a million tons of stores and ammunition—had been left behind in France.

The experience of the BEF had been catastrophic. There were many who maintained that despite everything that had happened, the performance of both officers and men under pressure had been above reproach, considering the circumstances. But there were others for whom the simple, unpalatable fact was that the British army had been driven into the sea and that it was too easy to hold the French exclusively to blame. Inevitably, there was some second-guessing about what should have been done and who should be held responsible. The irrepressible General Montgomery—who was convinced that Gort was a total incompetent—insisted on a private interview with Chief of Staff General Dill to tell him that certain officers were not fit to command. Dill subsequently felt obliged to put a stop to the backbiting in a message to all divisional commanders.

> I learn there is a certain amount of rather loose criticism going on among commanders of the BEF regarding the manner in which their seniors, their equals and their juniors conducted the recent operations in France and Belgium. Such criticism is calculated to shake the confidence of the Army in its leaders of all ranks, and I need not emphasise the dangers, particularly at a time like the present. I look to you to put a stop to all this. Any failings of commanders or staff officers should be submitted confidentially through the proper channels but on no account must they be discussed unofficially.

It would be a long time before some of the men who had
gone through the horror of Dunkirk would recover their emotional balance. Many had seen their comrades killed and had
almost been killed themselves. Many could not easily shake free
of the recollection of terror at being dive-bombed or strafed or
floundering in the water after rescue vessels had been blasted
from under them. Some were subject to terrifying nightmares
for long afterward. Some who during the retreat and on the
beaches had behaved in ways they preferred to forget at the expense of their comrades or the men who served under them had
trouble coming to terms with themselves. They had seen the
face of war and had been confounded, frightened, and humiliated by it. Many withdrew within themselves for weeks and
months after their homecoming, seeming dazed and saying little.
Pretentious newspaper claims that all the returned soldiers
wanted now was "another crack at Jerry" were the fabrications
of people who had no idea of what the men had gone through.

Despite all of this, army morale was on the whole much
better than might have been expected. The nation was in danger, and a sense of urgency and commitment in preparing to
repel the enemy prevailed. Inevitably, many feared for the future. But though deeply worried by what might lie in store, the
people of Britain and their leaders, buoyed up by the rescue of
their army, were generally confident that whatever happened,
all would work out well in the end. This would be called the
Dunkirk Spirit, the belief in ultimate triumph regardless of the
odds and no matter how forbidding the long, bleak corridor that
had to be traversed. Most important for practical purposes,
RAF Fighter Command, believing its own vastly inflated kill
claims, had emerged from the operation convinced that, despite its losses, it was more than a match for the German air
force, against which it would soon have to defend the skies over
Britain.

Nevertheless, in cold, practical terms, the outlook for the
country generally was not at all promising. France was about to
be forced to its knees and the British knew they were about to
stand alone against the might of Nazi Germany whose triumphant, better equipped forces sat perched a mere twenty miles
away across the Channel. The Luftwaffe had already taken possession of airfields a few minutes flying time from the English
coast. For all its confidence in the final outcome, Britain anx-

iously awaited a rain of death from its skies and ruthless ma-
rauders at its shores.

It was left to Churchill, who would have been destroyed
politically if Operation Dynamo had been a fiasco, to offer a
public summing-up of the situation when the House of Commons assembled a few hours after the conclusion of the operation. He confessed that it had seemed to him that the "whole
root and core and brain of the British Army . . . [had been]
about to perish upon the field or to be led into an ignominious
and starving captivity." But he would not let his people delude
themselves into believing that in having to be rescued from annihilation, the BEF had achieved a victory. "Wars," he declared,
"are not won by evacuations." Nor did he permit the deliverance of the British army to detract from public awareness of
the great danger which still confronted the country.

However, he did invoke the remarkable achievement of
Operation Dynamo to shore up public confidence in final victory
in the war no matter what difficulties lay ahead. In one of the
most memorable public speeches of modern times, he proclaimed unwavering defiance of Nazi Germany.

> Even though large tracts of Europe and many old and fa-
> mous States have fallen or may fall into the grip of the Ges-
> tapo and all the odious apparatus of Nazi rule, we shall not
> flag or fail. We shall go on to the end. We shall fight in
> France, we shall fight on the seas and oceans, we shall fight
> with growing confidence and growing strength in the air, we
> shall defend our island, whatever the cost may be. We shall
> fight on the beaches, we shall fight on the landing grounds,
> we shall fight in the fields and in the streets, we shall fight in
> the hills; we shall never surrender, and even if, which I do
> not for the moment believe, this island or a large part of it
> were subjugated and starving, then our Empire beyond the
> seas, armed and guarded by the British Fleet, would carry
> on the struggle, until, in God's good time, the new world,
> with all its power and might, steps forth to the rescue and
> the liberation of the old.

In the weeks that followed, Churchill was able to employ
his extraordinary personal qualities to prune away remaining
doubts in Parliament, the Foreign Office, and the War Office
about his ability to lead Britain in its moment of supreme peril.

The most articulate exponent of the Dunkirk Spirit, the prime minister was soon a hero even to men who had scorned his abilities a few weeks before. Like the weary, hungry Tommies who had peered anxiously out to sea from the Dunkirk beaches and who had scooted along the eastern breakwater to be embarked, the man who would lead Britain back from the edge of defeat had been rescued by Operation Dynamo.

Postscript

As the last of Operation Dynamo's rescue vessels reached port in England, the German army command proclaimed that the triumph of its forces in northern France and Belgium would "go down in military history as the greatest battle of annihilation of all time." Hitler could boast that his armies had scored a tremendous victory. In less than a month, the British had been driven out of Europe and France was staggering toward capitulation. But though he did not know it, and though further notable victories lay ahead for him, the German leader had more reason to be downcast than elated. The escape of the British Expeditionary Force from Dunkirk was the first step toward the defeat of his armies, the collapse of his Nazi empire, and his own suicide five years later. Dunkirk was the beginning of the end of the Third Reich.

Ifs and buts are uncomfortable factors in any equation. But from what had gone before and from what was to follow, it is not unreasonable to conjure up the elements of an alternative scenario, a what-might-have-been if Hitler had not stopped his panzers on the Canal Line for three days, if Gort had not made his decision to withdraw to the coast, if the weather in the English Channel had been as blustery as it usually is, or if the Royal Navy and Royal Air Force had not made the great escape possible.

Before Hitler learned that the BEF had been extracted from the Dunkirk trap and that Britain still had an army, he confidently told one of his senior generals that he expected the British to come to a "sensible peace arrangement" so that he could turn his attention to conquering the Soviet Union. Even afterward, when France was forced to capitulate, the German dictator bombarded Britain with a spate of armistice proposals through neutral intermediaries. If Operation Dynamo had been a fiasco rather than the masterstroke of improvisation it turned out to be, Britain, the bulk of its army in captivity, would have had to give very serious consideration to whatever peace terms Hitler was prepared to offer.

Churchill's uncompromising determination not even to examine whether an honorable compromise settlement could be negotiated with triumphant Nazi Germany had already exasperated Lord Halifax. Other senior figures in London also wondered whether acceptable terms could be found that would spare Britain the death and devastation Hitler's air force promised to deliver. In their search for a way to extract Britain from the war, they would have been joined by countless others of their countrymen and countrywomen worried about the fate of a quarter of a million British young men who would have been held hostage by the Germans.

Having been chosen prime minister to lead the British to victory, Churchill would instead have led them to the most ruinous rout in their history within weeks of taking office. His position would have been untenable. With prominent figures critical of his leadership, it is likely he would have had to step down. If victory in the war appeared unattainable and devastation imminent, popular pressure for peace on whatever "honorable" terms could be extracted from Hitler would have been well-nigh impossible for any British government to resist.

If Britain had been removed from the war at that stage, the situation would have been fundamentally altered as well for the Soviet Union and the United States. For the Soviet Union, the consequences would have been grim indeed. The Battle of Britain, in which the Germans tried but failed to seize mastery of the skies over Britain, would not have taken place. During that historic battle, which commenced six weeks after the conclusion of Operation Dynamo, the Luftwaffe lost 1,882 aircraft as well as great numbers of its most experienced pilots and bomber crews. Had they not been lost, Hitler would have had an air force more than half again as large as the one at his disposal when his blitzkrieg against the Soviet Union was launched the following June.

In addition, he would have been able to dispatch up to forty more divisions of troops against Russia, ones which he would not have needed to deploy on his Atlantic Wall, elsewhere in Western Europe, and in combat against the British in the desert sands of Western Egypt and Libya. Even without those additional divisions and aircraft, the German army took some three million Soviet prisoners of war during the first four months of its invasion of Russia. Within the first five months, it occupied territory inhabited by 40 percent of the entire Soviet population. Before winter set in, the Germans had cracked Moscow's outer defenses and the Soviet government had felt obliged to begin abandoning the city.

It is not difficult to imagine even greater Soviet reverses if the German armed forces had not had to contend with the consequences of the escape of the British army from Dunkirk. They might have launched their invasion of Russia early in May of 1941 instead of late in June and covered much more ground before the weather turned. Moscow might have fallen. Leningrad too. And the historic winter battle of Stalingrad, which foretold the doom of Nazi Germany, might well have had a different conclusion.

During the first winter of the German invasion of the Soviet Union, the United States began shipping desperately needed war equipment to the Russians to help them bring the German advance to a halt and then go on the offensive. But if Dunkirk had been a fiasco and if Britain had been forced out of the war as a result, it is likely the United States would have stuck to its earlier determination not to be drawn into the European conflict. According to Secretary of State Cordell Hull, "Had we had any doubt of Britain's determination to keep on fighting, we would not have taken the steps we did to get material aid to her." And if not to Britain, certainly not to Communist Russia. This is not to suggest that the Soviet Union, the largest nation on earth, would necessarily have been crushed. But a different outcome to the war, and to the character of postwar Russia, might indeed have resulted.

The fall of France three weeks after the BEF had been rescued came as a great shock to Americans. But the determination of Britain to hold out against Nazi Germany, the blossoming of the Dunkirk Spirit, aroused admiration, sympathy, and growing support across the United States. The day after the conclusion of Operation Dynamo, the *Washington Evening Star* reflected government and popular feeling in America in asserting, "It is a matter of inestimable importance to our own security that we should instantly remove all restrictions on the rendering of realistic, material aid to the Allies." A few days later, Secretary of the Treasury Morgenthau confided to an official, "We are doing everything we can, within and without the law," to get the flow of arms to the Allies going. After that, direct American involvement in the war, essential for blocking Nazi domination of the western world, became inevitable.

All things considered, the escape from Dunkirk was one of those rare events when, in a matter of only a few days, accident and design conspired to check and ultimately turn the tide of history.

Acknowledgments

Thanks are due to a great many people whose assistance was of great value in the writing of this book. They include the late Harold Robinson, who, as general secretary of the Dunkirk Veterans Association, offered wise and informed advice. Of great help in London were the staffs of the following: the Documents and Printed Books Divisions of the Imperial War Museum; the British Library at the British Museum; the London Library; the Colindale Newspaper Library; the documents section of the National Maritime Museum at Greenwich; the Public Record Office at Kew; the much-neglected, excellent Special Collection at the West Hill Branch of the Public Library in Wandsworth; and the Reading Room of the National Army Museum in Chelsea. The staffs of the Military Reference section of the National Archives in Washington, D.C., and of the Franklin Delano Roosevelt Library at Hyde Park, New York, were also most helpful. My thanks too to Eric Munday of the Air Historical Branch of the Ministry of Defense in London; Paul Melton of the Royal Navy Historical Branch; and K. W. Scott of English Heritage for showing me around the remains of Operation Dynamo headquarters in the cliffs of Dover.

Particular thanks to the survivors of Dunkirk, including those I met during the Dunkirk Veterans Association pilgrimage to Dunkirk in May 1988, who were good enough to permit me to probe their memories and who, in some cases, lent or showed me personal diaries, letters, photographs, and other unpublished materials, especially John Agate, Stanley Allen, General John Carpenter, Sid Dodd, James Else, F. R. Farley, Harry Genders,

Leslie Ginsburg, Tom Griffiths, Patrick Hennessy, Arthur Hopkins, Professor William Kershaw, Richard Maycock, Major Richard Merritt, Commander Stanley Nettle, Tom Noyce, Ernest Richards, Victor Slaughter, Frank Tabrar, Cyril Thompson, Albert White, Major Bernard Whiting, General Ashton Wade, and Bill Warwick.

I am grateful to Lieutenant Colonel Michael Burkham, Royal Welsh Fusiliers, who was good enough to read the manuscript of this book and offer wise and helpful criticism, though any errors that remain are my own.

Thanks most of all to my wife, Barbara, for her advice and moral support.

Notes

Abbreviations:

FDR - Franklin Delano Roosevelt Library, Hyde Park, New York.
IWM - Imperial War Museum, London.
NA - National Archives, Washington D.C.
NAM - National Army Museum, London.
NHB - Navy Historical Branch, London.
NMM - National Maritime Museum, London.
PRO - Public Record Office, London.

The ranks by which the Dunkirk veterans cited below are identified are those they held at the time of the Dunkirk evacuation.

15. "I should count it a privilege": Cadogan, p. 327.
18. The soil of Europe: Adolf Hitler, *Mein Kampf* (London: Hurst and Blackett, 1939), p. 541.
19. "I spend my nights": Gilbert, Vol. 5, p. 850.
20. "He would be a rash man": CAB 23/90, PRO.
20. "Heaven knows": Hearden, p. 156.
22. "every resource of material": London *Times,* March 20, 1936.
22. "Aircraft do not decide": Chapman, p. 22.
23. "the mistake of living": Jordan A. Schwarz, *Liberal: Adolf A. Berle and the Vision of an American Era* (New York: The Free Press, 1987), p. 131.
25. "no belief whatever": Feiling, p. 403.
26. Former President Herbert Hoover: John Caughey and Ernest May, *A History of the United States* (Chicago: Rand McNally, 1964), p. 572.
26. William Dodd, the American ambassador: Arnold Offner, *American Appeasement* (Cambridge: Belknap Press, 1969), p. 104.

26. "I have seen war": *The Public Papers and Addresses of Franklin D. Roosevelt,* Vol. 5 (New York: Random House, 1938), speech, August 14, 1936.

27. "Germany does not have": Hearden, p. 160.

27. Walter Lippman advised: Nathan Miller, *FDR: An Intimate History* (Garden City, N.Y.: Doubleday, 1983), p. 421.

28. Charles Lindbergh was warmly received: Wayne Cole, *Roosevelt and the Isolationists* (Lincoln: University of Nebraska Press, 1983), p. 280.

28. Hugh Wilson, the American ambassador: Offner, op. cit., p. 177.

28. "What an avalanche": Langer, p. 470.

29. "Considering the situation": Shirer, *Third Republic,* p. 262.

29. "The Germans, after all": Offner, op. cit., p. 142.

32. "like little boys": Bullitt, p. 287.

32. "Like frightened householders": Malcolm Muggeridge, *The Thirties* (London: Hamish Hamilton, 1940), p. 291.

33. "in future warfare": Lord Carver, *Twentieth Century Warriors* (London: Weidenfeld & Nicolson, 1987), p. 27.

34. "Czechoslovakia has ceased": Shirer, *Third Republic,* p. 448.

34. "effectively defended": *Trial of the Major War Criminals Before the International Military Tribunal* (Nuremberg: International Military Tribunal, 1948), p. 606.

35. "at once . . . lend": *Hansard,* March 31, 1939.

35. "to tear each other to pieces": Cowling, p. 302.

35. "With the Germans we risk": Horne, p. 79.

37. On August 31, 1939: *Nazi Conspiracy and Aggression,* Vol. 5 (Washington: Office of the United States Chief of Counsel for Prosecution of Axis Criminality, U.S. Government Printing Office, 1946), p. 391.

37. "The Polish State," Hitler explained: *Documents on British Foreign Policy,* Vol. 7 (London: Her Majesty's Stationery Office, 1954), p. 473.

38. "nearer to real panic": Joseph Harsch, *Pattern of Conquest* (London: Heinemann, 1942), p. 37.

38. "At twilight the air raid siren": Joseph Barnes, *New York Herald Tribune,* September 2, 1939.

38. "The people cannot": William Shirer, *Berlin Diary* (London: Hamish Hamilton, 1941), p. 161.

39. "It now only remains": London *Times,* September 2, 1939.

39. "Speak for England, Arthur": Angus Calder, *The People's War* (London: Cape, 1969), p. 33.

39. "crumpled, despondent and old": London *Daily Express,* September 4, 1967.

40. "Here is one war": London *Times,* September 4, 1939, quoting *New York World Telegram.*

41. "except in one or two": Sumner Welles, *The Time for Decision* (New York: Harper, 1944), p. 75.
41. "every effort will be made": *New York Herald Tribune,* September 2, 1939.
41. "As long as it remains": Basil Rauch, *Roosevelt—From Munich to Pearl Harbor* (New York: Da Capo Press, 1975), p. 138.
41. "precipitate action": CAB 65/1, PRO.
42. "to arouse the Germans to a higher morality": Churchill, Vol. 1, p. 330.
42. "Are you aware": Spears, Vol. 1, p. 32.
42. "That means the war is really on": Albert Speer, *Inside the Third Reich* (London: Weidenfeld & Nicolson, 1970), p. 165.
43. Some reservists who had gone off: Interview with Lance Corporal Albert White, Royal Signals, October 1987.
43. "In London, the universe": MID 2060-1130/100, NA.
44. "During September": Westphal, p. 71.
45. "minor attacks": Turnbull, p. 32.
45. "Our duty as an ally": François Fonvielle-Alquier, *The French and the Phoney War* (London: Tom Stacey, 1973), p. 94.
45. "There is not a village": London *Daily Mail,* September 4, 1939.
45. "French Army Pouring": London *Daily Mail,* September 7, 1939.
45. "Soldiers of France": Shirer, *Third Republic,* p. 501.
46. "people began to say": Alfred Duff Cooper, *Old Men Forget* (London: Rupert Hart-Davis, 1953), p. 206.
46. "After listening to it all": *Foreign Relations of the United States, 1939,* Vol. 1 (Washington: U.S. Government Printing Office, 1956), p. 441.
47. "Joe has always been an appeaser": Henry Morgenthau, Jr., *Presidential Diaries,* Microfiche, Card 4, FDR.
48. "even begin to know": Ironside, p. 83.
48. "not very clever man": Spears, Vol. 1, p. 34.
48. "had no confidence": Bryant, p. 41.
50. "higher headquarters": Halder.
50. "My chief endeavor": Shirer, *Third Reich,* p. 641.
50. "for an attacking operation": Ibid., p. 644.
51. "to exploit favorable weather": Ibid., p. 656.
51. a total of eleven times: Liddell Hart, p. 117.
51. It was a savage winter: Interviews with Gunner Sidney Dodd, Royal Artillery, August 1987; Sergeant Richard Merritt, Royal Artillery, January 1988; and others.
52. "that such a catastrophe": Gilbert, Vol. 6, p. 47.
52. "judging from his record": Colville, *Fringes of Power,* p. 29.
55. "The enemy," Hitler said: Liddell Hart, p. 60.
55. "the protection of the Reich": Shirer, *Third Reich,* p. 697.
57. "advising and giving orders": Shirer, *Third Republic,* p. 547.

57. "lack of brains": Bullitt, p. 411.

58. "You have sat too long": *Hansard,* May 7, 1940.

62. "So there's to be": Bartlett, p. 47.

62. "The battle which begins today": Horne, p. 198.

63. "Everything wonderful": *The Rommel Papers,* ed. B. H. Liddell Hart (London: Collins, 1953), p. 7.

63. "reports on the whole": Halder, p. 3.

63. "by means of sirens": BBC broadcast, May 10, 1940, BBC Archives Centre.

64. "It is now France's turn": Ibid.

65. "speedily become more or less": Birkenhead, p. 269.

65. "It was only the realization": Cowling, p. 383.

65. "I cannot yet think": David Duff, *George and Elizabeth* (London: Collins, 1983), p, 174.

66. "I hope it is not": W. H. Thompson, *I Was Churchill's Shadow* (London: Christopher Johnson, 1951), p. 37.

66. "The Tories don't trust": Gilbert, Vol. 6, p. 327.

66. described him as "useless": Cadogan, p. 277.

66. "has not got the stability": Ironside, p. 248.

66. "We had known of Churchill": Sir Ian Jacob, *Atlantic Monthly,* March 1965.

66. "the mere thought of Churchill": John Colville, in John Wheeler-Bennett, ed., *Action This Day* (London: Macmillan, 1968), p. 48.

67. "the country had fallen": Ibid.

67. "You ask," he told Parliament: *Hansard,* May 13, 1940.

68. "Quite intolerable": Birkenhead, p. 457.

68. "There seems to be": Gilbert, Vol. 6, p. 327.

68. "The battle is joined": Horne, p. 191.

68. "We shall see": Baudouin, p. 27.

70. "It is not often": Calder, op. cit., p. 85.

70. "the German hordes": Gilbert, Vol. 6, p. 306.

71. "So far so good": Pownall, p. 309.

71. welcomed by the cheering, waving: Interview with Private Cyril Thompson, Suffolk Regiment, May 1988.

71. "Are they letting us": Baudouin, p. 28.

71. "An offensive on the scale": London *Daily Mail,* May 11, 1940.

71. "no defense works": Goutard, p. 110.

72. "A long battle": Ironside, p. 302.

72. "This time at least": London *Times,* May 11, 1940.

74. trouble getting into his car: André Maurois, *Why France Fell* (London: The Bodley Head, 1941), p. 89.

74. Several of its most senior officers: Goutard, p. 104.

75. "Bouillon is a summer resort": Horne, p. 194.

75. "avoid bombing": Ibid., p. 196.

76. "main thing is our and French troops": Cadogan, p. 282.

76. "to get accurate information": Baudouin, p. 28.

77. "Almost the whole": Cooper, *German Air Force,* p. 115.

77. "The gunners stopped firing": Goutard, p. 133.

78. "If I am obliged": Shirer, *Third Republic,* p. 625.

79. "means victory or defeat": Goutard, p. 138.

79. "The atmosphere was that": Bond, *France and Belgium,* p. 102.

80. "I confess": Shirer, *Third Republic,* p. 596.

80. "Almost every evening": Bullitt, p. 423.

81. "There was no intelligence": Interview with Flight Lieutenant Frederick Rosier, December 1984.

82. "One aircraft!": Interview with Flight Lieutenant Sir Archibald Hope, January 1985.

82. "ten times more than Britain": BBC broadcast, May 11, 1940, BBC Archives Centre.

82. "we cannot continue": Richards, p. 119.

82. "these calls . . . will continue": Ironside, p. 308.

83. "bled white and in no condition": Richards, p. 123.

84. "report at once": London *Daily Sketch,* May 11, 1940.

84. "The only thing to tell": Alexander Kendrick, *Prime Time* (London: Dent and Sons, 1970), p. 197.

85. "to defend by every means": *New York Times,* May 11, 1940.

85. "an orgy of destruction": Ibid., May 14, 1940.

85. the United States must be prepared: Langer and Gleason, p. 473.

86. "The voice and force": PREM 3/468, PRO.

86. "vigorously contested": *New York Times,* May 13, 1940.

86. "if things kept up": Lash, p. 123.

86. "There are no real leaders": Harold L. Ickes, *The Secret Diaries of Harold L. Ickes,* Vol. 3 (New York: Simon & Schuster, 1954), p. 146.

87. "holding the bag": *Foreign Relations of the United States, 1940,* Vol. 1 (Washington: U.S. Government Printing Office, 1959), p. 222.

88. "unless . . . things got": Lash, p. 128.

88. "The question of whether": Ibid.

91. "The German advance": Horne, p. 298.

91. "When the destiny of France": Ibid., p. 278.

91. "No information": Chapman, p. 152.

91. "I spent more than an hour": Bloch, p. 28.

92. "No one really wanted": Goutard, p. 181.

92. "were quite frankly": Major O. A. Archdale, War Notes, IWM.

94. "Taxis hooted": Clare Booth, *European Spring* (London: Heinemann, 1941), p. 270.

94. "The German army has pierced": Paul Reynaud, *In the Thick of the Fight* (London: Cassell, 1955), p. 310.

95. "We are beaten": Churchill, Vol. 2, p. 38.

95. "seen a good deal": Ibid., p. 39.
95. "What you tell me": Pertinax (pseudonym), *The Gravediggers of France* (Garden City, N.Y.: Doubleday, 1944), p. 75.
95. "unless God grants": Shirer, *Third Republic,* p. 659.
95. "in an indescribable disorder": Spears, Vol. 1, p. 146.
96. "If this goes on": Baudouin, p. 30.
97. "obvious that the situation": Gilbert, Vol. 6, p. 349.
97. "Where is the strategic reserve": Churchill, Vol. 2, p. 42.
97. "The hard point": Baudouin, p. 32.
98. "We had a right to know": Churchill, Vol. 2, p. 43.
98. "into a warlike mood": Colville, *Man of Valour,* p. 197.
98. "the first necessity": CAB 65/13, PRO.
100. "drained away": Francis Mason, *Battle over Britain* (London: McWhirter Twins Ltd., 1969), p. 115.
100. "whatever the need": Gilbert, vol. 6, p. 366.
101. "It was no uncommon occurrence": CAB 65/13, PRO.
101. water level so low: Pertinax, op. cit., p. 76.
101. Belgian civilians who had welcomed their arrival: White interview.
102. wrong turning: Nicolson and Forbes, p. 22.
102. it became one retreat after another: Merritt interview.
102. "withdrawal party prepare": A. M. Bell MacDonald, War Journal, IWM.
102. "We weren't given": Merritt interview.
102. "We have slept": letter home from Sapper A. J. Hooker, IWM.
102. "Germans have broken through": Bell MacDonald, op. cit.
102. "in no mood to halt": W. G. Blaxland, Personal Journal, IWM.
103. "endless mining towns": Bell MacDonald, op. cit.
103. subjected to the attentions of Stuka: Merritt interview; interview with Corporal Harold Robinson, Royal West Kents, May 1988, and others.
103. "It seemed all hell": L. H. Vollans, Personal Journal, IWM.
103. The wretched refugees: White interview and others.
104. "The Fuehrer is terribly nervous": Halder, p. 17.
104. "frightened by his own temerity": Guderian, p. 109.
105. "My country has been beaten": Shirer, *Third Republic,* p. 677.
106. "I am shattered with fatigue": Archdale, op. cit.
106. "be at liberty to appeal": Ellis, p. 11.
106. "singularly stupid and unhelpful": Pownall, p. 323.
107. "bomb trap": CAB 65/13, PRO.
107. the "unlikely" possibility: ADM 199/792, PRO.
109. "a scandalous—i.e. Winstonian": Pownall, p. 323.
110. "in a state of complete depression": Ironside, p. 321.
110. "Situation desperate": Ibid., p. 328.

110. "Worst of all": Sumner Welles, *The Time for Decision* (New York: Harper, 1944), p. 119.

111. "absolutely reliable" informant: *Foreign Relations of the United States, 1940,* Vol. 1, p. 224.

111. A stiff return message: President's Secretary's File, Safe Box 5, FDR.

111. "I think it may possibly be": Bullitt, p. 427.

111. The British ambassador in Washington: Lash, p. 135.

112. "If members of this administration": Roosevelt-Churchill Correspondence, May 20, 1940, FDR.

114. "not only that our codes": Lash, p. 137.

115. scamper unceremoniously back: Interview with Guardsman Thomas Griffiths, Welsh Guards, January 1988.

115. Guderian's newly committed: Guderian, p. 114.

116. "The only complaint": Baudouin, p. 39.

117. "at the earliest moment": Ellis, p. 111.

117. "Can nobody prevent him": Pownall, p. 333.

117. "criticism . . . that the BEF": Colville, *Man of Valour,* p. 215.

117. "Clearly at home": Pownall, p. 340.

118. "tell the government": John Cairns, "Great Britain and the Fall of France," *Journal of Modern History,* December 1955.

118. put on half rations: Interview with Guardsman Thomas Noyce, Grenadier Guards, December 1987.

118. living off the land: Interview with Second Lieutenant John Carpenter, Royal Army Service Corps, February 1988.

118. "a sort of licensed pillage": Bell MacDonald, op. cit.

119. "gathered the impression": Bryant, p. 119.

119. Blanchard was overheard: Bloch, p. 110.

119. Blanchard incapable of command: Colville, *Man of Valour,* p. 214.

119. Marshal Pétain also suggested: Spears, Vol. 1, p. 230.

120. "overcome by the defection": Baudouin, p. 45.

120. "criminal" to have sent: Ibid., 46.

120. "incredible mistakes": BBC broadcast, May 21, 1940, BBC Archives Centre.

120. "always made for harbors": Horne, p. 478.

120. "In the voice of a seasick passenger": Spears, Vol. 1, p. 189.

121. "any relatively advantageous offer": Baudouin, p. 53.

121. It was his contention: Ibid., p. 54.

122. "We know nothing": Blaxland, p. 184.

122. "I must know at earliest": Gilbert, Vol. 6, p. 394.

122. "Gort seems—inexplicably": Cadogan, p. 289.

123. large white balloonlike objects: CAB 80/11, PRO.

123. "there appeared to be": CAB 120/439, PRO.

123. "might be faced with a situation": CAB 65/13, PRO.
124. "His Majesty's Government are confident": Gilbert, Vol. 6, p. 395.
124. "Nothing but a miracle": Bryant, p. 117.
124. "On many occasions": WO 197/119, PRO.
125. a British liaison officer: Blaxland, p. 250.
126. "the ring around the British": Masefield, p. 90.
126. "looking rather bewildered": Archdale, op. cit.
127. "The defection of the English": Baudouin, p. 56.
128. They included medical orderlies: Robinson interview.
130. Panzer Group commander von Kleist: Hans-Adolf Jacobsen and Juergen Rohwer, *Decisive Battles of World War II: The German View* (London: Andre Deutsch, 1965), p. 54.
130. "The principal thing now": Ellis, p. 150.
130. "would give an unconditional assurance": Walter Warlimont, *Inside Hitler's Headquarters* (London: Weidenfeld & Nicolson, 1964), p. 98.
131. "occupy the territory": Jacobsen and Rohwer, p. 56.
131. "divergence of views": Halder, p. 35.
131. "It was forbidden to cross": Guderian, p. 117.
131. "which has no enemy before it": Halder, p. 35.
132. "Are we going to build": Goutard, p. 230.
132. ordered to withdraw them: Liddell Hart, p. 139.
136. "for our soldiers in dire peril": London *Times,* May 27, 1940.
137. she had shouted "Peace": *New York Herald Tribune,* May 27, 1940.
137. "I have had information": PREM 3/204, PRO.
137. ". . . in the meantime": Ibid.
138. "I must not conceal from you": Ibid.
138. "I never thought I'd lead": Richard Collier, *1940: The World in Flames* (London: Hamish Hamilton, 1979), p. 16.
138. "This bridgehead": Divine, p. 83.
138. examine possibilities for "reembarkation": Ellis, p. 174.
139. Darlan's reflexive response: Goutard, p. 238.
139. "suddenly realized . . . that": Spears, Vol. 1, p. 192.
139. Morale among British troops: Thompson interview.
139. Frontline regular infantry units: Noyce interview.
139. "It's every man for himself": Interview with Gunner Victor Slaughter, Field Artillery, May 1988.
139. "as though we were an army": Gun Buster, p. 173.
139. ". . . the Germans may try": Ironside, p. 335.
139. "so that you can take": Harold Nicolson, *Diaries and Letters: 1930-1964,* ed. Stanley Olson (London: Collins, 1980), p. 186.
140. "will seem trifling": Anthony Weymouth, *Plague Year* (London: Harrap, 1942), p. 87.

140. "within a few weeks": *Washington Post,* May 26, 1940.

140. "great secret weapon": Ibid.

140. "I believe that the British": Microcopy, M982/740.0011/3274/8/10, FDR.

140. Churchill prepared to plead: CAB 80/11, PRO.

141. Reynaud said that he feared: Gilbert, Vol. 6, p. 403.

142. "We must take care": Cosgrave, p. 213.

142. "we would not": Gilbert, Vol. 6, p. 404.

142. whatever happened to France: Ibid.

142. "possible to get out": CAB 65/13, PRO.

143. "postulate the destruction of our independence": Gilbert, Vol. 6, p. 404.

143. "too rambling and romantic": Ibid.

143. "If we could get": Collier, op. cit, p. 68.

143. "The only one who understands": Baudouin, p. 58.

144. "Prime Minister has had": Ellis, p. 174.

145. "forbids evacuation": Ellis, p. 165.

145. "for the sake of": Ibid.

145. "Whether we ever get to the sea": Pownall, p. 342.

145. "we shall be lucky": Bryant, p. 134.

146. "nearly reached the limit": *Belgium—The Official Account of What Happened* (London: Evans Brothers, 1941), p. 46.

146. "Our armored and mechanized forces": Halder, p. 37.

146. "Operation Dynamo is to commence": T.S.D. 64/48, NHB.

147. "It is imperative": Ibid.

147. He thought the BEF: Ironside, p. 234.

147. "two vessels every four hours": ADM 792/199.

149. "In war," Morrison told people: *The Listener,* May 30, 1940.

149. "whether the Allied forces": MID 2016, 1297/107, NA.

150. code-named Rainbow: Conn and Fairchild, p. 34.

150. "protective occupation": WPD 4157-7, NA.

150. ". . . if the bad boys win": Letter from Charles H. Baker, Jr., to President Roosevelt, May 16, 1940, FDR.

151. ". . . if [the British colony of] Bermuda": President's Official File, 335/Box 2, FDR.

151. control of several commercial airlines: London *Daily Mail,* June 1, 1940.

151. "initiate conversations": WPD 4115-14, NA.

151. "The only sure way": Ibid., 4115-15.

152. "You're going to need it": *New York Times,* June 4, 1940.

152. six thousand Nazis: Watson, p. 95.

152. code-named Pot-of-Gold: Ibid.

152. "Tonight over the once peaceful": May 26, 1940. *Public and Private Addresses of Franklin Delano Roosevelt,* 1940 volume, FDR.

153. a charade meant to scare the American people: *New York Times,* May 28, 1940.

153. The Army had: Watson, p. 305.
157. a proposal from Weygand: Ellis, p. 198.
157. "extremely difficult": ADM 199/792, PRO.
158. "the only authority": Ibid.
158. Early that morning: D.W. Hughes, *History of Tough Brothers of Teddington,* IWM.
158. "There they lay": Ibid.
159. "personal appeal": Ellis, p. 198.
159. "Situation demands hard hitting": Ibid.
159. "quite clear that sole task": Divine, p. 96.
160. "Until French ships materialize": ADM 199/792, PRO.
160. "I have been sent by Lord Gort": Goddard, p. 251.
161. Massacre at Paradis: Blaxland, p. 286.
162. "At every position": Ellis, p. 191.
162. "BRITISH SOLDIERS": Barker, p. 145.
162. "We sat down on chairs": Howard and Sparrow, p. 49.
163. "Large ships are being made fast": Jacobsen and Rohwer, p. 65.
163. "The [withdrawal] plan": Supplement to *London Gazette,* October 17, 1941.
163. "It is no good": Pownall, p. 344.
164. "ensure the protection": *RAF Narrative,* p. 323.
165. "We were jumped": Interview with Pilot Officer Peter Brown, April 1984.
166. The flight and combat tactics: Interview with Flight Lieutenant Robert Stanford-Tuck, December 1984.
166. Criticism of the RAF: Merritt interview and others.
167. Communist coup: Baudouin, p. 59.
167. Britain's "refusal to fight": Spears, Vol. 1, p. 235.
167. "This is awful": John Reith, *The Reith Diaries,* ed. Charles Stuart (London: Collins, 1975), p. 254.
167. "most of the cards": Gilbert, Vol. 6, p. 408.
168. "there are signs": Colville, *Fringes of Power,* p. 140.
168. "Suppose," the foreign secretary said: CAB 65/13, PRO.
169. "evil must be met by force": London *Times,* February 28, 1940.
169. "long and rather confused": Birkenhead, p. 458.
169. To Cadogan he declared: Cadogan, p. 291.
169. "If the Germans made Britain": *Foreign Relations of the United States, 1940,* Vol. 1, p. 233.
169. "Those were the days": Welles, op. cit., p. 149.
170. "practically no help": Gilbert, Vol. 6, p. 410.
170. Bermuda rather than Canada: Colville, *Fringes of Power,* p. 141.
171. "to pick up the bits": Gilbert, Vol. 6, p. 413.
171. "blood, toil, tears and sweat": *Hansard,* May 13, 1940.
172. "several men [there]": Rhodes, p. 215.

173. "Please send every available craft": "The Evacuation of the Allied Armies from Dunkirk and Neighbouring Beaches," Supplement to *London Gazette,* July 15, 1947.

173. "Dunkirk is in enemy hands": T.S.D. 64/48, NHB.

174. "with utmost despatch": Ibid.

175. "The galleys [of the destroyer Gossamer]": James Dow, "Dunkirk 1940—an Eye-Witness Account," *Journal of the Royal Naval Medical Service,* Spring 1978.

176. "[The king] wishes": Ellis, p. 198.

177. "seem to have vanished": Gilbert, Vol. 6, p. 414.

177. "No one in this country": *New York Herald Tribune,* May 27, 1940.

177. Now Duff Cooper urged in Cabinet: CAB 65/7, PRO.

177. "The situation is past belief": Chalmers, p. 73.

196. "You can rummage through": Hanson Baldwin, *The Crucial Years* (London: Weidenfeld & Nicolson, 1976), p. 119.

196. "They must now stand by us": Spears, Vol. 1, p. 253.

196. "might sting the French": CAB 65/7, PRO.

196. "The move back": Howard and Sparrow, p. 37.

197. "because the middle of the road": *Account of Movements and Actions Fought by 1st Battalion Welsh Guards in France and Flanders from 17th May to 1st June 1940,* NAM.

197. These officers soon discovered: Interviews with Commander Stanley Nettle, July 1988, and Petty Officer John Agate, August 1988.

199. "Then, and not until then": E. Hamilton-Piercy, diary, NMM.

200. "I . . . begged General Blanchard": Ellis, p. 209.

201. Massacre at Wormhout: Leslie Aitken, *Massacre on the Road to Dunkirk* (London: Kimber, 1977).

201. "From every house": Gun Buster, p. 183.

202. "crawled underneath the wreckage": Ibid., p. 214.

202. "We kept enough transport": Bartlett, p. 112.

202. "New wireless sets": Gun Buster, p. 185.

203. "like thousands of sticks": Divine, p. 145.

203. "The beach was an extraordinary sight": Hadley, p. 137.

203. "followed the crowd": Interview with Lance Bombardier Richard Maycock, Royal Artillery, May 1988.

203. "We all had one idea": Rhodes, 225.

203. "odds and sods": Maycock interview.

203. "You don't belong to us": Ibid.

204. "It would start off as a queue": Slaughter interview.

204. where they felt safer: Carpenter interview.

204. the sand muffled the bomb explosions: Noyce and White interviews.

204. "I saw a man suddenly": Rhodes, p. 228.

205. "Tired, wet and hungry": Sergeant W. C. Brodie, diary, IWM.
206. "in urgent need of repair": Ellis, p. 208.
206. "A tank attack": Ibid.
207. Sir Roger Keyes returned that day: CAB 65/7, PRO.
207. "I expect to make a statement": *Hansard,* May 28, 1940.
208. "We must not ignore the fact": CAB 65/13, PRO.
208. "We should find": Ibid.
208. "nations which went down": Ibid.
208. It should be done, the former prime minister said: Ibid.
209. "Quite a number": Churchill, Vol. 2, p. 88.
209. "supreme control": *Keesing Contemporary Archives 1937-1940,* May 27, 1940.
210. Fighter Command flew 321 sorties: *RAF Narrative.*
210. "Our men can find no words": BBC broadcast, May 31, 1940, BBC Archives Centre.
210. "For all the good": Interview with Flight Lieutenant Alan Deere, April 1984.
210. "I and the Forces": Chalmers, p. 97.
210. "Rightly or wrongly": Richards, p. 132.
211. "The sky is a big place": ADM 199/788, PRO.
211. "fighter defenses were almost": CAB, 65/7, PRO.
211. "a curious old thing": Ironside, p. 346.
212. "There can be no doubt": CAB 120/247, PRO.
212. The BEF commander asked London: CAB 65/13, PRO.
212. "We have every confidence": Ibid.
213. "It will be necessary": London *Daily Sketch,* May 29, 1940.
213. "The British Expeditionary Force": *New York Herald Tribune,* May 29, 1940.
213. "Poor chap": Pownall, p. 352.
215. "Personnel vessels": Supplement to *London Gazette,* July 15, 1947.
215. "exercising navigational caution": ADM 199/792, PRO.
216. "On arrival alongside": T.S.D. 64/48, NHB.
217. "in an endeavor to take charge": Ibid.
217. Some soldiers did row back: Interview with Gunner Patrick Hennessy, Royal Artillery, May 1988.
217. often brandishing a weapon: Agate interview.
217. "I took my revolver": Nettle interview.
218. "At three this morning": Bartlett, p. 120.
219. "dispense with full cover": ADM 199/792, PRO.
221. "On our way to the coast": Interview with Sapper Leslie Ginsberg, Royal Engineers, September 1988.
222. "A fresh traffic block": Barlone, p. 56.
222. "A party of about twenty French troops": Brodie, op. cit.

223. "a big fuss": Pownall, p. 353.
223. "to hold on to Dunkirk": Ibid.
223. "every Frenchman embarked": ADM 199/792, PRO.
223. "While it is eminently desirable": Ibid.
223. "We wish French troops": CAB 65/7, PRO.
224. "a rabble . . . panicking": Gilbert, Vol. 6, p. 428.
224. "absurd state of affairs": Baudouin, p. 63.
224. "the British government should be informed": Ibid., p. 62.
224. Orders, he said, had been given: Cosgrave, p. 225.
225. less than completely forthcoming: Ibid. p. 223.
225. "should be able to obtain": CAB 66/8, PRO.
225. omnivorous strain of grasshopper: *New York Times*, May 29, 1940.
226. "We do not consider": CAB 80/12, PRO.
226. "In these dark days": PREM 4/68/9, PRO.
227. Dill was worried: CAB 65/13, PRO.
227. "relinquish the struggle": Ibid.
227. Churchill disagreed: Ibid.
227. "If you are cut from": Ellis, p. 218.
228. "Every road scoring the landscape": Gun Buster, p. 184.
228. "Weariness came down": Howard and Sparrow, p. 47.
229. "We continued towards Malo-les-Bains": Gun Buster, p. 242.
229. "[It hung] like Death's hovering wing": Ibid., p. 214.
230. "In the basements of the houses": P. G. Ackrell, Personal Journal, IWM.
230. One soldier stumbled across: White interview.
231. "sea-going ships and vessels": ADM 199/792, PRO.
232. "Just as it would have been": Les Shorrock, Diary, IWM.
232. more "suitable motor boats": T.S.D. 64/48, NHB.
233. "had been affected by the events of the day": ADM 199/792, PRO.
234. "As soon as we have reorganized": CAB 65/7, PRO.
235. "Ships out there were sinking": Interview with Petty Officer John Agate, August 1988.
235. "not immediately engaged": BBC broadcast, May 30, 1940, BBC Archives Centre.
236. "It was a dirty, tired army": *Sheerness Times and Guardian,* June 7, 1940.
236. "Saturated with sea water": *East Kent Times,* June 5, 1940.
236. "dog-tired, wounded and unkempt": *Washington Post,* May 31, 1940.
236. "shattered remnants of the BEF": *Washington Post,* May 30, 1940.
236. "The news is bad": *Manchester Guardian,* May 30, 1940.

237. "Invasion of England": *Washington Post*, May 31, 1940.

237. Admiral of the Fleet Sir Dudley Pound: Gilbert, Vol. 6, p. 434.

237. "had the right to do": CAB 65/7, PRO.

239. "Any organization for forming groups": ADM 199/788, PRO.

240. "A destroyer going full out": Ibid.

241. "the water was like a millpond": Maycock interview.

241. "God had work for the British": Interview with Ordinary Seaman Stanley Allen, May 1988.

242. "The snag was": Divine, p. 134.

242. a man stark naked: Lieutenant R. N. Irving, Journal, MS 67/050, NMM.

243. at the port of Ramsgate alone: ADM 199/792, PRO.

243. engineer troops, among the comparatively few: Ginsberg interview.

243. "Fifteen or more lorries": Sergeant H. J. Cornwall, Journal, IWM.

244. "in the very best spirits": MS 67/050, NMM.

244. "He was told to consider": Ibid.

245. "every Frenchman embarked": Pownall, p. 356.

246. "for the good of the common cause": Gilbert, Vol. 6, p. 431.

246. "congested mass of disorganized Frenchmen": CAB 65/7, PRO.

246. "if the German armored divisions": Sir Ian Jacob, op. cit.

246. "the perimeter would be broken": Ibid.

246. A renewed plea: Spears, Vol. 1, p. 282.

246. The War Office in London: Blaxland, p. 329.

247. last "reasonable date": ADM 199/792, PRO.

248. "Continue to defend": CAB 65/7, PRO.

248. "was in an unfit state": Nicolson, *Alex*, p. 103.

249. he broke down and wept: Ibid., p. 104.

249. A report by Sir Charles Tegart: Fisk, p. 121.

250. "the Germans have concerted": PREM 3/130, PRO.

250. London was told: Ibid.

250. "until [Ireland] abandons her attitude": CAB 66/8. PRO.

251. "have the greater part": CAB 80/12, PRO.

251. "under conditions specially favorable": Ibid.

251. "ineptitude of the navy": ADM 19/792, PRO.

252. "countless thousands of the enemy": Halder, p. 43.

252. "effects of the blunders": Ibid.

252. "no one is now interested in Dunkirk": Ellis, p. 390.

252. "fighting back very stubbornly": Ibid., p. 225.

254. A newspaper cartoon: London *Daily Mirror*, May 31, 1940.

255. "a nasty surf": T.S.D. 64/48, NHB.

255. "My crew and myself": Irving Journal, op. cit.

255. "Majority of boats": ADM 199/792, PRO.

256. "Dunkirk our only hope": Ibid.
256. "Long columns of men": Sapper A. J. Hooker, Personal Journal, IWM.
256. "We have been continuously": T.S.D. 64/48, NHB.
256. "Half way along the mole": Signalman L. H. Vollans, Personal Journal, IWM.
257. Wake-Walker sent messages: ADM 199/792, PRO.
257. "Why the jetty was not blown": Letter from Sublieutenant Roger Wake published in *Kings Royal Rifle Corps Chronicle*, 1941, NAM.
257. Gort reported from La Panne: CAB 65/7, PRO.
257. In an extraordinary phone call: Ellis, p. 231.
257. Gort wanted to know: CAB 65/7, PRO.
258. his main concern had to be: Ibid.
258. Reynaud urgently renewed: Spears, Vol. 1, p. 292.
258. King George felt inclined: *The Second World War Diary of Hugh Dalton,* ed. Ben Pimlott (London: Cape, 1986), p. 31.
258. "as fresh as a daisy": Spears, Vol. 1, p. 293.
259. "But how many French": Ibid., p. 295.
259. "We are companions": Ibid.
259. "arm in arm": Baudouin, p. 69.
259. "I will not": Spears, Vol. 1, p. 308.
259. "His emotions were leading him": Ibid., p. 309.
260. "England did not fear": Gilbert, Vol. 6, p. 444.
260. "if one of the two comrades": Baudouin, p. 73.
260. "England has already coolly assumed": Ibid.
262. "realized in his heart": Spears, Vol. 1, p. 319.
262. no troops on the shore: ADM 199/792, PRO.
263. "Our motor yacht": Agate interview.
263. "A horrible stench of blood": Gun Buster, p. 245.
264. "The Kurfuerstendamm jammed": Shirer, *Berlin Diary*, p. 308.
264. "It was always impossible for me": ADM 199/792, PRO.
265. "to imperil the safety": CAB 44/69, PRO.
265. "no further organized evacuation": Ibid.
265. "His idea": William Morgan, "With Alexander to Dunkirk," *Army Quarterly,* London, April 1972.
265. Abrial threatened to use his authority: Blaxland, p. 331.
266. "General," he scolded: John Cairn, "Great Britain and the Fall of France," *Journal of Modern History,* December 1955.
266. "did not take into account": CAB 44/62, PRO.
267. "as rapidly as possible": Ibid.
268. "The streets of La Panne": *Diary of the 2nd Battalion, The Bedfordshire and Hertfordshire Regiment in France, May to the Early Part of June 1940,* p. 23. NAM.

268. "'Off the streets'": Private F. R. Farley, Middlesex Regiment, Memoir.
269. "cannibals or murderers": M982 740.0011/3416, NA.
270. stricken with a form: ADM 199/788, PRO.
271. "jocular, robust men": Smith, p. 52.
271. The minesweeper *Hussar*: Ibid.
271. "mass hysterical epilepsy": Ibid.
271. "It was evident that my crew": ADM 199/788, PRO.
272. "The effect of the consequent plunging": Commander H. Light-oller, Memoir, MS 67/050, NMM.
272. "force them back to their duty": ADM 199/792, PRO.
272. "We were running this RAF launch": Agate interview.
273. Spotting a tug making for Dover: ADM 199/792, PRO.
274. Navy personnel on the shore: ADM 199/792, PRO.
274. "To my right and left": Farley Memoir, op. cit.
274. 0243—Minesweeper *Gossamer:* T.S.D. 64/48, NHB.
275. "A-Company, Green Howards": Gun Buster, p. 243.
275. "I saw what appeared to be": R. B. Brett, Memoir, MS 67/050, NMM.
275. "have a go": Interview with Private F. R. Farley, Middlesex Regiment, August 1988.
276. "A solid block of troops": CAB 44/62, PRO.
276. "The litter on the beach": Nicolson and Forbes, p. 41.
277. "The troops on the shore": K. C. McGriffie, Memoir, MS 67/050, NMM.
277. "Get out of here": Smith, p. 59.
277. "she turned turtle": ADM 199/792, PRO.
279. Gort doubted if many French troops: CAB 65/13, PRO.
279. Profoundly alarmed by the punishment: CAB 65/7, PRO.
280. "already considerably below": CAB 80/12, PRO.
280. The War Cabinet was told: Ibid.
281. "The critical point of the evacuation": PREM 3/175, PRO.
281. "to decide for himself": Ibid.
281. "the abysmal collapse": Spears, Vol. 2, p. 7.
282. An officer of the 5th Borderers: Lord, p. 232.
283. "hold on as long as possible": CAB 44/69, PRO.
284. "It was almost like a motorway": Ginsberg interview.
284. "In these circumstances": ADM 199/792, PRO.
285. "There have been trapped armies": *New York Herald Tribune,* May 31, 1940.
285. "So long as the English tongue survives": *New York Times,* June 1, 1940.
286. A ballot was taken: Divine, p. 205.
287. "We entered the town": MID 2016-1297/118, Part 1, NA.

287. "That the British": Ibid.

288. Equally unsuccessfully: Divine, p. 209.

289. "A still close dark night": CAB 44/62, PRO.

289. "After which everyone": Ibid.

289. Twenty-four men: Ibid.

290. "Looking shoreward": ADM 199/792, PRO.

290. The men farthest along: CAB 44/62, PRO.

290. "We had been told": Quilter, p. 34.

291. "The final evacuation": T.S.D. 64/48, NHB.

292. Armed guards were posted: Ibid.

293. "The British Expeditionary Force": *The Listener,* June 6, 1940.

293. "bomb trap": CAB 65/13, PRO.

293. "long, dreary processions": Hugh Dalton, *The Fateful Years* (London: Frederick Muller, 1957), p. 341.

294. "we lost the luggage": Ibid.

294. "the armed forces": Gilbert, Vol. 6, p. 452.

294. "certain 'specialized troops'": *Chicago Herald American,* June 4, 1940.

294. "MYSTERY NAZIS MASS AT CHANNEL": Ibid.

294. Preparations were made: CAB 66/8, PRO.

294. Ironside noted in his diary: Ironside, p. 348.

295. "Very few friends": *Manchester Guardian,* June 5, 1940.

295. A picket of men: CAB 44/62, PRO.

296. "Operation completed": T.S.D. 64/48, NHB.

297. At half past midnight: Supplement to *London Gazette,* July 17, 1947.

297. "Plenty of ships": Ibid.

297. The destroyer *Vanquisher:* Ibid.

298. "Is anyone there": Nicolson, *Alex,* p. 113.

299. "I hoped and believed": T.S.D. 64/48, NHB.

299. "After nine days": Ibid.

300. The prospect did not please: CAB 65/7, PRO.

300. Forever sounding the alarm: CAB 65/13, PRO.

301. "Had this rate continued": Ibid.

301. rate of eight to one: Ibid.

302. "We are coming back": PREM 3/175, PRO.

302. "a double game": Baudouin, p. 76.

302. "cannot resist the call of the ports": Ibid.

302. Late in the day: Divine, p. 219.

303. Among the vessels: Supplement to *London Gazette,* July 17, 1947.

304. "swarming with French fishing craft": T.S.D. 64/48, NHB.

304. "The congestion was chaotic": Ibid.

304. "Lord help us": Wake, op. cit.

306. An alarm was raised: ADM 199/792, PRO.

307. Later that morning: PREM 3/175, PRO.

307. ". . . by the time we left": Wake, op. cit.

308. "It was quiet now": Private W.B.A. Gaze, Personal Journal, IWM.

308. "like waking from a dream": ADM 199/792, PRO.

309. "Operation Dynamo now completed": T.S.D. 64/48, NHB.

310. "Had a combined staff": ADM 199/792, PRO.

311. The irrepressible General Montgomery: Montgomery Papers, IWM.

311. "I learn there is": Ibid.

313. "whole root and core": *Hansard,* June 4, 1940.

313. "Even though large tracts": Ibid.

315. "go down in military history": Cooper, *German Army,* p. 236.

315. "sensible peace arrangement": Joachim Fest, *Hitler* (London: Weidenfeld & Nicolson, 1974), p. 641.

317. "Had we had any doubt": Cordell Hull, *The Memoirs of Cordell Hull,* Vol. 1 (Hodder & Stoughton, 1948), p. 775.

318. "It is a matter of inestimable importance": *Washington Evening Star,* June 5, 1940.

318. "We are doing everything": Hearden, 155.

Selected Bibliography

Account of Movements and Actions Fought by 1st Batallion Welsh Guards in France and Flanders from 17th May to 1st June 1940. B Echelon Diary. Welsh Guards Archives, Guards Museum, London.

Barker, A. J. *Dunkirk: The Great Escape.* London: J. M. Dent, 1977.

Barlone, D. *A French Officer's Diary.* London: Cambridge University Press, 1942.

Bartlett, Basil. *My First War.* London: Chatto & Windus, 1940.

Baudouin, Paul. *The Private Diaries of Paul Baudouin.* London: Eyre & Spottiswoode, 1948.

Birkenhead, Earl of. *The Life of Lord Halifax.* London: Hamish Hamilton, 1965.

Blaxland, Gregory. *Destination Dunkirk.* London: William Kimber, 1973.

Bloch, Marc. *Strange Defeat.* London: Oxford University Press, 1949.

Bond, Brian. *France and Belgium 1939-1940.* London: Davis-Poynter, 1975.

Bryant, Arthur. *The Turn of the Tide, 1939-1943.* London: Collins, 1957.

Bullitt, Orville, ed. *For the President, Personal and Secret: Correspondence Between Franklin D. Roosevelt and William C. Bullitt.* Boston: Houghton Mifflin, 1972.

Butler, Ewan, and Bradford, J. Selby. *Keep the Memory Green.* London: Hutchinson, 1950.

Cadogan, Alexander. *The Diaries of Sir Alexander Cadogan—1938-1945.* Ed. David Dilks. London: Cassell, 1971.

Carroll, Joseph T. *Ireland in the War Years.* Newton Abbot: David & Charles, 1975.

Chalmers, W. S. *Full Cycle: The Biography of Admiral Sir Bertram Home Ramsay.* London: Hodder & Stoughton, 1959.

Chapman, Guy. *Why France Collapsed*. London: Cassell, 1968.

Churchill, Winston S. *The Second World War*. Vols. 1 and 2. London: Cassell, 1948, 1949.

Collier, Richard. *The Sands of Dunkirk*. London: Collins, 1961.

Colville, John. *The Fringes of Power: Downing Street Diaries 1939-1955*. London: Hodder & Stoughton, 1985.

Colville, John. *Man of Valour: The Life of Field Marshal the Viscount Gort*. London: Collins, 1972.

Conn, Stetson, and Fairchild, Byron. *The United States Army in World War II: The Western Hemisphere: The Framework of Hemisphere Defense*. Washington: Office of the Chief of Military History, Department of the Army, 1960.

Cooper, Matthew. *The German Air Force*. London: Jane's, 1981.

Cooper, Matthew. *The German Army*. London: Macdonald and Jane's, 1978.

Cosgrave, Patrick. *Churchill at War*. Vol. 1. London: Collins, 1974.

Cowling, Maurice. *The Impact of Hitler*. London: Cambridge University Press, 1975.

Divine, David. *The Nine Days of Dunkirk*. London: Faber & Faber, 1959.

Duggan, John P. *Neutral Ireland and the Third Reich*. Totowa, N.J.: Barnes & Noble, 1985.

Eden, Anthony. *The Eden Memoirs: The Reckoning*. London: Cassell, 1965.

Ellis, L. F. *The War in France and Flanders 1939-1940*. London: Her Majesty's Stationery Office, 1953.

Evacuation from Dunkirk of the British Expeditionary Force and French Troops. London: Tactical and Staff Duties Division, Historical Section, Naval Staff, Admiralty, 1947.

Feiling, Keith. *The Life of Neville Chamberlain*. London: Macmillan, 1946.

Fisk, Robert. *In Time of War*. London: Andre Deutsch, 1983.

Gilbert, Martin. *Winston S. Churchill*. Vols. 5 and 6. London: Heinemann, 1976, 1983.

Goddard, Victor. *Skies to Dunkirk*. London: William Kimber, 1982.

Goutard, A. *The Battle of France, 1940*. London: Frederick Muller, 1958.

Guderian, Heinz. *Panzer Leader*. London: Michael Joseph, 1952.

Gun Buster (pseudonym). *Return via Dunkirk*. London: Hodder & Stoughton, 1940.

Hadley, Peter. *Third Class to Dunkirk*. London: Hollis & Carter, 1944.

Halder, Franz. *The Halder Diaries*. Vol. 4. Washington: Infantry Journal, 1950.

Harman, Nicholas. *Dunkirk: The Necessary Myth.* London: Hodder & Stoughton, 1980.

Hearden, Patrick. *Roosevelt Confronts Hitler.* Dekalb: Northern Illinois University Press, 1987.

Hoehling, A. A. *America's Road to War, 1939-1941.* New York: Abelard-Schuman, 1970.

Horne, Alistair. *To Lose a Battle.* London: Macmillan, 1969.

Howard, Michael, and Sparrow, John. *The Coldstream Guards.* London: Oxford University Press, 1951.

Ironside, Edmund. *The Ironside Diaries.* Ed. Roderick Macleod and Denis Kelly. London: Constable, 1962.

Langer, William L., and Gleason, S. Everett. *The Challenge to Isolation.* New York: Harper, 1952.

Lash, Joseph. *Roosevelt and Churchill.* New York: Norton, 1976.

Lees-Milne, James. *Harold Nicolson: A Biography.* Vol. 2. London: Chatto & Windus, 1981.

Liddell Hart, B. H. *The Other Side of the Hill.* London: Cassell, 1948.

Lord, Walter. *The Miracle of Dunkirk.* London: Penguin Books, 1984.

Masefield, John. *The Twenty-five Days.* London: Heinemann, 1972.

Nettle, S. A. *Dunkirk: Old Men Remember.* Frome, Somerset: March Press, 1988.

Nicolson, Harold. *Diaries and Letters.* Vol. 2. London: Collins, 1967.

Nicolson, Nigel. *Alex: The Life of Field Marshal Earl Alexander of Tunis.* London: Weidenfeld & Nicolson, 1973.

Nicolson, Nigel, and Forbes, Patrick. *The Grenadier Guards in the War of 1939-1945.* Aldershot: Gale & Polden, 1949.

Pownall, Henry. *Chief of Staff: The Diaries of Lieutenant-General Sir Henry Pownall.* Ed. Brian Bond. London: Leo Cooper, 1972.

Quilter, D. C. *No Dishonourable Name: The 2nd and 3rd Battalion Coldstream Guards.* London: S.R. Publishers, 1972.

RAF Narrative: The Campaign in France and the Low Countries, September 1939–June 1940. London: Air Historical Branch, Air Ministry, undated.

Rhodes, Anthony. *Sword of Bone.* London: Buchan & Enright, 1986.

Richards, Denis. *Royal Air Force 1939-1945.* Vol. 1. London: Her Majesty's Stationery Office, 1953.

Taylor, Telford. *The March of Conquest.* London: Edward Hulton, 1959.

Turnbull, Patrick. *Dunkirk: Anatomy of Disaster.* London: Batsford, 1978.

Shirer, William L. *The Collapse of the Third Republic.* London: Heinemann, 1970.

Shirer, William L. *The Rise and Fall of the Third Reich.* London: Secker & Warburg, 1960.

Smith, Peter. *Hold the Narrow Sea*. Annapolis: Naval Institute Press, 1984.

Spears, Edward. *Assignment to Catastrophe*. Vols. 1 and 2. London: Heinemann, 1940.

Vince, Charles. *Storm on the Waters*. London: Hodder & Stoughton, 1946.

Watson, Mark Skinner. *United States Army in World War II: Chief of Staff: Prewar Plans and Preparations*. Washington: Department of the Army, 1950.

Westphal, Siegfried. *The German Army in the West*. London: Cassell, 1951.

Williams, John. *The Ides of May*. London: Constable, 1968.

Index